The Use of Man

Aleksandar Tišma

The Use of Man

Translated by BERNARD JOHNSON

HARCOURT BRACE JOVANOVICH, PUBLISHERS
San Diego   New York   London

HBJ

English translation copyright © 1988 by Harcourt Brace Jovanovich, Inc.
First published in the Serbo-Croatian language in 1980 by Nolit Belgrade

This translation has been made possible (in part) through a grant from the Wheatland Foundation, New York.

Library of Congress Cataloging-in-Publication Data
Tišma Aleksandar, 1924–
The use of man.
Translation of: Upotreba čoveka.
I. Title.
PG1419.3.I8U613   1988   891.8'235   88-2250
ISBN 0-15-193203-4

Designed by Dalia Hartman
Printed in the United States of America

First edition

A B C D E

The Use of Man

Chapter 1

Fräulein's diary was small and oblong, with a coarse-grained red binding of imitation snakeskin, and in the top right-hand corner was the inscription "Poésie" in embossed gold letters. It was one of those albums that little girls used to be given as presents, to keep the memorable jottings of their nearest and dearest. But in a small town such as Novi Sad on the eve of the Second World War, this was the only tasteful, attractive, and yet intimate kind of notebook money could buy.

Anna Drentvenšek, known to her pupils as "Fräulein," bought it one spring day at Nahauer and Son's on Main Street, the stationer where she regularly made such purchases. The store was the biggest and best stocked, and in addition belonged to a German, which pleased her, a German herself, and inspired her with confidence. She turned the massive iron knob in the shape of a drooping fern leaf and opened the glass door between the two display windows, in which were set out, in neat, regular rows, textbooks, note pads, fountain pens, pencils, paper knives, and two typewriters, an Adler and an Underwood. She entered the long, narrow, pharmacy-like solemnity of the shop's semi-darkness, with its smell of wood and glue. She made her way around a stocky customer who was methodically rearranging, on the counter, the heavy tomes handed him by a lanky, saffron-haired assistant wearing a protective black apron and perched on a stepladder. She stopped in front of a second, much older, assistant with silver-rimmed spectacles. "May I help you?" he asked, a smile barely moving his thin lips as he linked his fingertips across a small, round belly that bulged beneath the same kind of serge apron worn by the first assistant. Or, rather, he said, "Sie wünschen?," knowing she was German and preferred to be addressed in her own language. This was not the case with all the Germans in Novi Sad in the thirties, when, with the arrival of the first refugees and the first Kulturbund uniforms, there was already the feel of another war in the air and the settling of old scores. Shyly, for it would be the gratification of a secret wish, she raised her head—shaded by a broad-brimmed hat—and pointed a finger in a black silk glove at the shelves above the assistant's head, to where her gray eyes had timidly risen. "A notebook, but with fine paper, please."

He bowed slightly, with an expression of comprehension appropriate to the price of the article requested, for such was the demand of his calling and of his experience. It was this all-knowing expression that won the confidence of his lady customers, who vaguely and with timid, hesitant gestures asked to be served. He turned to the shelves and, stretching nimbly, began to take out and lay on the counter two, three, seven, eight different notebooks and jotters, with hard and soft covers, slim and thick, till finally, tapping the back of the shelf to make sure he had taken down the whole selection, he spread the notebooks out, opening them and riffling their pages, as a shoe salesman bends back soles and uppers to show their lightness and suppleness. Fräulein's eyes, slipping over the gray and dark-olive bindings and the squared and lined pages, came to rest on the one with the gold letters "Poésie" printed in the top corner. She picked it up and opened it; its thick, yellowish vellum pages crackled. "How much is this one?" When the assistant told her, she replaced it on the counter. "I'll take it." She dug into her handbag and paid after he had swiftly wrapped the book in thin, silky, white paper. She put it in her bag and took it home. Once there, she opened the package, turned to the first of the book's stiff yellow pages, then sat at the table and, dipping her pen in the inkwell, wrote, "May 4, 1935" and, below, "With God's help"—all, of course, in German.

The notebook was now a diary. Gradually it filled with the words Fräulein used to give form and sense to the important happenings in her life—until one day, November 1, 1940, when she wrote the words "A new illness," as she had done many times before, but this was the last time, for the new assault on her body was to exceed her reason's power to describe it. She would go from doctor to doctor, stretching out on low tables covered with white oilcloth, and with eyes glued to the ceiling would suffer the painful and embarrassing probings of expert fingers. In Dr. Korkhammer's laboratory, they would take blood from her vein and from her finger, and urine in a glass vessel. She would take their findings to Dr. Boranović's sanatorium. Finally, Dr. Boranović, a surgeon then at the height of his powers, a thickset, lumbering, fifty-year-old man, told her that she had an inflammation of the gall bladder with an attendant stone, and immediately proposed a date for the operation. "Does that suit you?" His small gray-green eyes, set deep in rolls of fat, looked up at her from the calendar on his desk. She was shocked by the nearness of the date, and asked for time to think. "Well now," he said with a crookedly pitying smile, "if you take too long to think it over, I may not be able to take you into my clinic at all, because I like my operations to be successful." The veiled threat hit like a thunderbolt.

Fräulein went home to pack her things, as if for a journey. Nightdress, underwear. Something warm in which to lie with her arms outside the covers, as she had seen on a recent visit to the hospital. But what? A cardigan? None of them was suitable; they were all too dark, utilitarian. She rushed into town between lessons—telling her pupils she would be gone only temporarily—to buy a warm, yet feminine piece of clothing. But everything available was made of coarse material in loud colors. She was dropping with fatigue, running from shop to shop, until she finally found a *liseuse*, as she discovered it was called from the kindly proprietress of the Lady boutique, Mrs. Ekmedžić, to whom she confided everything. The *liseuse* was a light-mauve woolen bed jacket, thin, without buttons, and with wide sleeves, which were a little too short, so that when she tried it on at home they rode up to her elbows. Now she had everything she needed.

Evening found her, cold, in her tiny room. The piercing light from a naked bulb mercilessly exposed all these clothes thrown onto the bed, ready to be packed into a bag as if into a coffin: the pink nightdress, the slightly darker *liseuse*, the panties, pink and white, and the snow-white bra on which she had just reinforced a button that had been loose for some time. Everything went into the bag. If anyone should see her on the way to the sanatorium, they might think she was going shopping (perhaps to the market, which was on the way). And what about the diary? Her eyes went to the wardrobe, where she kept it in the shadow of hanging dresses and an abandoned spring coat. She opened the wardrobe door and moved the dresses aside. The little red book was there at the very bottom, and she bent to pick it up and add it, like an overlooked valuable, to the things she would take with her. But would she want, or even be able, to write anything in her diary under the eyes of the doctors and the good sisters? If she just kept it with her—under her pillow, say—someone might find it when she was distracted or on the operating table, and read it uninvited. She shuddered, as if someone had surprised her naked. And what if . . . ? Trembling, she imagined herself dead and the diary left to the prying eyes of all. But if she left it at the bottom of the wardrobe, who might find it then? Mrs. Šimoković, with whom she intended to leave the key to her room, or her sister, urgently summoned by telegram? (She had written uncomplimentary things about her sister in it, too.) Whoever it was, it would be terrible. But inevitable, because she would no longer be able to protect or hide it. She saw herself lying dead, far from this room, very far, alone, lying still and colorless, knowing nothing, but her diary would still be there, her secret. The thought was so unbearable that she stooped down, clasped it to her chest, and threw herself on the bed, sobbing. For the first time, she fully realized that she might die, and what that meant: complete isolation, complete abandonment, complete oblivion, powerless to do anything for herself. She wept deep into the night, alone in her room, the small iron stove long since grown cold. She knew that crying was harmful to her, but she couldn't help it. Finally, worn out, she crawled, still dressed, beneath the eiderdown and fell asleep, still shaken by sobs and sighs.

The next morning, she had to make the fire quickly, wash, dress, divide among her neighbors the duties she herself would no longer be performing, say good-bye to everyone, pack her things, and go. But the decision about the diary remained to be made. Should she burn it then and there, on the bright morning fire? She held back superstitiously from such an act, which seemed almost like extending an invitation to death: Here I am, I've nothing left, come for me. Then she thought of writing something in the notebook under that day's date, a note about her departure, something businesslike to blunt the earlier effusions of tenderness, which revealed, perhaps, too much. But she was afraid of bursting into tears again, of not having the strength to leave the room (that might even be for the best), but since no time remained for hesitation, she walked out with the problem unresolved, turning back to bid farewell once again to Mrs. Šimoković, who, caught with a tub full of washing, wiped her hands quickly on her apron before responding.

Fräulein felt she was already forgotten, but that was not the case. In the poor quarter in which she lived, where people took little note of important happenings, the news of her departure spread like circles in a pool of water, soon reaching Slavica Božić, the mother of one of her pupils. Mrs. Božić continued to inquire around, eventually discovering that Fräulein had had her operation, performed by Dr. Boranović himself, and that she had regained consciousness at the proper time, which meant that the operation had been a success. The ambitious thought struck Slavica, who was normally at a disadvantage compared with the well-to-do parents of Fräulein's pupils, that she should make a show, if not of position and wealth, then at least of concern. She took her son's best suit from the wardrobe and brushed it, ironed his white shirt, picked out white socks, and thought of buying a large bouquet that would add the final touch to such a display—seasonal flowers. She had just seen them in the market—autumn roses. When asked for his approval, Milinko obediently agreed, as always. At school he took his friend Sredoje Lazukić into his confidence, and, at their evening rendezvous, his girlfriend, Vera Kroner. Sredoje and Vera spread the word to their own homes, and there, too, the step met with approval, and the projected bouquet increased threefold (autumn roses—all exactly alike).

Eventually, a whole delegation of pupils trooped along to see Fräulein in her white-walled hospital room on the first floor of the two-story sanatorium. She received them that day, Thursday, because she had neither the means nor the strength not to, although the night before, her wound had begun to pain her and now she felt the pain spreading through her whole body. Her cheeks burned, her chest felt heavy, she had no appetite, only thirst, but water gave no relief, her lips remaining dry and hard even after she drank some. Weak as she was, she was torn by a desire to leap from her bed and run away to a place that was cool and painless.

The children crowding around the bed made it harder still for her to breathe, and the good sister, instead of holding them back, was so delighted by the profusion of flowers that she rushed off to find a larger vase. The children were noisy as well, asking Fräulein to tell them how she felt, if she was in pain, how soon she would be allowed up. Fräulein was suddenly struck by how senseless it all was, how unreal—that she was going to die after all. She closed her eyes, and the whiteness of the room at once became a glimmer of red under a drawn-back curtain of hanging dresses—the very same sight she had seen not long before. Fräulein started, opened her eyes, and saw the good sister—whose return she had not noticed—frantically motioning the children to leave. She saw them looking at her in surprise from a great distance, and raised her hand in farewell. At the same moment she understood that she was parting with other human beings for the last time in her life, that this was her last opportunity to do something about her nightmare, and she called, or she thought she called, for her lips could only whisper: "Vera darling! Come here." And to the girl who approached from the doorway, drawn not by the feeble whisper, which had been unintelligible, but by the intense, staring eyes, she said, "Come closer," and whispered (now intentionally), "If I die, go to my room, take the little book from the bottom of my wardrobe, and burn it." The effort of speech exhausted her. With no saliva to moisten them, she could barely move her lips, and more in an exhalation than a voice, she asked, "Will you?" Vera nodded. Fräulein closed her eyes and sank into a heavy fever, no longer aware of the nurses' anxious bustling, no longer aware that they were stripping her, injecting her. She died that same night.

Vera got the news from Milinko the next day, and the funeral was held the day after. She attended it reluctantly, as a matter of form, along with her mother, observing all the while just who greeted her mother (if they were men, how they did so) and also how her mother behaved, whether she was pretending sorrow like the rest of the ladies (like Sredoje's mother, elegantly pale and ugly), and whether anyone noticed that her mother was different from the rest. Tension prevented Vera from being sad or even shaken by the knowledge that the person she had spoken with only two days before was now prayed over and lowered into the ground, a person whose hand she had touched and from whose lips she had received a last request. The request was constantly on her mind, and as soon as the earth was rounded into a mound over the grave, she left her mother with the dry remark that she had something to do in town, and set off in the direction of Stevan Sremac Street, more to think the request over than to carry it out.

Once she found herself in front of Fräulein's house, however, she had no choice but to go through with it. Of course she had to wait for Mrs. Šimoković, who had also attended the funeral but who needed twice as much time to return home, arm in arm with her cousin and pausing frequently to pass remarks (among them, the mumblings of the priest that the dead woman's sister hadn't made it to the funeral). Mrs. Šimoković was pleased to see Vera, for the girl's visit made the day's events last longer, and she gladly and not without curiosity opened Fräulein's room for her. They both stopped short at the door: it proved to be colder in the room than in the courtyard. ("And it's only been a week since she had a fire in here," Mrs. Šimoković said with surprise.) They turned the light on, and Vera went straight to the wardrobe and opened the door, as if she had done this many times before and knew exactly where to find what she was looking for. And indeed she immediately saw the bound red notebook at the bottom of the wardrobe. She picked it up and casually opened it, moving her eyes and lips as if to convince anyone around of her right to the article; then, with a smile, she made her way past Mrs. Šimoković, who was too awed by the written word to entertain suspicions of any kind. Neither of them spoke as they parted, yet Vera felt like a thief. That feeling stayed with her all the way home and troubled her even when she read the diary that night in bed. She was not supposed to do this, she knew very well, but she could not bring herself to burn it unread. Once it was read, the knowledge of its contents prevented her from burning it at all.

Vera had the feeling that the diary contained a whole human being—someone unknown to her until now, or known in a completely different way—and that if she destroyed it, she would never again have the chance, once the shock of surprise had faded, to come to know that human being more clearly. She was seized by a fear she had not felt at the funeral: Was it possible for the content of a whole long life to vanish so easily, so abruptly? (From her own vantage point, it seemed very long indeed, more than forty years!) She told Milinko of her hesitation, but he, forever upright, advised her to be true to her promise. She couldn't bring herself to do it, but hit upon a compromise: She wouldn't read the diary any more at present, but would put it out of sight, for a later, more mature decision. Looking around for a hiding place, her eyes fell on her own wardrobe, but she drew back instantly, almost superstitiously, from such a blatant repetition. No, it would be better to put it in her book cabinet, where no one ever looked. She found the right place for it, between two textbooks— introduction to biology and math—which had been abandoned and were of no further use to anyone. But before doing so—burying it, as it were, instead of cremating it—she thought she should validate her decision—which she experienced as both a denial and a betrayal—by recording it. With this in mind, she sat down at her desk, opened the diary, and, as a continuation of the confidential entries in Fräulein's firm, slanting hand, wrote on the next empty page, in her own rounded characters, the succinct, stark, tombstonelike inscription: "Anna Drentvenšek died December 19, 1940, after a gall-bladder operation."

In fact, it was this inscription that persuaded Sredoje Lazukić to take possession of the diary when, quite by chance, he came upon it four years later as a soldier of the Partisan army. His group had marched through the streets of the town that had once been his own, through the triumphal arch that displayed greeting to its liberators—and he was a liberator, accepting chaste kisses on the cheek from the beautiful buxom girls who rushed off the sidewalks to shower the soldiers with flowers and then vanished as quickly as they had appeared. He had merged with a crowd in the main square, to listen to a speech by an unknown officer wearing the three-cornererd hat of the Spanish Civil War veteran.

That evening, he settled into the barracks and later went to a dance to try to make time with Nurse Valerie, from Slavonia, until her girlfriend spirited her off to a small room next door, where the officers—the brigade commander at their head—were making merry. Through the half-open door he caught sight of the commander flailing his arms as he danced on a table covered with a white cloth. Sredoje sensed vaguely that a horde of uninvited guests, himself included, was trampling on something that was his, and the feeling did not leave him the next day, when, while waiting to be transferred to the front, he wandered through the streets of Novi Sad.

Everywhere there was filth, burned-out ruins, bedraggled bunting from the celebrations, noise. He went, in spite of himself, as if to a cemetery, to the house that had once been his, a house standing like a lone tower, with a dome that his father had been much taken with when it was being built. He looked at it furtively, from around a corner. Then he rang the doorbell and realized with relief, once faced with an unfamiliar young woman with a child in her arms (to protect herself, it seemed), how much he had been afraid of finding one of his old neighbors settled there, someone who remembered how his mother had been led away to be shot—who perhaps had even been involved. It was easy to tell the young woman who he was, and natural to accept her frightened invitation to come in. He proceeded to walk around the rooms as if carrying out an inspection, his eyes passing quickly over the belongings of others, noting how entirely they changed the space that had once belonged to him. He passed through the house to the garden, now stripped of everything but the three pine trees that his father had planted, one for each of his sons. Then he turned on his heel and left.

This excursion into the past drew him ever deeper into the past's entangling coils, however, and instead of going back to the barracks or to the square to enjoy himself, he set off toward other familiar places, in whatever order he happened upon them: the Swan pastry shop, the park, the cathedral, the high school. He dropped in at Milinko Božić's house and from Milinko's mother learned that his old classmate had recently become a soldier. He peered through the windows of Fräulein's old room and finally arrived at Vera Kroner's house. He had never been inside it before the war (though he had very much wanted to be), so he paused, undecided, at the gate. But the disorder in the yard and the wide-open front door convinced him that the house had been abandoned and that he was free to enter it, only to find furniture strewn about haphazardly, carpetless scuffed floors, the remains of smashed crockery. Silently he walked through the debris, searching for Vera's old room. He recognized it at once, though he had never seen it before, by the white furniture and a scrap of white curtain, caught on the latch of the open window, that fluttered there like a tiny flag of surrender. He opened the wardrobe and found that it had been looted. He pulled open two drawers, and they, too, were empty. His eyes fell on the small cabinet high on the wall, its white doors hanging open, and behind them textbooks in orderly rows on the shelves. No one had touched them, of course, he observed with a wry smile, but when he looked closer, he was suddenly moved by the narrow letters printed on their spines—the very same books he himself had had to toil his way through! Rummaging among them, he spotted a small volume with an unusual red cover, opened it, and was surprised to find it written in German. He was unable to recognize the hand, although it seemed familiar, until he reached the last page, where the change in script was at once recognizable as Vera's. "Anna Drentvenšek died December 19, 1940, after a gallbladder operation."

Sredoje's whole past swept back into him like an underground river. He tucked the notebook into his uniform jacket and returned to his barracks. But when he read it there, he was disappointed. Fräulein, whom he had known as self-assured to the point of obduracy, was suddenly revealed to be fragile to the point of helplessness in the face of life. Nevertheless, he held on to the diary, as if it were the sole belonging saved from a fire, and burned it only five years later, at the insistence and with the agreement of one other person, for whom it also had some meaning. He was not to know that there was yet another person still alive who was invisibly involved in the circle of the diary's existence.

That person was Milinko Božić, a patient in the veterans hospital in Sauerkammermunde. Armless, legless, eyeless, his eardrums and vocal cords shattered, Milinko lay covered up to his neck with a blanket, from beneath which a rubber tube led to a receptacle on the floor. At intervals he was unable to determine, someone attended to him, let in fresh air (which sometimes stung his face with cold), and the smell of its freshness was mixed with the scent of that person—an odor of sweat, soap, and skin which Milinko recognized to be that of a woman. The woman lowered the blanket and removed the tube from his penis; a sponge filled with warm water moved over his face, neck, chest, and torso, to be followed by the touch of hands, sometimes soft and warm, sometimes hard and chilling, which took hold of him and rolled him onto his stomach, passed the sponge over his back and buttocks, rolled him back over, replaced the tub, and pulled the blanket up over his body. Then another tube was put in his mouth, and soon, as he sucked, he began to receive, drop by drop, warm nourishment, at once sweet and salty. He had no way of indicating when he had had enough, but he had the impression that someone else could judge, since the food usually stopped flowing through the tube as soon as his hunger was satisfied, to be followed by water. Then everything came to a halt till the next visit, when again he would sense the familiar wave of scent slowly ebbing and flowing around him and try to guess what kind of woman it belonged to—fragile and dark? plump and mousy-haired?

Occasionally he felt that the woman tending to his needs was a redhead, and, remembering Vera, would let out a silent scream, painful and protracted. He could not go beyond that scream, for he knew nothing else: where he was, how he had got there, or why he was anywhere in the first place. As for Anna Drentvenšek's diary, he remembered only that once (but what did "once" mean?), somewhere (but what did "somewhere" mean?), it had been mentioned in the street, when he could still use his legs (if he had ever had legs), by a girl (if she ever existed), who spoke to him about a diary (but he no longer knew what speech was). And then he would scream again, the scream being the only response of which he was capable.

Chapter 2

Habitations. First, the Lazukić house, with its dome, set on concrete pillars in the fine, restless Danube sand, sand forever shifted by the winds. The façade, with its three semicircular bays of casement windows. A wrought-iron fence facing the street, with a gate that shuts with a clang. On the courtyard side, a terrace with twin flights of steps leading left and right into the garden, onto a lawn with three pines planted in a triangle. The air full of the smell of water and rust. Above the roof, a white gull's flight and its near-human cry and laughter. Cleanliness, the rooms too well aired and drafty even in summer, and in winter warm only near the tiled stove, which go cold by dawn. Spare new furniture, polished to a high gloss. People calling to each other from room to room, echoes that deceive. Misunderstandings, weariness.

The Kroners' house in the old center of Novi Sad, in a short, narrow cul-de-sac behind the Baptist church, where sewer and water pipes made their appearance later than in the suburbs. A solid, rectilinear frontage, unequally split by a wide, vaulted gateway, always open, that leads into an asphalt courtyard strewn with casks, crates, bits of carob pods, and, in winter, orange peels. Large rooms on both sides of the house, gloomy because of their narrow windows and cluttered with worm-eaten old furniture alongside expensive new pieces, all jumbled together. Vast, cold kitchens, larders with mounds of empty bottles and jars; a bathroom where towels are left hanging anywhere and more often than not end up on the floor. At the back of the courtyard, a detached, sorry-looking storeroom with dusty, many-eyed windows, a line of concrete blocks like an apron around its waist, and a wooden lean-to office.

The tenement containing Milinko and Slavica Božić's apartment, behind the cavalry barracks. The roadway here graveled, bordered by ditches full of mud and rubbish, and in summer, choked with grass like the hair growing out of an old man's ears. A low building at the back of the courtyard next to clapboard sheds and communal toilets. Swarms of flies and bees; pigeons on the roofs. At the entrance to the apartment, a kitchen with a shiny scoured stove, a sewing machine, and a sink that is repainted white every year. Beyond the kitchen, the main room, with twin beds; in the center, a table and straight-backed chairs; a dresser with rows of jars containing fruit and paprika preserves, each with a label giving the year.

Two streets farther on, in a small, low house, Anna Drentvenšek's tiny apartment. One room and a kitchen. An old bed, a wardrobe, a table covered with green baize, a shelf of books—mainly textbooks and dictionaries falling apart from long use, but also an occasional novel and an anthology of German sayings, *Geflügelte*

Worte. On the wall, a landscape in oils bought from the painter himself, a young man who sold his work from door to door one winter. In the kitchen, a half-rusted iron stove, a cabinet, table and stools, a hot plate on which Fräulein does most of her cooking— hastily, impatiently, because the room is permanently cold.

In Belgrade, a bachelor apartment on the third floor of a large four-story building with entrances on two streets. Massive, heavy objects, a clock with a chime, a dozen icons on the walls, an atmosphere of neglect impregnated with cigarette smoke.

Taverns in Novi Sad and Belgrade, established in low houses whose once-spacious courtyards have gradually been filled with summer kitchens, sheds, laundry rooms, rooms for assignations, courtyards where refuse has choked the grass, weeds, and the last unpruned fruit tree.

The hospital at Sauerkammermunde on a hilltop, 1,636 feet high, with an asphalt driveway ending at its gate. A high brick wall, behind which stand four square buildings, identical and equidistant, like the four spots on a die; each two-story building containing thirty-two rooms, of which one is the doctors' office and another a small medicine storeroom. Behind the buildings, through a doorway in the brick wall, surrounded by trees—the forest yields to their advance—mounds with nameless wooden crosses.

The concentration camp at Auschwitz, near Cracow. Acres of flat land encircled by a high barbed-wire fence and heavily built up with long squat huts; an administration building with an upper floor, grimy workshops, a low whitewashed brothel, a hospital, a prison with torture chambers in its cellars and walls suitable for shootings and hangings—all overshadowed by slender observation towers and the round chimney of the cremation oven, the crematorium.

Chapter 3

Fräulein's arrival in Novi Sad: a shipwrecked sailor arriving on dry land. But this dry land was modest, a place of cart drivers and bricklayers, day laborers who worked too long and for too little money to be able even to give themselves over totally to vice. Every Saturday they washed in a tub in the kitchen, which their wives filled with hot water; then they changed into clean clothes and went to the taverns, returning drunk to beat their wives and make them pregnant. The downtrodden remainder carried within themselves the poison of their frustration: they were striving toward something. They read the Sunday picture magazines and dreamed of becoming millionaires, or, at least, police inspectors, so they could set themselves up with fabulous brothels, or else prevent others from doing just that.

But Fräulein did not share their views on class distinctions, even though she lived in cheap rented rooms in Novi Sad, right in the midst of the innocent working class. The world she came from was another, far different, one: the wine-growing hillsides of the Zagorje, the farthest slopes of snow-white mountains, a small town with clean streets, and a house with green shutters, a house obsessively aired. A town where on Sundays people discussed with the parish priest the indestructibility of the faith and their children's progress at school. A German woman surrounded by Slovenes and Croats, she was the daughter of a lame watchmaker, whose wife had abandoned him when Fräulein and her sister were five and seven, respectively. She was extraordinarily careful of her behavior and of the way she spoke, and insisted on having what was hers, asserting herself despite her isolation and the moral shadow hovering over her. Because of this self-assurance, which he perhaps took as a telltale indication that she was well off, the eye of a solicitor's assistant clerk fell upon her: he was a Slovene, tall and angular, with a deep tan and a hooked nose protruding above a wayward ash-blond mustache. As soon as they were married, he persuaded her (he was most resourceful in bed) to ask that her part of her father's inheritance be added to her dowry, which had proved inadequate, so they could move to Zagreb and set up an independent business. The "independent business" was to be a kind of lawyer's office—or, rather, an advice bureau, for Janez Drentvenšek had no law degree, but simply a liking for the field. The office turned out to be a basement in a side street of the Old Town in Zagreb, with a sign in gaudy colors over the entrance at sidewalk level: "Legal Aid! The solution to your problems lies behind this door." This Drentvenšek had copied from an article on American business practice. But no one brought his troubles down the creaking steps of that long-empty former cobbler's workshop, despite the new and alluring sign, and the only financial transaction made there was the payment of the rent. Still more rent was required for a furnished room, which the newly-weds took not far from the "office." Anna Drentvenšek cooked barley and fried groats and frankfurters on an old iron stove refurbished with silver paint. She had learned from her aunt, who had brought up the two sisters in their runaway mother's absence, that although cheap, this was "hearty food," which men enjoyed. But Drentvenšek was not so Spartan; he like luxury, Wiener schnitzel, and beer, bright and warm rooms where music played, and he avoided coming home, pleading the press of business. In fact, he spent his time looking at the window displays on Ilica, the main street, and dined in taverns.

In one of them, he got to know a cloakroom at-tendant, a woman in her thirties with big breasts and hairy lips, and took up with her, mainly because it gave him the right to sit around until closing time, waiting for her in the smoke and animation of the tavern rather than being cooped up at home, bored. In their fur-nished, room Anna languished, tearful, for he no longer even came to her bed, though she waited up for him all night, the groats on the still-burning stove slowly char-ring to cinders.

In the daytime, when she emerged from her lonely room, she found solace in the company of her landlady, the widow Tkalec, who also was German and also had been deceived in marriage. Her husband had been a talented musician and something of a composer, but had contracted a disease of the lungs and died without leaving her any offspring, having first driven her to distraction with his cantankerousness. The only bright spot in the landlady's recollection of married life was at its very beginning, when, just married to the trumpet major Tkalec, their honeymoon was spent traveling by boat, in a cabin, all the way from Vienna to his first place of employment, Novi Sad, far to the east, but still on the Danube. At Novi Sad, as in Vienna, German was widely used, and there was a large military compound opposite the town. It seemed to her that everything in Novi Sad swam in rosy reflections, as if bathed in eau de Cologne. The Danube was rosy at dusk, the air rose-tinged early in the morning, the orchard blossoms roseate in spring, and her husband's voice floated from a rose-filled garden, where he taught violin and trumpet to youngsters whose parents had to queue to pay for their lessons.

These colorful memories wove inexhaustible patterns through Anna Drentvenšek's lonely days, and unexpectedly transformed themselves into a way out for her when Janez disappeared altogether, surreptitiously taking his personal belongings in their jointly owned suitcase. Previously he had sold all the furniture from the office, which, as it turned out, had two months' rent still owing. His young wife was left without any means of support in a town where she had been subjected only to humiliation. Although her own small town was not far off, she could not possibly return to it. It seemed more natural, more necessary to get farther away. As far as possible. To a place where people were still uncomplicated, where prosperity and generosity still prevailed. Weeping, she got ready for the journey; weeping, her landlady gave her her blessing, envying her the youth which would bloom once again in that gentle and beautiful place. But when Anna arrived in Novi Sad (by train), a summer rainstorm had turned the unpaved station yard to mud, and she sloshed through it on high heels to the nearest inn, which was full of peasants and salesmen. From her room on the second floor, she listened until dawn to the wailing of a singer in the room below, and to the laughter of waitresses bringing guests upstairs.

The next day, she went to look for a room to rent, and took one on the outskirts of town—prices there were more reasonable—in a one-story house that had a well, a pump, and a clapboard privy. This town was to be the center of her existence to the end, as well as the cause of her dissatisfaction, headaches, and loss of appetite. In this setting of sand and sticky black earth, thoughts of her wine-growing Zagorje, with its gravelly soil and swift, clear waters, would always make her homesick, and her eyes would search in vain for the promised rosy hues on gray sidewalks—sidewalks burning hot in summer and at all other seasons covered with mud—or in the unbridled growth of the gardens, or in the wind-torn milky sky. The food she was able to obtain tasted of the sand that was driven through the streets and deposited in handfuls under the cracks beneath doors and around windows. The neighbors, sluggish and cunning, watched her, trying to fathom the secret of why she had come to live among them. Her defense was to recall her healthy childhood, her worthy father, who had not gone to pieces after he was faithlessly abandoned with young children, but had stubbornly gone on, dragging his lame leg from the house to the market, from the market to the house, from the room to the workshop, from the workshop to the room, and to the church and the Town Hall, protecting his two girls, standing in front of them with his head held

high and his chest stuck out like a fortress of right-
eousness. Now she herself was that fortress, of necessity
refortified, so that nothing could crush it.

She was courteous to the people around her, but kept
the distance nurtured by her different upbringing. She
looked for work, which she found through the adver-
tisements in the local newspapers, usually as a govern-
ess for the children of the well-to-do, to take the place
of their spoiled mothers. But she continued to dream of
giving lessons in the privacy of a garden, like the one
in Mrs. Tkalec's stories, and for the strident and piercing
notes of the trumpet and the violin, she would substitute
the harmonious sounds of her mother tongue. It was
now her turn to place an advertisement in the paper,
and as soon as the first pupils appeared, she gave up
her positions as Kinderfräulein and from then on became simply Fräulein.

Giving lessons obliged her to move into her own
apartment—cheap though it was and in the same poor
area—and to buy furniture, if only secondhand and on
credit. At the same time, the abundant, home-cooked
food she had enjoyed while looking after children was
no longer to be had. Most often now she ate only bread,
and drank, since her stomach was already beginning to
trouble her, camomile tea—prudently gathering the
flowers late in the summer, in the wild meadows outside
town, and drying them in her section of the attic. Sometimes she would be sick with hunger, but always, when
she was on the point of despairing, a neighbor or the
mother of one of her pupils would invite her for supper,
or send over cakes for her to sample. As time went on,

her conscientiousness, the progress made by her pupils, and her modest fee became widely known in town among parents who cared for their children's future. Besides, the rise in importance of the power that she unintentionally represented by her spoken language contributed to the growth of her reputation. In a professional sense, she began to stand on her own feet.

It was at this time that Janez Drentvenšek turned up on her doorstep, gaunt, his mustache scraggly and drooping, wearing a threadbare suit and coat and sporting a greasy green hunting hat. He had just been released from prison, where he had been sent for fraud. He begged Fräulein's forgiveness, promised to behave irreproachably, to find work, and she, however disillusioned, could not refuse him. For two or three days he was polite and submissive, taking long walks during her lessons and greeting the neighbors with a ceremonious sweep of his hat. Then he began to ask her for money for cigarettes and newspapers, and finally for the tavern, since one could not find work, as he put it, without getting to know the right people. In time he allegedly became acquainted with such people, and obtained any number of useful ideas from them—though each idea required a certain cash investment. The old quarrels and anxieties revived, with the difference that Fräulein could no longer be taken in. Having to work six, seven, or eight hours a day giving lessons caused her nerves to give way, she stopped eating, and she began to vomit bile. At the same time, her landlords informed her that they had no wish to listen to heated arguing all night long.

Fräulein told her husband he must leave, and he agreed, provided she give him enough money for traveling expenses and to begin a new life elsewhere. Once again she had to borrow. She was forever paying back or saving for something, and she always managed to keep doing so by her own hard work, except that this thriftiness, both with money and with herself, ate away at her enjoyment of life. More and more often she was ill, and her illnesses made ever more remote her secret longing for Mrs. Tkalec's rose-tinted fantasies and for that masculine voice murmuring in the garden, which she ascribed now to one man, now to another, among her acquaintances and admirers. At last she came to understand that having achieved her independence, she was going to be left too independent, in fact, completely alone, and that she was not up to such solitude. With no one in Novi Sad, that rancid, hostile city, to confide in, she began to keep a diary.

Chapter 4

The presence of a German teacher in Novi Sad provided Nemanja Lazukić with the means of employing an ancient ruse—infiltrating the enemy's camp with a Trojan horse. The Germans were the enemy of his people, and therefore his own. With the backing of the newly powerful Third Reich, German immigrants had usurped the most fertile land in the Vojvodina from the Serbs and on it built huge houses, which they filled with their own progeny—a seemingly anemic and puny brood, but doggedly determined when it came to work and advancement.

In that region of mixed population, Lazukić, too, was a newcomer, but from Serbia. Not only did he not understand German, but he could not conceive that that harshly guttural language (which he had first heard as a young soldier in the trenches, over the sights of a rifle) could be pronounced without shame. And, indeed, from the moment he arrived in Novi Sad, referred to sometimes as "the Serbian Athens," he had been astonished that a civilized person, one apparently normal and human-looking, could speak like that, and actually within earshot. (Lazukić was also irritated by Hungarian, a more widely used language there, but felt no danger from that quarter. "We'll eat the Hungarians for breakfast," he would say.) With undisguised hatred he watched everything the Germans did, publicly and privately; he watched them getting rich, strengthening their position through patriotic organizations, spreading their ideas of conquest, their pictures, emblems, banners. They were doing everything that the Serbs should have done in that borderland, a land won by the sword and with his own—Lazukić's—participation and sacrifice. But alas, the Serbs had not done, nor were capable of doing, what was needed. And, most painful of all, he himself proved incapable of it.

He had arrived in Novi Sad after finishing his studies, which were protracted because of the war, on a private mission to Serbianize the city. Nevertheless, he accepted, and for a long time remained in, the position of clerk to Dr. Matković, a lawyer who was a Catholic from Croatia and who openly mourned the passing of civilized Austria-Hungary. For the most part Dr. Matković represented Germans and Jews, because they were the most prosperous citizens. In addition to Lazukić's wages, Dr. Matković provided him with his accommodations, a room furnished with a soft couch and heavy green baize curtains, which kept out the morning light and noise of the street. In the half-light of this room and the shady courtyard onto which it opened, the lawyer's daughter, Klara—past thirty, pale, fragile—seemed to him a vision of purity, and he allowed himself to be drawn into the marital web which her parents, despairing over their only daughter, spun around him.

Lazukić counted on her old Herzegovinian blood combining with the fresher, younger fire of his own to produce a flood of offspring. He intended to have three sons by her, three heirs to his name, and as many daughters as necessary until that goal was reached. But after the second son, his wife was taken ill, and an operation on her womb, carried out in Zagreb, put an end to his hopes. It was then that he openly turned against the Germans, like a knight whose shield has been knocked from his hand and whose only remaining option is attack. He left his father-in-law's firm and addressed himself to a different clientele: Serbs, Serbian companies, Serbian politicians. Successful in a number of important cases, he built—on credit—a villa outside the town, near the Danube, where the new ruling class was settling. But above and beyond his own well-being, he cared about the destiny of his nation, and enthusiastically joined the small government-supported Nationalist Party, writing in the pages of its newspaper scathing attacks on German baseness and worthlessness.

These articles had no real effect, for instead of being supported by concrete facts, which their scanty readership expected, they were no more than incoherent cries of anguish and empty posturing. When he asked himself why this was so, Lazukić was forced to admit that unfortunately he knew very little about the enemy that he hated so fiercely. Realizing that it was too late to remedy this deficiency in himself and his elder son, Rastko—who had turned out, like his mother, puny in body and morose in spirit—he decided to equip the younger son, Sredoje, for hand-to-hand combat. Headstrong, dark-skinned, obstinate, Sredoje was his true heir. As a first step, Lazukić sent him to Fräulein to learn German.

Similarly, though for opposite reasons, Robert Kroner sent his daughter, Vera, to Fräulein—he could not persuade his son to go—because German, or, rather, the local Austrian dialect, was his children's mother tongue, just as Yiddish, a dialect of German, had been his own. But both dialects were corrupted, in his eyes, by unacceptable contractions and distortions—divergences from the rules, from what was correct—just as he felt his whole life had been.

Portents of disaster crept around Kroner's house like rodents. His mother, her shaven head covered, silent, in the dark cubbyhole of her room gave herself over to prayers, fasting, and the ritual lighting of candles, as if by exaggerated zeal she could atone for the sins of her son and grandchildren, dishonored by the blood and proximity of a Gentile daughter-in-law, who had been not only a maid but a whore. And that daughter-in-law, uneducated and with an unclean past, her white body drained by hundreds of sweating nights, exhausted by countless couplings, smelling of the smoke of endless cigarettes, was useless for anything except sex—and yet no longer possible for Kroner to use for that purpose. At home, he was both prosecutor and criminal. Both there and in the office of his wholesale business next door, he experienced his divergence from the norm as a wild race of frenzied wheels under the foundations, wheels that would carry him wildly, uncontrollably to a shameful catastrophe. He closed his eyes. All the more painful to him now was the faulty speech, shrill and garish, of his children, of his wife, of his mother. The monstrousness of their verbalizing both personified and emphasized for him the underlying disorder of their behavior.

After finishing business school, Robert Kroner had spend four years in Vienna, to which he had been sent by his farseeing and generous father to be a trainee and then bookkeeper with a firm of his father's acquaintance, Adelstädter and Son. On Saturdays, his day off, at the Burgtheater, and on weekday evenings at lectures at the Junior Chamber of Commerce, he had the opportunity to learn correct, literary German. He was quick to make use of his improved pronunciation and vocabulary whenever he went to visit his employer's home on Sunday afternoons, chatting with the two grown daughters and young son, all seated at a little table in the living room. Behind the table stood a large bookcase containing the works of writers whose names were printed in gold letters on the spines: Körner, Goethe, Herder, Schiller. He would borrow these books to peruse during the week. Although unable to understand much of their contents—he read aloud to himself in bed before going to sleep, as if reciting a prayer learned from his mother—the disciplined succession of printed angular Gothic letters transported him into a state of profound tranquillity.

It was during this time that he decided to stay forever in dignified, orderly Vienna, even if he had to spend his whole life as a minor clerk rather than as a boss in marshy, indolent Novi Sad. Even now it seemed far away, its squat houses engulfed in mist and bulrushes like an oppressive dream. But his father fell ill, died, and after the funeral his mother held on to him, sobbing on his shoulder, and between her tears issued directions on how to conduct the business, which his father had left him in his will.

His ability to resist was broken. Now he was in

despair at the backwardness into which his life had fallen, at his hopelessly bad marriage, which was perhaps the result of that despair, and finally at the muddled babble of speech into which the marriage had plunged him. By sending his daughter to this new teacher, he was extending a hand, belatedly, to the life that had eluded him.

Chapter 5

Evening separation. Only Milinko Božić and his mother, Slavica, were spared that painful division of individuality. They were together in the evenings—indeed, only then were they truly together. Although from the time of his adolescence the son had been sleeping in the bedroom and the mother on a couch in the kitchen, the minute they were in bed they got going—loud enough to hear each other but not so loud the neighbors could hear—on the conversation they had not had time for during the day. "Do you have gym tomorrow?" "Do I have to get bread in the morning?" "You did less homework today than yesterday." It was not only the words that joined them. After the words, their unspoken thoughts came together like roads that intersect, like fingers that intertwine.

At the Lazukić home, the parents were completely absorbed in each other. Klara Lazukić—straight calves, ankles swollen with age, pale puffy lids above bulging eyes, hollow cheeks, and sagging breasts—was still enthralled by having been saved from spinsterhood and by her serious, heroic savior; while Nemanja, though his wife had not fulfilled his hopes of an abundant fam-

ily, could see, as in a nimbus above her head, the blessings of wealth and luxury. They lay together in bed
every night and caressed each other, slowly, patiently,
gently, as if the other might break, with whispered apologies, and an almost tearful parting before falling asleep.
But their ministrations were more audible than they knew.
For all their care, the bed sighed and moaned for a whole
hour, and the parquet floor creaked at the step of the
first one, then the other, as they felt their way, without
switching on the light, to the bathroom, from which
issued at length the splashing and hissing of water in
both toilet bowl and bath. Their sons, accustomed to
these noises since early childhood, had long ago arrived
at the correct interpretation of their meaning. They had
become simply a disturbance. Rastko, always into some
novel or other, or a history of an exotic country, or news
reports on wars and revolutions, scowled because they
broke his concentration. Sredoje—who immediately put
out his light to give himself over to dreaming—having
failed to force his imagination into an almost tangible
form, would burst into laughter.

Fräulein was truly alone. She listened to every noise
in the darkness, thinking she could hear a mouse gnawing in the corner of the room or a cat (or perhaps burglars) creeping around in the courtyard, under the
window. She thought of her father, of the people she
had run into during the day (occasionally a man), and
of the day to follow, with its succession of lessons. All
the words she had to utter seemed to loom insurmountably high, like a soft, crumbling mountain that would
collapse and bury her.

At the Kroners', only the grandmother was alone,
in her own part of the house, separated from her son's

by the vaulted gateway. She still felt herself to be living in the master's quarters, not in this servant's room, to which she had relegated herself of her own free will when her son announced that he was marrying and whom. Her thoughts were there, not here, her imagination stronger than her senses. She could see the daughter-in-law sprawled on the bed, legs thrown wide and hanging over the edge, the bush of red hair between them giving off the stench of the poison perfume that was choking, withering, dissolving her son (whom she could visualize only as a line of pain). Her grandson, Gerhard, who spent his days hanging around with other boys on the street, fell asleep as soon as his battered head touched a pillow.

Apart in her white room, Vera compared—like two pages of a book—the street scenes, the neighbors' faces, the teachers' reprimands, the children's shouts, with the faces and behavior of the members of her own household and came to the painful conclusion that an abyss lay between the two. What should she do for it to be bridged, to be filled in? She sensed that something vague, something hidden would never allow that to take place, that making of peace.

Meanwhile, Vera's mother slept. She had seen that Gerd, her son, had what he wanted; her room was warm, the bed soft, no one would wake her; tomorrow she could get up later than her husband. In his study, into which he had had his couch moved (ostensibly to have his books close at hand when he felt the need for them late at night), Kroner tossed and turned in the exasperated knowledge that she was sleeping peacefully, that she was not waiting for him, did not want him. Did she want anyone, in her daydreams or her sleep? He didn't think so. He knew her for what she was: content as long as she was close to her son and enveloped by security. But that security was in the process of being destroyed, and her son was beginning to distance himself (he could see this already). Once those pillars of support were gone, he knew that she would wriggle away, slippery as a fish, just as she had wriggled free of her previous life and into his.

Chapter 6

For his physical pleasures Robert Kroner went to the house of Olga Herzfeld's girls. It was not far from his own, on a busy street behind the Baptist church. The house was solid, tall, jutting out on the corner with an entrance now bricked up: it was once the jeweler's shop belonging to the late Philip Herzfeld, Olga's husband. Even when he had no intention of going there, Kroner's thoughts would stray to that corner, behind whose bricked-up wall his amorous assignations were kept. These visits were arranged beforehand, usually for an evening when, obscured by the gathering dusk, he could get away on the pretext of a walk before supper. When he got to Olga's house, a girl would be waiting for him, one of the three or four of her "boarders," who would stay with her for several weeks or months before ceding their place to others, or a girl or woman from the town whom Olga had persuaded to sell her charms. These "chance acquaintances"—women he had never seen before, to whom he was not introduced until they went to bed with him—were the ones he liked best; they gave him the thrill of the unknown, of surprise, providing the fulfillment or disappointment of an anticipation stretched to the limits of possibility. An anticipation including even love, for Kroner was prepared each and every time to find love, constancy, fidelity, with any woman who responded to his inner need, to his hunger for a missing feeling, a feeling that for a brief moment would flare up in him at the touch of a woman, only to fade away just as quickly each time.

Such a chance meeting had deceived him with an illusion of permanence when, in a similar fashion, in a similar brothel in the tavern opposite the Vrbas Railway Station, he had found his wife-to-be. He caught sight of her upon entering the vast, smoke-filled, noisy tavern, carrying his suitcase, intending to take a train. Her figure was fuller then, her face white with pouty red lips, to which she pressed the rim of a wine-filled glass that clinked audibly against her large white teeth before the pungent, fiery liquid plunged down the curve of her throat. He whispered the name, Reza, not daring to believe that it was really she, the German servant girl with whom he used to have pillow fights in the back room of their shop, and who used to lie down fully clothed next to him, her red plaits stretched out over the white pillow, to allay his fear of the dark until his parents came back from Sombor or Senta on market days. At the time, Reza, nimble and sturdy, looked like a tomboy compared with him, an undersized schoolboy dressed for bed in a long white nightshirt. When they had a fight, though, and he became angry, he was surprised at how easy it was to throw her down, helpless with laughter, onto her skinny shoulder bones. She had almost no breasts then, only small twin hummocks on the flat chest against which he lay, victorious, pinning her arms to the floor with his own, his legs pressing her thin, sinewy calves into the carpet to keep her from squirming free and throwing him off.

But there in the tavern, she was amply rounded, her white breasts bulging out of the open neck of her yellow silk blouse, her white teeth evenly set between her taut lips. When she got into bed with him in the room behind the kitchen, where she had led him as soon as the price had been agreed upon and the owner was paid, she gave herself to him with all the voluptuousness of a fully grown woman. Telling his mother that his frequent journeys to Vrbas were for the payment of bills, he went on visiting Reza in the station tavern, enjoying her debauchery and shamelessness, until finally he married her—after vacillating between moments of disgust, when he swore to break with her, and bouts of exaltation at her childlike tenderness, which brought back to him those nights when they were left alone in the Jewish merchant's house, where a little German girl, a Christian, a Gentile, was never anything more than a servant, a being of a lower order, but still enigmatically dangerous and therefore kept at a distance.

For Robert Kroner, thin and morose, Reza was the only thing that stimulated him to play, to self-forgetfulness—before, during his childhood, and now that he was grown and seeking play and self-forgetfulness in the creation of new lives. He could not imagine having children with anyone else, even though, filled with remorse, he knew that that was something he should undertake with a woman of his own religion. But all the Jewish girls he met or who were set in his way by the schemings of his anxious mother only served to freeze in him any inclination to play, to go to bed, to procreate.

It was as if all of them were older relatives with whom he would be committing incest. With the vision of their menacing, crooked smiles in his head, he continued traveling to Vrbas, to the station tavern, and taking Reza, slightly drunk on wine, to bed, a bed that was dirty and shameful but where she spread wide for him the red warmth of her hair and offered her tongue and her belly. But after he married her—bringing shame on himself and his mother, obliging the latter to move into the servants' quarters so as not to be under the same roof, although even that could not keep her from being a neighbor of her former maid, whom she had once dismissed for some minor misdemeanor and by so doing had, so to speak, driven the girl down the wrong path, into immorality, and now, as punishment, got her back as her daughter-in-law—after he married Reza, Kroner no longer found in her his earlier playful companion.

By becoming a member of his family, it was as if she had lost all the freedom and capriciousness that play demands, as if she, too, had assumed the responsibility that weighed down those people whose main concern was survival. She took her pregnancy seriously, as a kind of duty: in bed with Kroner, she kept her eyes fixedly on the darkness above her, avoided abrupt movements, and remained unresponsive to his embraces, as if she had to account to someone else for her behavior. And that was indeed the case; that someone was her son, her first-born, Gerhard Kroner, a tyrant from the moment he was born, summoning her with his loud crying at those very times Kroner most wanted to be with her.

She would push Kroner away from her and run without thinking to her son, and Kroner would be left standing by the bed, pensive, listening to her loving cooing in the next room, the gurgling laughter into which the infant's cries and her anxious response dissolved as soon as they were together and she clasped him to her breast. Kroner would stand waiting for a long time while she cradled her son in her arms, rocking him to sleep, and waited in vain, for she often fell asleep, kneeling by her son's cot with her head on the edge of the blanket, her arms beneath it around the child and his pillow, her red hair spread out across his cheek, which trembled blissfully at its touch. Kroner would beg her to come back to the warm bed, or sometimes cover her from her shoulders to her bare feet with a blanket, so that she could stay like that, in the position of an Indian fakir, which for her was wonderfully comfortable, her face and that of the child creased where they were pressed together.

He was losing her, and for him that process of loss was both a cause for despair and a cause for perverse pleasure, for perhaps, he thought superstitiously, it absolved him of the guilt of having married a woman unworthy of him. Sometimes he would get angry and, to remind her of her marital obligations, would force her to stay with him while the child in the next room cried— it was as if he sensed exactly when to start, anticipating the moment she would become unfaithful to him—but a few such episodes sufficed to estrange her from him completely, his embraces became repulsive to her, and she avoided them even when the child gave no cause for her to do so. Kroner understood that he no longer had a wife. The woman for whom he had paid the price of his humiliation, of his fall, was abandoning him. Now, to atone for his actions, he slipped even further down the same slope on which he had found her—by becoming a regular visitor to Olga Herzfeld's "establishment."

Olga Herzfeld was a Jewess, but an emancipated Jewess. Her husband, a freethinker and Esperantist, much older than she, had left her childless and accustomed to an independent life. In place of motherhood she developed a penchant for organizing and facilitating amorous trysts. For this she felt herself a benefactress, as if she were not being paid for her services. Consequently she was upset by any departures from the standards of behavior she expected from those who made use of her good offices. Every girl she took into her double-fronted residence and gave one of its large, gloomy, chilly rooms was obliged to play the role of wife-mistress to the hilt: to be a good cook and housewife but, whenever it was demanded of her, to show brazen proof of her femininity and passion.

Madame Herzfeld hoped that her temporary boarders would make miraculous conquests of their gentlemen callers, who in gratitude would then shower her, Olga, with presents and attention. Instead, her boarders were lazy, slovenly, and often, when she asked one of them to leave, she discovered that the woman had been stealing from her for some time. They promised everything when they came to her, usually needing money urgently—for an abortion, say, or to repaint their apartment—but as soon as they saw that it was not possible to earn large sums quickly, or as soon as they had taken care of their immediate needs, they left her in the lurch, exactly as their clients, who proved generous only before taking their pleasure, did to them.

Such was the gist of the complaints Olga presented at length to Kroner, her honorable and proper compatriot, while waiting in the semidarkness for an assignation with one of the unfamiliar ladies from town who was late, or shortly following an assignation and during the arrangement of the next, which put them in each other's company, contented, and with time on their hands.

They did not notice the shadows lengthening around them, for their conversation grew more profound than the shadows. Indeed, they went into the most intimate details. Kroner quite openly pointed out the women who especially pleased him, describing the exact physical qualities that made them attractive to him; and she, in turn, told him of her early marriage to the elderly Herzfeld, who, preoccupied with his humanitarian principles, had failed to satisfy her either as a wife or as a young woman of poor background desirous of moving up in the world. The two understood one another—not needing to speak in complete sentences, for often a facial expression, a gesture, or a potent word in Yiddish sufficed to convey a whole scene, a situation. These tête-à-têtes gave voice to a vaguely common past that both separated them from the rest of the world and brought them closer to one another.

Sometimes during the course of the conversation there was even physical contact between them. Madame Herzfeld, short and fleshy, with thinning, straw-colored hair and a small pointed nose, would lean forward in her armchair, and her plump warm hand would take hold of Kroner's, which lay on his knee. Then the rest of her would follow, pulling him down onto her, onto the floor and between her heavy breasts, across which her housecoat would suddenly, miraculously open wide. After they coupled rapidly, they got up, went one at a time to the bathroom to wash themselves, then came back and, lighting cigarettes, resumed their conversation as if nothing had interrupted it. This short-lived joining of bodies in no way interfered with their friendship; on the contrary, it seemed to strengthen it. Kroner carried on with his descriptions of the charms of other women, and Madame Herzfeld continued to recommend certain partners and dissuade him from others as if only these intimacies gave her the insight into the finer details of his desires.

Chapter 7

Once, just before the war, Sredoje Lazukić, too, found his way to Madame Herzfeld's house, which in Novi Sad marked the high point of his achievement among the tortuous ways of love for money. Indeed, in that sphere of activity, the house was foremost in the town, perhaps even represented, if pleasure in love can be accepted as the most powerful of all experiences, a summit for the whole of Novi Sad. Truly, what could surpass it? Balls, dances, even those of the most select company, the doctors' or the journalists'? Or church services, in the fifteen or twenty churches in the town—Orthodox, Catholic, Protestant, and the denominations with fewer followers, like the Jewish and Armenian, as well as sects like the Adventists, the Anabaptists, and who knows what else—all calling themselves into doubt by their very diversity? Or learning, nurtured in two high schools—one for girls, one for boys—and in two or three vocational and business schools under the direction of teachers for whom their posts meant assured daily bread after the starvation of their student days? (Not to mention all the voluntary groups and classes, of which one was mentioned in Fräulein's diary, likewise hotbeds of doubtful, haphazardly undertaken learning distorted by prejudice.) In all these noble pursuits, too, were hidden the temptations of the flesh, infecting them with a lust for money and power that inevitably and quickly, in the restricted circumstances of a small community at the crossroads of Pannonia and the Balkans, exhausted itself in disappointment and self-ridicule.

To prey on others or be preyed upon, to use or be used, if this was the range of possibilities for inflamed desires, then it was certainly easier, and more direct, to translate them into sensual pleasure, into games of cards and beer-drinking under the shade of trees in summer or in a warm, well-lit tavern in winter, into marbled meat, warm potatoes, cold watermelon, fragrant wine, woolen underwear, and lined shoes.

What else was there? Boredom, which caresses you like a blind and bloated rich aunt? Streets on which nothing happens, until, say, a cat jumps out of a cellar window and runs across the road, surprised by a maid with a lighted candle and a basket for firewood. That maid with the basket is the only thing that might break the boredom. Her body leaning forward, the quivering light distorting her cheek, her forearms. A woman. While women long for men and cunningly, almost imperceptibly, entice them toward their sex by scent and movement, men, more impatient, simply buy them.

To Herzfeld's establishment went local government dignitaries, those who summoned their employees by pressing buttons on their desks. The biggest mill owner came, once at eleven o'clock at night, after his card game with the same male friends and before going home; the local landowner, too, handsome and elegant, so proud that not even the theaters and taverns in Belgrade could entice him to cross the Danube, since, for him, Central Europe ended right in Novi Sad. At Madame Herzfeld's they all laid aside their vanity and greed; a touch of youth and smooth pink skin beneath their fingers intoxicated them, and for a moment or two they forgot that one day they would all be dead, rotting in the ground, no matter what they did or achieved now above it. That same forgetting—of self, of death—was present even in Sredoje Lazukić's amorous ecstasies, although his youth kept him from being conscious of it.

He was not yet sixteen when he went to "see the girls" for the first time, with his schoolmate Ćapa Dragošević, who was slightly older. Until then, girls, and that meant all females, had tormented him by their unattainability. They had legs, arms, lips, a belly, teeth; these parts of their bodies were necessary, like those of his own, to carry out certain functions, but they also desperately craved to be touched, to be hugged, to be penetrated until it hurt. Girls and women, however, pretended to have no inkling of this other aspect of their bodies. They used their bodies as if they were only bodies. They crossed their legs to make themselves more comfortable when they sat on chairs, and only the unconscious gesture of pulling a skirt down over bare knees betrayed any sign of awareness that besides making themselves comfortable they were making a point. When they laughed, they displayed teeth and red tongues, as if by opening their mouths they were merely reacting to a joke, yet their teeth and tongues produced an effect quite different from those of a male acquaintance. But no one admitted this. Had Sredoje tried to put his lips onto a girl's lips, everyone would have been shocked, even though her lips were heavily rouged to draw attention to their fullness, a fullness that could be verified only by touch. In the end, this perceived hypocrisy drove him to hatred.

Sredoje could no longer envisage relations with a woman as anything except a violent demolition of this hypocrisy. Since he knew from experience that it was not only widespread but entrenched, he had to create situations in his imagination that dispensed with all normal behavior, all resistance and pride, and even the slightest pretense of self-esteem. Gradually he developed a capacity for sadistic fantasy. The girls who caught his eye during the day were summoned to his bed at night, when the dark had erased every vestige of reality, to put on a show—not as ordinary girls and women, the real-life daughters and sisters of his fellow citizens, but as obedient subjects of his will. And for him to be able to imagine them convincingly subservient to his every wish, he also had to transform himself from a lustful schoolboy to a full-grown male of overwhelming power. In these fantasies, constantly being reembroidered, he was now a millionaire, now a hypnotist, now a jewel thief, until finally he hit upon the character that suited him best, a career that was the perfect personification of violence and power: captain of a pirate brig.

There opened up before him an immense variety of fiercely amorous prospects and practices. He saw himself in the midst of the fire and smoke of a sea battle,

sword drawn, at the head of a crew of ferocious buc-
caneers. Dripping blood, he would jump over the rail
of a proud schooner and fight alongside his men, urging
them on, shouting orders to cut down the enemy. His
eyes having turned to the lower deck, where, trembling
and wringing their hands at the sound of battle and its
uncertain outcome, the ship's passengers huddled together—soft-skinned, elegantly dressed women and
girls—he would carve a passage through corpses toward
them. Or, after the guns of his ships had forced a seaport
to hoist the white flag and its defenders had been disarmed, with a group of his most trusted followers he
would search its houses, looking for white females to
carry off as slaves. It was always that first stage, the
battle, that led to the second, the surrender, for he knew
that women obtained as booty through the massacre of
their protectors, women broken by the horrors of battle
and fearful for their own lives, would readily strip off
their veils of hypocrisy and restraint and throw themselves at his feet, begging to be spared at any price.
With such women, he could do anything he pleased at
last, and he drove his fantasy to create ever newer images of male dominance.

But these scenes, however elaborately played out,
brought satisfaction only to the mind, not the body.
Mere phantoms, they took his body to the brink of delight only to leave it tied in knots. Afterward, there was
nothing to be done but to repeat them, to force them to
new and greater agonies of frustration.

Thus when Ćapa, pockmarked and long-necked,
his thin, chapped lips twisted in a smirk, explained to
Sredoje that only money was needed to achieve carnal
power over a girl, that very afternoon—without a sec-

ond thought—Sredoje took thirty dinars from his mother's drawer in the dining room and scampered off to meet his new guide.

They took a streetcar to the marketplace, entered a run-down tavern opposite its abandoned stalls, sat at a table by the wall, and, noting with relief that they were almost alone, ordered pear brandy from the dark, heavily built woman who had tottered toward them from behind the counter. Ćapa, more shamefacedly than his earlier bravado might have led one to expect, asked for a certain Živka. They waited, looking around furtively, embarrassed at every loud noise from another, distant, table, where three railwaymen were drinking. Finally Živka arrived, young and thin, with bulging eyes, her skirt above her knees. She sat down between them and hoisted her legs onto the table, so that her skirt rode up to the top of her stockings, showing her bandy thighs. Ćapa, with a wink, accepted this invitation with a grubby fist. After a drink was ordered and drunk, Ćapa and Živka came to a whispered agreement, got up, and left through a door behind the counter. Ten minutes later, Ćapa came back and told Sredoje that the girl was waiting for him in the courtyard. Going out obediently, Sredoje almost bumped into Živka by the door, in the semidarkness of early evening. She took his hand, led him across the rubble-strewn, sodden ground of the yard to a low building, into a room that smelled of laundry and damp rot, unbuttoned the front of his trousers, pulled him down onto the bed, spread herself beneath him, and drew him in. He felt a sudden release of all his pent-up tensions—and from that moment became the slave of taverns and houses that catered to such encounters. A slave of that submersion, after one's own,

51

in someone else's orgasm. In its depth, of course, it was disappointing as well. Cold fingers, cold embraces, cold beds, coarse words, coarse haste. Or indifference, or anger, but always the expectancy of the next coupling, of the next woman, who by some miracle might receive him, submissive and elated, clean and sweet-smelling, ready just for him.

Chapter 8

Although Milinko Božić was his friend, Sredoje Lazukić never spoke to him of his excursions into the demi-monde. Milinko was too resolutely upright for anybody to think of involving him in such a subject. Besides, at the time of Sredoje's adventures, Milinko was in love with Vera Kroner, and so taken with her that he would probably not keep anything secret from her, not even a friend's confessions. He had sailed into love like a ship into a harbor—not a pirate ship, as in Sredoje's imaginings, but a white ocean liner docking proudly before a crowd gathered on the quayside.

During the evening promenade with Vera, Milinko strutted, squaring his shoulders, his dark-brown eyes darting back and forth in search of acknowledgment. Yet he was not in the least surprised that Vera had taken to him (it was Sredoje who was surprised), having become convinced that diligence and honesty made one worthy of everything, even of the favor of an exceptionally attractive girl. For that favor he had worked hard, from the moment he had first caught sight of Vera, just as he worked for good grades at school, or for his own pleasing looks by caring for his hair and teeth and working out in his spare time. Milinko had the gentle but resolute nature of his mother, whose ally he had previously been in bringing one war in the family to a victorious conclusion—his father's suicide.

Milinko's father had been completely unlike the two of them: inflexible, short-tempered, weighed down by the credit he had accumulated by denouncing pro-Hungarians in the days of the formation of Yugoslavia. As reward he had received only the position of plainclothesman, the pay for which was barely sufficient for him to get married and set up house. He liked the responsibility of detective work, but, in hanging around taverns and street corners in order to keep an ear to the ground, he had begun to drink, and promotion had passed him by. The rebuff had embittered him. He adored his son and dreamed of securing for him a high social position, but an inadequate salary, much too much of which was spent on alcohol, dragged him steadily downward. His wife was ready to come to his aid. She had studied domestic science in school and could sew, but he forbade her to apply her skills to make money, in the belief that it would detract from his dignity as a policeman. So in secret she began to alter old dresses for her neighbors, for insignificant sums. With his investigative flair, he eventually uncovered the subterfuge, viewing it not only as disobedience but also as a kind of betrayal. On coming home drunk, he would drag the culprit from bed by her hair and force her to confess how many dresses she had worked on and what she had been paid, as if it were a question of adultery for money.

Awakened by the shouts and crying, Milinko would sit up in bed and watch wide-eyed these settlings of accounts. As soon as his father's rage subsided, he would spring up and run barefoot in his nightshirt to his mother, to help her to her feet and bathe her bruises. His father by then would be holding his head in his hands, and for him Milinko had not even a glance of understanding. In time, the policeman could no longer endure it. After one such angry dispute, he ran from the house (it was in December and snowing), rushed to the shed, smashed in the door with a blow of his fist, entered, pulled out his revolver, and shot himself in the temple.

This spectacular end left no scar whatever on Milinko, as it would have on many other, less sensitive, children. Instead, it simply strengthened his conviction that evil must always succumb to virtue. Moreover, his mother's life and his own, after his father's death, took such a turn for the better that the conviction was unavoidable. The policeman's salary came to an end, of course (being replaced by a paltry pension), but so did all those wasteful expenses that had piled up debts and quarrels. Mother and son left their cold two-room apartment overlooking the street in a middle-class neighborhood, where they had been held in contempt because of the shouting matches and bloody battles, and rented another place, much cheaper, at the back of a large courtyard, among modest working people who respected them, and who formed a suitable milieu for the work of the humble, conscientious seamstress that Milinko's mother willingly became.

Her sewing machine, which had come to her as part of her dowry, hummed all day by the window in her kitchen and until late in the evening, while in the only other room Milinko sat at a table studying. For him, too, to be able to work alone, without his father's outbursts, was akin to bliss. He sat at a high, oval walnut table, the surface of which was protected by blue wrapping paper held down by thumbtacks. With his books, note-books, and pencils arrayed closely around him, he felt like a hero behind the ramparts of a besieged town, a hero who was acquiring the knowledge that would allow him to save it.

Very early, as far back as elementary school, he had understood the importance of time for successful learn-ing: how time inevitably—as if independent of one's will—contributed to the achievement of one's aim, but only if beforehand the connecting link between the source and mouth of the river of knowledge was correctly es-tablished, just as the needle of his mother's machine had to be correctly positioned on the cloth. He felt him-self to be the master of time and therefore the master of knowledge, and since he believed that knowledge opened the door to all ambitions, he felt himself to be the master of his destiny as well.

This feeling fostered a self-assurance that made him attractive. He never hurried, but always looked at others calmly, with smiling dark-brown eyes; at school, his responses were restrained, for he knew that there would be ways and time enough to show his ability, and his teachers valued him highly. His classmates did not hold him less in their esteem for that. He thus became friendly even with Sredoje, who was a less-than-average pupil, but who, thanks to his home circumstances—particu-larly his mother's penchant for surrounding herself with beautiful things and good books—possessed an extra-curricular knowledge unavailable to Milinko. This at once aroused the latter's interest. "How do you know that?"

he asked in surprise when Sredoje informed him that a certain term in tennis was pronounced differently from what the rules of the Serbian language prescribed. And how was one to acquire a legitimate opinion about matters of this sort outside school, which avoided such dilemmas? Where was one to look? That was how he found out about encyclopedias, those repositories of knowledge that Sredoje had skimmed through even before he could read, attracted by their colored pictures.

The possibility that Milinko, too, would be able one day to open such a book was crucial in his getting close to Sredoje and coming to tolerate the latter's bouts of indifference and mockery, which Milinko treated with a smile, as mischievous irrelevancies. His patience was rewarded one day when Sredoje invited him home to the villa, as the house with the dome was then referred to. There, Sredoje had his own room, on the second floor, with a view of a carefully trimmed lawn and three young pines. Not allowing himself to be corrupted by this luxury, Milinko waited impatiently for the afternoon to end, dutifully going over arithmetic exercises with Sredoje, whose attention was no more than apathetic. For doing so, he had been promised, after the ailing Mrs. Lazukić retired, that he could go downstairs and stand in front of the tall glass bookcase in the now-empty living room, where Sredoje would hand him the huge book.

Once opened, there glistened before his excited eyes long columns of information in small type. He took his time examining the book, reading here and there at random, to make sure that it was really what Sredoje had said it was and what he himself had imagined. He then turned to the front matter (something that Sredoje had never done) and carefully took note of the title and details of publication. The following day he recited these to the proprietor of the bookshop near the school, who returned in triumph from his storeroom carrying a copy of the very same book and more than happy to inform him of the price.

During the next few months, Milinko saved up to buy the *Minerva Encyclopedia of General Knowledge*. In time he became an avid encyclopedia collector, for an encyclopedia exactly corresponded to an ideal he had imagined but could not believe existed: a book containing nothing superfluous—as was often the case with schoolbooks, intended for the dull, average pupil—but only the most essential facts all so arranged that they could be located without reference to chronology (as in history books) or taxonomy (as in texts on natural science), but according to one's needs.

But Milinko's discovery, however much it fed his imagination, served also to undermine his self-assurance. It alerted him to the danger of overlooking other important sources of knowledge, simply by being unaware of them. He no longer dared lose touch with Sredoje. He sought his friendship during breaks between classes; he made a point of sitting next to him; he flattered him, and decided that his visit to the Lazukić villa should be reciprocated.

So it was that Sredoje found himself in a courtyard as big as a lake, surrounded by one-room apartments, among which Milinko's was just another pebble on the shore. Something was going on in each of these apartments, in full view of the other tenants. Heads were sticking from windows; someone was standing or sitting at this or that door. Here everything hewed to its natural state, warm and homey: the rooms were places for the basics, for sleeping and cooking, and water was drawn in a bucket from a well whose shiny bottom could just be made out through the darkness. Sitting at the entrance door, where a three-legged stool had been placed for him, Sredoje found himself being offered warm pumpkin pie from a copper pan straight from the kitchen stove. Such elemental surroundings agreed more with his temperament—inclined not to knowledge, as was Milinko's, but to simple pleasures—than those of the remote villa at Liman, and he became a regular visitor.

Milinko, who would have been happier near the villa's serious books, came to terms with his role as host, for by keeping Sredoje at his side he could be sure of keeping abreast of everything he needed to know. Milinko's mother, too, felt gratitude toward Sredoje, even as her sharp eye took in the cut of his trousers, the styling of his hair, the weave of his warm clothes, and how many layers he wore. He became her model. And when one day he happened to remark with a scowl, "Pa wants me to take German lessons," mother and son (she stopping her machine, he raising his head from his book) glanced at each other meaningfully. "German?" asked Milinko, recovering from a rush of excitement that made his mouth dry. "But we don't take German till next year!" In their class at school, French was the only foreign language then required. Sredoje wrinkled his nose. "It has nothing to do with school. Pa says it's our last chance, if we want to keep on top of events." The seamstress and her son looked at Sredoje expectantly, waiting for him to explain this half-threat, half-promise, but since nothing more was forthcoming, she lowered the needle again and resumed turning the wheel of her machine, while Milinko resumed his reading.

But that evening they sat down by the lamp in the kitchen to talk it over. Milinko proudly opened his encyclopedia and read the entry under "Germany," an article three and a half pages long with two illustrations: a panorama of the city of Berlin and a portrait of Chancellor Bismarck wearing a pointed helmet. The next morning, they asked Sredoje who was going to teach him German. He could not tell them exactly but promised to find out. These inquiries went on for some time, until one day he brought along a piece of paper on which was written, in his mother's studied schoolgirl script: "Fräulein Anna Drentvenšek, 7 Stevan Sremac Street, courtyard, left." Milinko and his mother exclaimed on hearing it was in their neighborhood, but managed to hide their delight.

As soon as she could find time, the seamstress, dressed in her best, though not ostentatiously, set off, with scrap of paper in hand, down the first side street. She returned with the very best of impressions ("You know, she's not the least bit stuck up"); nor did the cost of the lessons exceed their expectations. Before coming to a decision, Milinko, it's true, reminded his mother of her intention to buy new bed linen, but she silenced him by saying that one good alteration could make up for the extra expense. And so Milinko and the lawyer's son began taking private lessons in German, and he was able to ask, on equal terms with his friend, "When do you have a lesson with Fräulein? Mine is tomorrow." The seamstress, too, was pleased to pronounce that strange foreign word and would remind her son, quite unnecessarily and contrary to her custom, "Don't forget you have a lesson with Fräulein." She felt, although she could not have expressed it, that, thanks to this new arrangement, the spirit of the great world had entered her courtyard quarters, putting it on equal footing with those homes that most valued progress.

This was to some extent a prophetic feeling, for by attending lessons at Fuäulein's, her son Milinko—and, for that matter, Sredoje Lazukić—was given the opportunity of meeting Vera Kroner, who came from just such a home. Fate therefore offered Vera to both of them, but, at the time, the offer was to be taken up only by Milinko.

Sredoje felt anything but attracted to Vera, who confused and exasperated him. Why did she mince along on those small, neat feet of hers, placing one in front of the other as delicately as if she were holding something between them? Why did she lower her long auburn lashes over slanting eyes, and then, once Sredoje had almost gone past, suddenly raise them to cast a swift, curious glance at him? Why did she twist her red hair into that long, narrow plait that bobbed up and down against the back of her black coat, so short it ended above her knees? He would have liked to punish her for all those artificialities, to shake them out of her, as one shakes dust from an old dress.

One winter, the second or third of their acquaintance, coming back from a lesson at Fräulein's, he caught sight of her in a side street, pressed against the wall by the onslaught of a dozen boys bombarding her with snowballs. A hand in a white woolen mitten was raised to protect her face and neck from the cold, wet blows. She had also half lifted one leg, sheathed in a white cotton stocking and high black snow boot, pulling up her knee as though to shield, however unavailingly, the middle of her body. The snowballs were hitting not only her but also the yellow wall of the house beside which she stood, leaving irregular white imprints with dull thuds. The boys worked furiously to pick up snow and press it into snowballs, throwing them as fast as they could and uttering hoarse cries of satisfaction, like beaters rousing game. Sredoje stopped, held his breath, and looked at Vera. He was not sure whether to run to help her (after all, she was a pupil of the same teacher) or, on the contrary, to join those who were attacking such an enticing target.

Then one of the boys, perhaps the ringleader, stopped his assault, ran up to Vera, threw his arms roughly around her neck, and pressed a loud kiss on her scarlet cheek. At that, they all rushed to follow his example, and the girl was suddenly surrounded by boys jostling each other to hug and kiss her, as if she were a piece of food that each had to take a bite of quickly and run off with a mouthful. Sredoje, still standing aside, sensed in those sudden movements, those short guttural cries, the warmth and softness of the virginal body squirming and yielding under their attack. He, too, rushed up to her, pushed aside two bigger boys, and pressed his lips to her hot cheek, wet with tears, snow, and saliva. Her skin gave beneath his kiss like a sweet, ripe plum.

At that moment hands seized him from behind and pulled him away from her with a jerk. He had only time to see her slanting eyes following him, curious and frightened. He had to defend himself against the boys who had attacked him and struck out with his fists; he received a blow behind the ear and hit someone in the stomach with his elbow. His anger flaring, he flailed out all around indiscriminately, and when there was no one left, for all the boys had run away, he saw that the place where Vera had been standing was vacant, too, that she had taken advantage of the scuffle to escape.

After Sredoje recounted the episode to Milinko, the latter, in accordance with his sober, antiviolent nature, took pity on Vera and began greeting her. Since more often than not this occurred while he was walking with Sredoje, for a long time she failed to respond—which amused Sredoje. When Milinko meekly bowed his head, and the red-haired girl turned hers the other way, refusing to look at him, Sredoje would double up with laughter. Noticing this, she suddenly changed her tune and returned the friendly boy's greeting in a reciprocally pleasant manner, being quick to notice what effect this favor had on his friend, who was not its recipient. Sredoje went on pretending that her ill will amused him; then, gradually, all three of them began to be amused by these encounters, where every gesture was so charged with meaning, or else meaningless. Finally, they could hardly wait for the next meeting, so each could observe the behavior of the others and compare it with the time before.

Sredoje and Milinko never let a day pass without talking about the girl, and she, having no confidante, recounted these events to herself every evening. By the time they were old enough, as seniors, for dancing lessons—held one week in the boys' and the next in the girls' high school—they were already well acquainted. When asked by the potbellied, frock-coated teacher to choose a girl with whom to practice the new steps, Milinko did not hesitate to make a bow to Vera. Keeping his arm tightly around her waist while dancing evolved into accompanying her home after the lessons, and soon they arranged to go to the lessons together. He became "her boy" and she "his girl." That meant that she belonged to him and he to her, and soon a circle of restraints grew up around them and brought them still closer together.

Sredoje, the nearest observer of all this, treated it with gleeful derision. By then, he was already making the rounds of the taverns on the outskirts of town, practicing, not dance figures, but far more intimate connections. And though it seemed to him that the former could make sense only as a preparation for the latter, he knew—was firmly convinced—that dancing was in fact a preparation for nothing at all, that all those nice little girls, after all those undulating turns to a waltz played by the teacher's small, dark, wavy-haired wife, went from their partners' embrace straight home—either alone or accompanied by an innocent boyfriend—to their mother, to have supper and go to sleep in a narrow, virginal bed.

To what purpose, then, was all that touching, that exchanging of glances, those pleasantly ambiguous remarks, that walk home? But, for all his mockery, he did not remain indifferent to those firm, supple hips on which, at the prompting of the piano, he placed his hand, nor to the warm, trembling fingers that rested, light as feathers, on his shoulder. Their touch aroused him, however, precisely because of his experience of a deeper and closer contact, even though it was with girls far less beautiful and delightful—girls from his illicit excursions, whom he could often call "girls" only in derision, so worn and faded were they, so irritable from drinking, almost always vulgar and ignorant, for it was that very vulgarity and ignorance, that social inadequacy, that had usually pushed them down to the bottom rung of the ladder in the first place.

How far removed from the slave girls who had preceded them in his imagination, sweet-smelling and beautiful and dedicated to pleasing him! But just as far removed from those fantasies were these girls at the dances, their movements strictly prescribed by the dancing master, their signs of submission studied, not an act of submission itself. That game of hypocrisy! Both kinds of girl came down to the same thing—a mere illusion—and he approached both with equal suspicion, sensing, in advance, disappointment, rejection, discord. Yet when he danced with Vera Kroner for the first time, quite by chance, finding himself opposite her at the moment the teacher told them to begin practicing a figure he had just demonstrated, it turned out that their movements harmonized so smoothly and so completely that they did not feel themselves to be separate individuals. Surprised at this, each stepped back a little to look the other in the eyes, but even this interruption did not impair the harmony of their movement, for, once they joined again, they continued to glide as one, as if tied fast with strings. They could not now deny the concord that bound them. Although they pretended not to seek each other out, they in fact did so, arranging to be opposite when couples were being formed, curious to see if that earlier rapport would repeat itself, and then, because they could no longer doubt it, they sought each other out for the sheer pleasure of that movement. It tempted them more and more as they mastered the art of dancing, progressing beyond the set steps, abandoning themselves to the rhythm that carried them along, joined together, like fast-flowing water. Now, for the first time, they enjoyed dancing for its own sake, but when they tried to experience the same pleasure with other partners, to their surprise they discovered they could not. Once again they turned to each other, trying to define this feeling that proved to be incomplete or a total failure with anyone else. Unable to find any explanation, they only became more necessary to each other.

At the end of the year, the theoretical part of the dancing instruction was over, and the lessons became only the practical application—two hours of rocking back and forth to the now-fast, now-slow numbers that the teacher's tiny wife hammered out with ever greater gusto, bounding up and down on the piano stool. Milinko, who at first had monopolized Vera's dancing time, had long since retired from the field, pushing his girl into Sredoje's arms in the belief that he had acquired sufficient knowledge of dancing and gladly renouncing the pleasure of putting that knowledge into practice. Unknown to him was the urge that at the first sound of music takes hold of bodies and pushes them toward each other, that liberating feeling of abandonment to a rhythm, to a beat, that intoxication that comes from swaying in a permitted embrace, in full view of everyone. For him, dancing was a social game, like chess or any other, entertaining and useful while being learned, but a waste of time if, without any possibility of further progress or perfection, it became simply repetition. Meanwhile, Sredoje and Vera danced, holding each other around the waist, around the shoulders, breathing against each other's cheeks, burning each other with the coals of their closeness.

Chapter 9

The dance lessons broke down the barrier Vera had put up between herself and others. She had felt herself to be quite unlike anyone else, even her brother, who alone, of all the people she knew, represented the same strange, discordant mixture of her father's and mother's worlds. Her brother saw that clash in the opposite way—as a special advantage, a privilege—and thanks to this assumption of superiority, felt a compelling need to put himself on the level of all sorts of people. He enjoyed striking up conversations much given to raillery with the phlegmatic old German merchants who sat on the crates in front of the Kroner storeroom while waiting for their carts to be loaded; he would draw them ever deeper into the oddities of their dialect, which he learned accurately to mimic. Or, just as fluently and with the same mocking delight, he would call to his father's toothless Serbian porter, Žarko, whenever the latter appeared at the gate dragging a handcart loaded with sacks, "I'll be darned!," for that was Žarko's favorite expression.

Robert Kroner and his wife had come to an agreement on the eve of their wedding in an attempt to protect their future offspring from the consequences of their indiscretion. Thus, Gerhard and Vera were brought up in, and officially registered as belonging to, the Orthodox Jewish faith. As a result of his instruction in that religion, Gerhard developed a zeal that far exceeded the wishes of his enlightened father, learning to intone the prayers and sing the psalms more correctly than Kroner himself and in an eastern cadence that so pleased Grandmother Kroner that she rewarded him financially for it. This recompense seemed to give the boy as much mischievous pleasure as his recital of the ancient ritual. Eccentricities attracted him. Whenever he came across someone whose behavior or mode of expression was odd, he literally gaped and grunted with astonishment. As soon as he could decipher its key, he joyfully took it for his own, bursting with pride if he managed to imitate it successfully.

Vera was just the opposite. Afraid of peculiarities of any kind, she avoided all those expressions, proverbs, superstitious sayings her mother had learned from her own peasant mother and made use of when she put Vera to bed, took care of her when she was ill, or punished her for disobedience. In the same way, with an almost physical revulsion, Vera was disgusted by the mystical curses that spewed out of the semidarkness of Grandmother Kroner's room. She was not interested at all in knowing what customs or accumulations of meaning lay hidden behind those provincialisms. She had difficulty in remembering any of them, and if one was forced upon her as having some special significance, she let it slip past as if there had been a mistake. She refused outright to attend the synagogue with her grandmother when she was old enough to do so, since her school friends didn't, and stubbornly screamed and hit herself on the temples with her fists until she was allowed to go to school on Saturdays like everyone else.

She thought religious customs, dress, and conventions outdated and silly, but at the same time dangerous, because they invariably classified people whether they liked it or not. For that reason, she never had any girlfriends, whereas Gerhard, who was fondly known among street acquaintances as Gerdi, was torn apart by passionate friendships and enmities. These he cultivated faithfully or bemoaned loudly, for he suffered as much, if not more, from being deprived of the company of those who regularly beat him as from the beatings themselves. But Vera, as soon as she noticed something different about the little girl or boy she happened to be playing with (more often than not brought along by an adult), something in their dress, hair style, or speech— a word, if the child was a Serb or Hungarian, or an idea unacceptable to her family, if the child was a German— she would prick up her ears in uncertainty or stare, not in order to imitate it, like Gerhard, or even understand it, but to shy away from it apprehensively.

Everyone believed blindly in the universal validity of their own customs. No one asked Vera: What about yours? But if she happened to ask herself that question, she was overcome by fright, for in her own house of mixed faiths, nationalities, and languages, the customs were ridiculously disordered; guttural German and sibilant Yiddish competed with one another, and the holidays were completely confused, since for each one— New Year's, Easter, Christmas—there were two or even three different dates, names, rituals. Yet nothing was genuinely celebrated, nothing genuinely believed in. She was infuriated by the madhouse in which she lived, of which she was inseparably a part, and by which—as she came to understand with ever-increasing horror—she was judged and her place defined. So she tried hard to hide the peculiarity of it (which was also her own) as much as possible.

The means to this end were as follows: not to allow herself to become involved in the peculiarities of others, which would have encouraged a closer examination of her own. But since one's personality is in fact made up of such peculiarities, it followed that her relations with people remained superficial. She went no farther than the threshold of a confidence, no farther than the threshold of a confession, never revealing her family circumstances, never recounting the scenes that took place at home, never bringing visitors home with her. It was neither her own decision nor her desire to go to the dancing lessons, but the choice of the school administration. The lessons, however, turned out to be a world of just the same sort of superficial contacts.

The piano played music for popularly accepted dances—the waltz, tango, or foxtrot—and the teacher in his tailcoat showed the students how to dance them. The girls tried them out by themselves first and then with the boys. Although these contacts were physically close, or perhaps because of it, they did not involve anything personal. They merely followed, as did the dance itself, a set of rules established for everyone, with steps that were to be performed in exactly the same way everywhere. The skill of the individual consisted in mastering this pattern of movement as precisely as possible and eliminating from it anything personal or particular. Vera threw herself passionately into this anonymous current with the unfailing instinct of a fugitive, for in it no one could recognize her as this or that individual, her father and mother's daughter, the one who lived in the house behind the Baptist church. Instead, people had to see in her those qualities expressed by her dancing alone. Whether she danced correctly or incorrectly, lightly or clumsily, freely or hesitantly, that was what Vera was judged by here, and at long last she could stand out without giving away anything of her real self, or her origins and past. The activity involved only her body, and she became aware that her body was an almost independent piece of machinery, capable, to an unexpected degree, of adapting itself to a pattern. At the same time, she was able to make the most of all the beauty she possessed, the shape of her hips, long legs, and prominent breasts, giving pleasure to herself and to others. At the dancing lessons, as she swayed to the music in the arms of a young man, her body was both aim and achievement, and everything else that signified her person receded from the sound-filled hall, pushed into the background and forgotten.

Chapter 10

Bodies. Vera's pearly complexion. The finely slanted slits of her dark-blue, almost violet eyes, her red mouth with its long pink tongue, the pinkish nostrils, the shells of her ears. Long limbs, hesitant roundnesses. Small languorous, pale nipples; a flat stomach; her mount of Venus low between her thighs, its red, silky hair. Sluggish circulation, a tendency to headaches, inflamed tonsils. Frequent cold sores on her lips; wounds that heal slowly; heavy perspiration when excited. A softer, gentler reflection of Tereza Kroner, née Lehnart.

Tereza, her thinner, more muscular arms and legs, which only after her second child became heavy, as did her hips. But breasts that were full from puberty, high, sharp, firm, milky. Moist lips, mocking blue eyes, a straight nose. An irascible nature, prone to extremes, quarrels, love, envy. An iron constitution.

Robert Kroner, slender, angular, stooping slightly from the waist upward. Long, agile legs, dark-yellow skin, greasy black hair, velvety black eyes. Uneasy blood, irritable, prone to melancholy, pessimism.

Nemanja Lazukić, tall and thick-necked, with square, bony shoulders, but narrow-chested, narrow-hipped, loose-limbed. Ashen skin. A man of thick, dry, dark, disobedient hair, watery blue eyes, a large, regular mouth and healthy teeth, full, wide nose, lesions beneath his ribs from pneumonia (during the war), his lungs and bronchial tubes full of mucus. An inveterate smoker, fond of wine and slivovitz, given to quick enthusiasm just as quickly sated, a determined lover, faithful to his wife, not attracted to other women, seeing in them disorder, imperfections. Particular also about food.

Klara Lazukić, heavy-legged and slow-moving, the top half of her body slimmer and more mobile. Small, empty breasts, drooping shoulders, a receding chin, a fleshy nose, soft green protruding eyes, fine graying hair. Suffering from varicose veins and bouts of fatigue. A mother for the first time at thirty-three, she never completely adapted to the state of motherhood, or indeed to marriage, but dedicated herself to both out of an exalted sense of duty.

Anna Drentvenšek, dark-skinned, tall, big-boned, with prominent cheekbones, clear gray eyes, sharply outlined broad lips, large white regular teeth, healthy skin. Sensitive nerves as a result of enormous effort and neglect; her resistance to cold weakened.

Slavica Božić, a fair, round, small head, inquisitive blue eyes, white skin, well-defined breasts and hips. Resilient, growing old with a slow and uniform rhythm.

Her husband, a crooked nose, low forehead, his upper lip long and turned up questioningly at the edges, an elongated body and short, crooked legs, indefatigable in any physical effort, but with explosive nerves.

Milinko, taller than his father, with darker, wavy hair, a well-balanced figure, patient and even-tempered.

Miklós Armanyi, very tall and lean, with a ruddy,

supple skin and a profusion of lines across his wide
forehead, a long straight nose, smooth firm cheeks, thick
lips, light-blue pensive eyes. Suffered in childhood from
mild epilepsy, which disappeared completely in later
life, but as a lasting memory of it, disposed to regularity
and discipline.

Gerhard Kroner, pale, a turned-up nose, jutting
forehead and cheekbones, hard, pinched lips, small ears,
big chest, strong legs. Frequent nosebleeds in infancy,
a slight tendency to asthma, but big and powerful muscles giving the impression of perfect health.

Chapter 11

The German offensive to the east, which reached Novi Sad and the Bačka in April 1941, had in the winter of that year its own representative in the Kroner house. Sep Lehnart, Reza Kroner's brother, had been given leave from the battles in Russia and very quickly exhausted any wish to pass his free time with his mother in their village, where his new black boots had nowhere to wander but the muddy, deserted streets. In the village, what he missed most were worthy listeners, for even in the heat of battle he had looked forward to telling his adventures. Not, however, to his sixty-year-old mother, who would pity rather than admire him, accompanying his words with sighs as the tears rolled down her wrinkled face. Nor to the well-fed peasants, who would squint at him doubtfully or ask him how things were over there where he had come from, what the houses and stables in Russia were like, the cattle and barns.

Sep himself had never been a true peasant. Left without a father, with an indulgent mother and an uncle who secretly tried to cheat him of his property, he went to work early, just as Reza had done, for a local Jewish merchant. Perhaps that Jew, the blond-bearded Solomon Heim, was the one person Sep could tell about his military exploits, showing him who he was now, and frightening him out of his wits, thus avenging himself for all the blows and heavy work he had been subjected to as a young apprentice. But when he got home, he learned that Heim and his twenty-year-old son, who was the same age as Sep and a bad example for him, twisted as he was by envy, had been killed by the Hungarian police in the course of the mop-up operation a few weeks previously, and that Mrs. Heim, after burying them, had gone off to her sister in town, leaving the house and shop boarded up.

Sep spent days hanging around that house with mixed feelings of curiosity and regret, asking the old customers who happened by exactly how his former employer had been killed, and where, and if he had died immediately from the bullets, and if he had cried out, and what his son had done—silently comparing what he heard with the experiences he had accumulated himself. When there was nothing left to hear, Sep packed his suitcase and left for the Kroners' in Novi Sad. He was prudent enough not to tell anyone in the village where he was going, but within the small circle of those who knew, it caused no little confusion: an SS soldier in a Jewish home!

The Kroner storeroom had already been requisitioned and its office occupied by a government official, Miklós Armanyi, of noble birth, to whom Kroner had been assigned as unpaid assistant. In the Kroner household, life was lived in uncertainty, as they received accounts of the killing of Jews and Serbs in the surrounding villages and watched the courtyard, now empty, deprived of its former bustle, as if stricken by plague. But now in that courtyard, early in the morning, oblivious of the frost, Sep Lehnart appeared, tall, slim, sinewy, his fair hair clipped close, his ears small and flat. Dressed in uniform trousers, shirt, and boots, he proceeded to go through his exercises.

First he would run around the yard three times. Then, standing at one end and with pauses for breath, he would begin the knee bending, arm and leg stretching, waist twisting, and head-turning workouts as if his neck were a piece of string. He would proudly tell his sister, after asking for breakfast in the kitchen, how much good all this exercise did him, explaining to her in detail which movement was beneficial for which part of the body, just as he had been taught in the army, and he would reproach her for not having encouraged her own children—his nephew and niece—to similar efforts, but letting them lie around in bed and begin the day as weaklings, which could only hurt them later in life. With all this, he seemed to have forgotten about the children's origins, which by the laws of racial purity condemned them to a life of slavery, if not, indeed, a premature and violent death. It was as if they were not half-Jews, but little Aryans, who tomorrow, like him, would carry a gun and the day after tomorrow, when peace reigned, take part in building the new Europe.

And truly, with half of his divided being—the half that against all caution had driven him to come to his sister's from the village—he believed this. Making his way into the elite German corps from his obscure village, he had enthusiastically embraced its teaching, which had raised him up—as once the tap of a sword on a knight's shoulder had done—among the predestined masters of the world. But because he considered that teaching to be perfect, he could not even begin to entertain the idea that it might harm anyone near to him. His niece, Vera, and his nephew, Gerhard, were close blood relations, the more so since he, as yet unmarried, had no children of his own, but also because the poverty of his childhood had made him proud that his sister had married a rich merchant, despite the fact that the merchant was a Jew.

"Jew," to Sep, meant a being rather like himself, an alien in Yugoslavia, but more mobile and more resourceful than his own kin, because independent of any nation. His service with Heim, the lessons and beatings Heim gave him, only served to confirm the idea of supremacy through fear; the SS instruction in the barracks had added darker, severer tones to this idea, but without changing its essence.

In Sep now there was a dualism of respect and fear, of envy and hatred. It was the gentle side that predominated when he looked at his own—so young—blood relations, his sister's children, and in the mornings he could hardly wait to see them up and dressed, although he scolded them for rising late and neglecting their exercises in the open air, the only lessons he could recommend with self-assurance. He was particularly fond of Gerhard, who bore a striking likeness to him—thin, muscular, and fair-haired, with a narrow face, straight short nose, and hollow cheeks. By his nature, too, Gerhard seemed to be of the same mold as the soldier, for like Sep he had little talent for complicated, patient work. It was for that reason that the boy had never even stolen a glance into his father's office. On the other hand, real exploits, actions demonstrating force and supremacy, inspired his utmost respect.

At that time Gerhard had finished his secondary schooling but was barred, because of his Jewishness, from continuing his studies, for which, in any case, he had no real interest. He had already come to an agreement with several other youngsters of similar outlook—to escape across the Danube before they were rounded up for forced labor, and join the Partisans. The arrival of Sep Lehnart provided an unexpected but perhaps welcome incentive to take that step as quickly as possible. When he told his friends, Franja Schlesinger and the Karaulić brothers, of his uncle's presence, he proposed at the same time that they kill him and seize his weapons, thus beginning their flight from the German Occupation with a deed of daring. None of the group could resist this attractive idea, which Gerhard put forward with all the passion of his highly purposeful being. So for them, the early days of the SS man's stay in Novi Sad passed in earnest discussions of how to get rid of him.

The Karaulić brothers and Schlesinger paid a special visit to Gerhard when they knew his uncle would be at home, so Gerhard could introduce them and they could look him over—take his measure, so to speak—which they did whenever he turned his back to go from one room to another. His revolver hung in its holster on a coat hanger in the entrance hall, underneath his cap and next to Robert Kroner's dark-gray overcoat and hat. Their eyes often moved in that direction and exchanged significant glances. Should they kill him with a bullet from his own gun? Or with rat poison secretly put into his food? Or stab him with a knife, in the back, as he walked in their presence? Deciding on this last solution, which would attract the least attention and make the least noise, they came up against the problem of how to dispose of the body.

There were a number of suggestions, but it was finally Gerhard's—to cut his body into pieces and bury that in the cellar—that prevailed. But how long would the body remain undiscovered? When a soldier didn't return to his unit from leave, how much time would the authorities need to establish where he had been staying, and hold the hosts responsible? The youths concluded that even if the four of them managed to make good their escape and link up quickly with the Partisans, the Kroner household—and most probably the families of the others as well—would bear the brunt of the reprisals. For this reason, the whole project was shelved. Thus it was that the uncle continued to strut around the Jewish merchant's house, totally unaware of the danger he had been in.

Because he did know, Gerhard, his cheek resting on his arms folded lazily on the table, observed his uncle with even greater attention, sitting with him gladly during the idle morning hours when his mother and the maidservant were cooking, his father was in the office, and Vera was putting creams on her face. He, too, noticed his resemblance to the man, a resemblance that was more than a resemblance: it was a prediction of his own adulthood. And probably of his occupation, for Sep Lehnart was exactly what Gerhard Kroner wanted to be: an armed killer.

He questioned his uncle ardently about the life of a soldier—the marches, the battles, what it felt like to wound or kill a man. Sep answered, but less willingly than he would have to a stranger or to someone he hated, for he knew that his words were filled with images too strong, too full of terror and temptation for a person as young as his nephew. He did his best to avoid telling him of the more gruesome scenes of war, emphasizing the humorous episodes, such as misunderstandings with the locals in Ukrainian villages through lack of knowledge of the language, or the adventures with girls who came secretly to a hut specially kept for that purpose to sell themselves for a can of food or piece of chocolate.

Gerhard found these boastful tales loathsome but did not reproach his uncle for them, because he was determined to draw out of him more and more information about Russia, the country on which the outcome of the war depended, and about the German army, which had to be outwitted and defeated. And, in any case, his attitude toward his uncle was a divided one, for along with the disgust he felt for his arrogance, he also had a certain sympathy for the man and for his principles. For Gerhard, too, the Occupation, despite its deprivations and humiliations, had been responsible for his first amorous encounter—with the wife of the Hungarian next door who had been called up into the reserves.

She came to take shelter, during the air raids, in the Kroners' cellar, which was more solidly built than her own. A gentle, easily frightened woman with round black eyes and a mouth that turned down at the ends, she trembled and clung to the person nearest her—and that happened to be Gerhard—at the first rumblings of distant bombs, and in the darkness of the cellar let him push his hand down between her breasts. From then on, he had only to bang on the fence that separated the courtyards of the two houses at any time of the day, and she would appear immediately at the gate, ready to go down to the cellar with him. Gerhard told his uncle of this affair, which he had kept secret from the other members of the household, during one of those long, unhurried conversations in the quiet apartment, unable to resist the need to counter one baseness with another. So nothing now was left unsaid between them, apart from Sep's experience as a killer and Gerhard's intention to kill him. But while Gerhard's secret in no way tormented him, since he shared it with Schlesinger and the Karaulić brothers, Sep wished desperately for someone to confide in, since he was unable to do so with his nephew.

Usually he spent the morning at home, hanging around the house and its courtyard, looking out through the windows, or trying to draw someone into conversation. But after lunch—which his sister served him separately, in the kitchen, as if to a servant—he got dressed, shaved (although his face was far from needing the attention of a razor every day), put on his cap in front of the mirror to make sure its peak came down over his low forehead exactly level with his brows, buckled on his revolver, and went out for a walk. He would walk for hours, paying no attention to the fact that the farther he went, the more painful it became to bend his left leg, where he had been hit by a bullet in battle. Often, he would buy a ticket for the first or second matinee and watch a film. Then he would sit down in a restaurant and order five *ćevapčići* or some other light snack, for although he was hungry, his innate stinginess begrudged spending his soldier's pay on what he could get free a few hours later at his sister's. But he did not keep so strict a curb on his drinking.

He watched as young people came into the restaurant in twos, in threes—sometimes even soldiers—but all complete strangers to him. They were relaxed, noisy; though his own age, they seemed more assured, more nonchalant than he, perhaps because they were from town—this town or some other. They would casually remove their outer garments and hang them on a coatrack near the wall, take cigarettes out of their cases, and quietly negotiate with the waitresses, who bent low over the table to give them the menu. He would have liked to get to know them—at least the waitresses—but whenever he spoke to one, he always seemed to say something trivial, and it was received with a distracted half-smile. But he went on hoping that someone would approach him, and so stayed there slowly drinking his beer, which from time to time he had to reorder. Gradually the beer made him intoxicated; visions of war in which he was all-powerful began to rise before him. Looking around with new eyes, he thought bitterly that all these clever townspeople who paid him no attention had never been through such exciting experiences, nor were they capable of it. He got quite drunk.

They had all left the restaurant with their girls to go to other, previously arranged, appointments. Only he was left, sitting with his elbows on the table, straight-backed, meticulously shaven, motionless, numb. The waitress brought him the check, and he, angry that it amounted to so much, totaled it again to himself, screwing up his face. Spluttering, he paid, leaving no tip, for he was certain that he had been cheated. Then he put on his belt, made sure that his cap was at just the right angle on his head, measuring its position with reference to his part, and with ringing steps, careful that no one would notice him swaying, went out.

He headed for home, walking along frozen, empty streets, here and there running into someone hurrying home to bed, or lovers, or a married couple. The town was retiring, settling down in its houses. Behind the walls, behind the darkened windows it slept peacefully. Sep Lehnart was sure that nothing could disturb that peace, that calm, that indifference toward him as he made his way—with difficulty now, dragging his leg like a heavey walking stick—outside those walls. Nothing, no wish for change, no war, no amount of killing. He had the unpleasant presentiment that all the towns would survive all the killing, that no matter how many of their inhabitants were stood up in front of a machine gun or finished off with a bullet in the back of the head, tomorrow, when the army had finished its bloody, exhausting work, there would still be enough people left to lie around in those houses, to light fires, cook, wash, and clean, and do all those unwarlike things that diminish the vital forces and distract them from the march to victory.

He felt an impatient urge to kill. The hands that moved back and forth beside him as he walked shook with the desire to clench someone's throat; his index finger quivered to pull a trigger. But he could not shoot here. One could shoot only rarely, for even at the front, battles were infrequent. More often than not one marched, was transported, pitched camp, and when one did fire a gun, it was mainly into empty space, without a seen target, after the artillery and machine guns had obliterated ramparts of human bodies. Very rarely, into live human flesh, as at Dubno and Voryansk. Now once again those images of violence swam before his eyes, but ill-defined and reluctant, as if shaken up by his doubts along the way, and Sep arrived home ready to go to sleep but hesitant about himself as a killer. He unfastened the gate and the front door of the apartment and, trembling with hope that he would find someone to talk to, moved through the rooms. Everybody was asleep, his sister and the children; only Robert Kroner was still awake in his room.

Usually, when the others had gone to bed, Kroner listened to Radio London, but the news was bad: the German army was advancing in Russia, in Africa; England was being bombed; America had not entered the war. Switching off the radio, he hadn't the strength to undress and lie down beneath the quilt, for he knew his thoughts would torment him and not let him sleep and that lying down would simply remind him of the common grave that lay in wait for him and his family. In such a mood, the appearance of Sep Lehnart had the effect of an apparition. It was as if the perpetrator of his worst fears was standing at the door, the embodiment of horror, brutality, bloodthirstiness. The shaven face shone in the electric light; each hair of the carefully cropped head stuck out evenly around the narrow skull with its flat ears; the shoulder tabs gleaming with silver; the boots black; the jacket fitted close to the body. And at the same time, behind this uniform, he could make out the well-known shape of his brother-in-law, so like that of his wife, almost identical with the features of his son, and that made the whole vision somehow monstrous.

And the effect that Kroner produced on Sep was

also that of a flesh-and-blood ghost. Kroner sat there beneath the lamp, his Jewish features—long hooked nose; dark, dry skin—immobile, with sadness in his eyes, ready to give himself up to the knife or the bullet. As if he were already dead. The room around him was still; it, too, was dead, in harmony with the man to whom it belonged—like him, dark brown and faded from long usage. In one corner was the couch, prepared for the night, the upper corner of the quilt turned down, showing a white pillow and sheet like bared teeth. Beside it, the radio, a dark round ring on the mesh of its speaker, where over many years the currents of sound had left their mark. Behind, a wall filled with bookshelves, from which gilt titles in Latin and Gothic letters gazed down gravely, names of great writers Sep dimly remembered from his schooldays, an alien, inaccessible world one had to immerse oneself in for years to understand. Each object had its place, nothing could be moved without being noticed, everything was fixed forever, and not even death would be able to dislodge it.

Hesitantly, in a half-whisper, Sep asked his brother-in-law if he could sit down. He began by complaining that he had not had a good time in town today, that his leave had afforded him no fun or enjoyment. For this he blamed the townspeople. "They didn't want to have anything to do with me," he said slowly, expressing the thought with difficulty. "They avoid me; they don't want to sit at the same table with bloodthirsty Sep." His Adam's apple bobbed up and down his thin neck. "Bloodstained hands aren't wanted here. Here you have to have white hands, fine, noble hands, good manners, elegant ways. But no one asks if life has given Sep the chance to learn any manners." He spoke directly to

Kroner, with whom he had never been on intimate terms. "But you know, and you can tell them"—he bowed his head imploringly—"who Sep is and what he's been through. The Jewish hydra"—he hissed, aware that he should not speak too loudly because of those sleeping nearby, and troubled by the knowledge, dulled by alcohol, that he was talking to a Jew—"the Jewish hydra in the shape of the merchant Solomon Heim ensnared young Sep in its web, to squeeze him dry and drag him down into the vile slavery of the god Mammon, the filthy god of money, of Wall Street, of Jerusalem, the god of the rabbis. But the German genius came down from heaven, the blond angel of Christian purity, to save young Sep. He put a rifle in his hand and said: Kill! As the Holy Scripture says, an eye for an eye, a tooth for a tooth. For every hungry German, for every German girl defiled by a hairy Jew, hundreds of Jewish and Bolshevik heads, hundreds of their maidens in our soldiers' beds!

"Come on, Sep, wake up, the alarm's been sounded. Put on your uniform, grab your rifle, fall in, climb into the truck, go outside town where the grave's been dug— a grave as big as this house—one hundred and thirty young Jews dug it for a whole day, till midnight, and now they're kneeling at the edge of the hole. Floodlights are shining on them from all sides into the depths of the black pit. We get out of the truck and move toward the pit, in formation, behind the backs of the men kneeling; the command is given and we load our rifles, and then another command and we press the muzzles to the back of the young heads and we fire. Without a sound the bodies roll into the pit. We reload our rifles while hundreds more appear in the beams of the floodlights,

Jews, Jewesses, and little Jewish children. They come slowly toward us, like a chain that you let slip link by link through your fingers. They come and we load, waiting to see who we'll get, like a lottery. It might be an old man mumbling his prayers, or a young man as full of strength as a lynx; it might be a beautiful woman, a lovely girl with soft, golden-brown flesh, or a child who knows nothing and cries out to you: 'Uncle, uncle! Dear uncle, don't!'

"But you fire all the same, no matter who it is; you feel the shudder of that life, of that death, you feel that with every bullet you're wiping a monster, a piece of filth off the face of the earth, cleansing the earth of vermin, of greasy corruption, of serpents who tried to drag the Germans down into their dirty game of racial degeneration and subjection to naked materialism. But there's no end to them, Brother-in-law, no end at all. Do you know what it's like when there's no end to something? Even if it's something good, that you accept with all your heart? You know what it's like when you have too much good, honest food, and it fills your stomach—no, your whole being right up to your eyelids? That's what it's like, killing all night long. Bang, bang! A bullet in the back of the head. First you stand, then you have to squat, because of the ache in your legs, and you order them to squat, too. Then your hands begin to shake, and you feel there'll never be an end to all the flesh that comes up to the pit and passes before you, the scraping of shoes, the sighing, until the one intended just for you stops right in front of your rifle barrel. You fire, and the others fire, and in the flash of your rifle you see that down there, in the pit, bodies are moving. You don't know whether you're imagining it or not—that they're not finished off, not properly killed, that they're going to crawl out of the pit back into the floodlights, first their fingers and fists, then their blood-stained faces. They'll push down on their hands, haul their trunks to the edge, force their knees up over it, and crawl out on all fours like lizards. What do you do then? You fire into the pit out of fear. Then, not waiting for the chain to form again, you shoot at the first one over the edge, then indiscriminately, at everything that belongs to this monstrous breed. But there's no end to it, you see, no end to it, and when the truck takes you back into town at dawn, you see the houses and you're afraid that they're still full of that vermin and that you'll never be able to exterminate them for good."

He looked at Kroner plaintively, hoping for a word of comfort. Hoping for him to say: "No, no, you're wrong. One day they will all be wiped out." But Kroner merely looked at him dumbly, large beads of sweat trickling from the line of his smooth black hair down over his rounded forehead, like a crown of thorns. He was breathing heavily, almost groaning. The story just re-counted had been like a nightmare for him, a madman's vision. The madman was his own brother-in-law; and if he wasn't mad, if anything at all of this account had actually taken place, then it was the world that was mad, and Kroner could not believe that to be so, still feeling himself very much part of that world.

Instead of rejecting the gruesome story, as Sep had half hoped, Kroner asked for more details, as if he were faced with a sick man who had to be humored. He asked Sep first for one thing and then for another, where the pit was, how far from town and in which direction, what ammunition the soldiers used and who supplied it, if food was brought to them, how they coped with thirst, who buried the corpses. But Sep, without a moment's thought, though annoyed at being distracted from the essentials of the story, answered every question, and the madness of the tale was not only not refuted, but it began to take on the fullness of truth.

Kroner was seized by a fresh horror: a reality that assumed the features of a nightmare. Where could he escape? From the course the war was taking, he was firmly convinced that in the end the Germans would be defeated, but now he understood that that would not save him from the steam roller of their insanity. The insanity was already rolling; Sep was its herald; tomorrow it would burst into this town, into this house. Feverishly he tried to think of a way it might be stopped. What if there were a revolt? He imagined the whole of Novi Sad, all of those who were threatened, rising up seizing any weapons that came to hand, attacking the barracks of the killers. If everyone did that—even if only every second or third man between age twenty and fifty did that, responding to the duty of his adult years, just as those on the enemy side were forced into service— then the revolt would succeed. Then he, Kroner, too, would have to take up a weapon, the first that came to hand—the revolver that hung at Sep Lehnart's waist— and shoot at the first enemy he saw: Sep Lehnart himself.

Kroner looked at his brother-in-law and imagined that act. He stretched out his hand under the table and clenched his fingers, practicing the movement that would open the holster and pull out the gun. And then the shot! At Sep's heart! But the thought alone made his forehead bead again with sweat. He couldn't shoot at a living body; he was not prepared for it, not trained for it; he was a noncombatant, whose father had bribed someone to get him listed as such when he had had to go to Vienna, and he had been thankful to his father for that at the time. But now he felt that something was missing in his character. His inability to shed blood seemed like some kind of physical defect that made him inferior to other people. It was the defect of whole generations of his people, who regarded the soldier's trade as a waste of time, something that the Christian, who had a country of his own, might do, but not the wandering Jew. Suddenly he felt contempt for that people, who—like himself, as an individual—trembled at the thought of taking a revolver from its holster and emptying it into the enemy's heart.

Stinking, cowardly vermin! He hissed to himself, against the people to whom he belonged, in the very words of Sep Lehnart: stinking cowardly vermin, who deserved to be killed, since they themselves were unable to kill.

Chapter 12

Several months later, when the sun invaded the streets, the blinds on the windows had to stay down the entire day, and the small table lamp next to the radio was switched on for reading, Robert Kroner's room was the scene of very different conversations, even though they concerned the same, or similar, life-and-death matters. In the half-light, which the depths of the room dispersed into an uncertain haze, all that Robert Kroner and Milinko Božić could see of each other was the yellow surfaces of their cheeks, foreheads, and the backs of their hands, like blurs on a film negative. It did not bother them that they could not see each other clearly; in fact, they liked it, for each could talk freely, without fear of noticing any sign in the other that he had gone too far, either in what was said or in how it was said. They seemed to be unusually sincere with one another, which was remarkable considering their relationship: Vera's father and Vera's boyfriend.

They did not refer to that relationship—it would have made things difficult—and when they mentioned its source, Vera, it was almost as if their roles were reversed: Milinko was the one who worried about her and wanted to curb her independence, whereas Kroner warned him not to be too strict and too mistrustful. The moment they met, like two elements naturally and mutually attracted, there passed between them a current of such kinship that the real, vital issue was pushed into the background. Milinko, who previously had confided only in his mother, realized, looking at Kroner's thoughtful and attentive face, that till now his innermost thoughts had been thrown away into an abyss of incomprehension. And his father, whom he had already begun to forget, he now remembered again with new contempt.

Kroner, on the other hand, discovered in Milinko something that he had not found in either his son or his daughter: youthful appreciation. How had he destroyed this in his own children? He didn't know exactly, but believed that part of the blame was borne by his wife, who had been overprotective and kept them away from his influence. Out of anger toward her, and then in spiteful resignation, becoming at last corrupted by the comfortable convenience his isolation gave him, he withdrew completely. Growing up without his direct control, the children never got to know him, and became more and more distant.

Vera was calm and dreamily absent: she never caused trouble, but her participation in the life of the family was limited to carrying out her basic obligations, and meant, in practice, an independence greater than rebellion. When he spoke to her, she would look at him thoughtfully with her slanting eyes, eyes that troubled him with their impenetrable beauty and that for some reason made him think of the women he encountered at Olga Herzfeld's, so he would turn red and lower his own eyes. But when he watched her as she listened to her mother, he could read in her pouting profile, with its upturned nose, total indifference to what she was hearing, and he guessed that she listened to him in exactly the same way. He realized that what shone from her, and most strikingly from her eyes when she faced him, was not attention to what he was saying, but a wholly personal self-absorbed excitement. What that excitement was, he could never bring himself to ask, afraid lest her answer, if for once it was sincere, confirm his intimation of Mrs. Herzfeld's house. That was why, after she became grown up, he had tended to avoid her. He did not avoid his son, but there were always conflicts with him. Gerhard hid nothing, he expounded provocatively on whatever came into his head. He was always looking for someone to talk to, just like Sep, and he resembled his uncle also in the vehemence of his opinions. In their content, too, because he ridiculed—though on a higher, more intellectual level, since he was better educated than Sep—his father's humanitarian, moderate ideas.

Robert Kroner based his thinking on the broadcasts of Radio London, which called upon Europe to put up a resolute, long-term resistance against the barbaric Germans in the expectation of an Anglo-Saxon invasion of the Continent that would bring salvation and a new order, an order humanitarian, of course, and democratic. Hitler, infuriated by such beneficence, in his hoarse speeches called this appeal and promise the paranoid delusion of the Jews and plutocrats. Sep Lehnart, too, by his tales of massacres, which later became a reality in Novi Sad, gave the lie to the Allied chances of success, and Gerhard found both arguments convincing. Unlike the female members of the family, who were uninformed, Gerhard had access to his father's room even during those sacred hours when the radio, its volume turned down, followed the signal of three short dots and single dash by flooding the soft nighttime silence with a river of encouragement in the name of justice and people's rights. Rarely was he patient enough to hear out these assurances of his survival. "Hah!" He would laugh drily, curtly. "Nonsense!" He scoffed at any hopeful news and made remarks as the announcers, commentators, writers, or politicians spoke in their English-contaminated Serbian or German. This irritated his father, who was hunched over in front of the darkened circle on the speaker. "Shhh!" he would say, waving his bony hand. "I can't hear!" At which Gerhard would shrug disdainfully and wander around the room or the adjacent dining room, making sure that his shoes squeaked as loudly as possible. Nevertheless, he always remained within earshot of the broadcast, and his father always let him resume his uncompromising opposition after that nervous pacing. It was as if the two hoped that suddenly an item of news might provoke the same reaction from both. They went on listening, until Gerhard once again broke in, loudly deriding as naïve some forecast of a quick and favorable conclusion to the war, or fumed because of the exaggerated patriotism that London asked of its supporters on the Continent.

"We should be confident, eh?" he would repeat, taking malicious pleasure in the well-worn phrases, accurately mimicking the speaker's accent. "We should close ranks? Why don't you come over here for a while to show us how that's done? Don't be afraid. You'll go on getting your pay; it'll accumulate in English pounds, and if you get out of this alive, you can collect it all from the cashier. But bring a spare pair of underpants with you; you may fill the first." Kroner's narrow face twisted at such boorishness and his "Shhh, I can't hear" became more desperate and more forlorn. Then, when the broadcast was over and the silence of the summer night could again return to the room, they grew calmer, but only to express their opposing views more clearly. "Still, things are improving," Kroner would sometimes say. "They're no longer advancing on Moscow, and in the Caucasus they're even losing positions." "Losing!" retorted Gerhard. "It's all lies! Why should they suddenly start losing positions, when we know what the balance of the forces is?" "It's not what you think," Kroner returned. "Just a few days ago there were deliveries of American military supplies to the Russians; millions of tons are getting through, convoy after convoy." "But the Germans have all of Europe supplying them." "That's propaganda. What Europe? And even so, what is Europe compared with the combined forces of England and America?" "But your America isn't in any hurry to get into the war." "To all intents and purposes, America is in the war. A lot of the planes defending England are American-made. The tanks in Russia, too, are about a third American. And America hasn't even started its military production yet." "What about their men? Where are they?" "This war won't be decided by men, but by machines, don't you see?" "No war will ever be decided by anything but men. That's where you're deceiving yourself. You sit at home listening to Radio London and imagine that machines made in America will settle the war. But the Germans go on killing. They kill tens of thousands every day. When you count up how many they'll kill in a year, you can see that they'll wipe out everyone who resists." "No. Killing only gives rise to new resistance." "What resistance? From people like you?" "I'm a civilian. I have no weapons. And there's no front where I could go and fight." "If everybody took up a club and hit a German over the head, we'd be rid of them by now." "Don't be silly. A club. You talk as if we were in the Stone Age. This is the age of technology. Death spews from tanks, from bombers." "You won't frighten the Germans one bit with that kind of talk." "And you, with your criticisms, one would think you're on their side!" "I can detach myself from my personal fate. Yes, I'm impressed by the efficient way they fight, and all the fine talk of your experts on the radio disgusts me." "For God's sake, Gerhard, one has to prepare for a war." "One has to win a war, Father."

It was a running argument; they stopped only when they became weary, or when it was time for the next broadcast from London, in another of the languages Kroner could understand. He had memorized the schedule, and while he argued with Gerhard, he would cast furtive glances at the alarm clock, which was placed alongside the radio on a chest and set back a little, so that only he, in his armchair near the receiver, could see it. Suddenly his bony hand would reach for the knob, click it on, and behind the dark patch of the speaker, as if a wild beast were awakening, the silence would become heavy, expectant, then be shattered by the crackling, buzzing, and whining of distant static, which culminated in the familiar roll of that nighttime drum. For Gerhard, who was absorbed in the conversation, pacing from one end of the room to the other, these preparations often passed unnoticed, and he would stop dead in his tracks as if stung. "Again?" But his father would already be bent over the set and waving his hand above his head—"Shhh!" Gerhard would turn his back on him then in contempt and leave, slamming the door behind him, so that it reverberated throughout the house.

Milinko would never have acted with such rudeness, and not only because this was not his house. Here, as everywhere, he was acquiring knowledge, and therefore had to be attentive, watchful. He would take Vera home from their walk, shyly kiss her good night in the twilight at the gate, his arm around her narrow waist, pressing her body against his, and afterward linger there alone, his eyes straying to the door that led down a long hallway to the living quarters. In this loitering there was, in part, a young man's desire to steal secretly into a certain room with a white virginal bed, where, hidden from all eyes, he would be able to hold that warm, supple body truly close. But he was intimidated, felt too great a respect for the people and circumstances that stood between him and his beloved. Only here, at this gate, through which carts drawn by heavy, sweating horses thundered during the day, and handcarts filled with crates were pulled by Žarko the porter, this gate turned by the evening stillness into an antechamber to such lofty pleasures as reading, listening to the radio, playing the piano, and quiet conversation—it was only here that he understood how much his own home, squeezed in a communal courtyard ruled by housewives, was unenlightened, exposed, disorderly. The realization made him value even more the one he had come to visit. He would never forget the moment when, at the very start of his friendship with Vera, he came to call for her and, after ringing the doorbell, was invited in by a middle-aged, ample-bosomed maid in a starched white apron. Room after room opened before him, spacious rooms, full of furniture, but also of objects of no particular use—vases, pictures, bowls. In one room off to the side sat a thin, angular, dark-skinned man with a book in front of him, reading. It was a scene full of calm and equilibrium, dignity, reason, like a sculpture, a work of noble beauty among the other ornaments of the house. From then on, when he came to see Vera, Milinko came also for that scene: the serenity acquired by knowledge. Even the Occupation, which thrust the Kroner family into a dangerous and humiliating position, could not ruffle that serenity; on the contrary, the danger and the humiliation only enhanced the special quality of this house. The Kroner house, besieged by the times, in extremity, was a kind of anvil of history.

Robert Kroner, vaguely aware of this role of his house, found confirmation of it only in the round brown eyes of Milinko Božić, eyes filled with reverence. One time, when the young man arrived early to call for Vera and was left for several minutes standing stiffly in the dining room, Kroner came out to offer him a chair. Noticing, as they chatted, that Milinko looked curiously and admiringly at the book-lined inner depths of his study, he invited him in. First they took down the encyclopedias and placed them on the table: the one-volume Yugoslav editions, a German one, Meyer, in twelve large tomes, and a Hungarian, Revay, in eight. Milinko realized then how narrow was the range of his information, based on only secondary sources and limited by the knowledge of only two languages. He shared this thought openly with Kroner, who, nodding in agreement, began to speak about the history of reference books and the law of influences.

"It's like people," he told Milinko, who was all ears. "Even nations borrow from each other. Nothing is born in a vacuum, nothing develops from itself alone, and anyone who claims otherwise—usually to laud the culture to which he belongs—is lying. All life is imitation. The way we live in this house is a copy of the way my father and mother lived in it, and they in turn patterned themselves on others. This kind of home, these objects, the storeroom in the back, the courtyard through which one passes from the private world into the business world and back again, all existed long ago, before this house, and served as a model when it was built and furnished. You could probably trace the migration of this type of merchant's house, going back in time, from street to street, from the outskirts of town to the center, from town to city. Thus Novi Sad would perhaps lead you to Szeged, Szeged to Pest, Pest to Vienna, Vienna to Berlin. It might have been in 1862, or 1852, when this kind of merchant's house was first adopted in Berlin. The same goes for books, whether they contain artistic material"—for material, Kroner said "Stoff," the German word, unable to find an adequate Serbian term— "or whether they are of a scientific nature. Invariably you find traces of imitation. For example, an idea current in my youth in Austria and Germany, Dr. Freud's psychoanalysis, had only recently been mentioned in Novi

Sad, and then critically, but it will be accepted in the next generation. This is where the intelligent man has an advantage: instead of waiting for a new idea or style to reach him via its long geographical-temporal course, he can receive it at the very beginning, before everyone else. In Novi Sad, the merchant who first built himself an Austrian house had an advantage over the old-fashioned merchant who used the market stall. Similarly, the intellectual who reads the books that are current among the larger, more developed nations will have an advantage over the one who waits for innovations to come to him."

Here he paused, allowing Milinko to plunge into the books before him, and returned the volumes to the shelves when they were done with. But Milinko suddenly stopped and sighed: What was the use of looking at something he couldn't obtain? He would have to go to Austria to buy books of this kind—to Germany, that is, now that the two countries were combined— with his pockets full of marks. Not at all, Kroner said cheerfully. In every trade, even in the book trade, business could be done by correspondence, and Milinko had only to send a postcard to the publishers of the encyclopedias he wanted, and he would receive detailed catalogs and price lists. "Unfortunately, or let us say, in this case, fortunately"—his thin, mobile mouth in a wry smile— "Austria—or, rather, Germany—is now not only our neighbor but, so to speak, our second identity, which undoubtedly will make it easier for such purchases to be made." He went around the wide desk, opened a drawer, rummaged through it, and pulled out a bundle of brochures and booklets held together by a yellow rubber band. "These are some old catalogs I happen to have." He spread them out, arranged them on the desk. In addition to printed information, there were photographs of the books in rows of dark red, blue, green. "Brockhaus, Langenscheidt, Meyer, Knaurr—you'll find those the most interesting," pointing to each with his long, thin middle finger. "Of course they are out of date; you must ask for new ones." He tore a sheet of paper from a note pad and handed it to Milinko with a pencil. "I suggest you draft a simple request first, to fit on a postcard." He looked over Milinko's shoulder as the sentence was slowly and thoughtfully written. "I think it might be better to put *schicken* instead of *senden*. Sounds more businesslike," he remarked, but otherwise noted, with surprise, that Milinko's German was correct. "If only Gerhard or Vera could write a letter like that! How long have you been studying German?" When he learned that Milinko had been taking lessons as long as Vera and that, unlike Vera and her brother, he had never heard German spoken, Kroner was most impressed. Milinko, flattered, did his best to carry out these instructions, and on his next visit he reported to his adviser that the postcards were mailed.

Milinko waited for the replies, and Kroner waited with him, never once failing to ask about them when Milinko came to the house. The first reply arrived after ten days: a stiff, yellowish-brown envelope with a two-pronged metal fastener and a white address sticker with Milinko Božić's name and address neatly typed. From it slid a whole pile of triple-folded brochures describing expensive books: histories, geographies, encyclopedias, dictionaries, much more than Milinko had requested or expected. He immediately took the package to Kroner, who was not at home, but Milinko asked the maid to put the envelope in the study, and that evening he went back so that they could enjoy it together. They studied the catalogs, read them over each other's shoulders in half-whispers, but raised their voices when they came to important things: number of volumes, price, method of payment. Kroner took a pencil and underlined. Milinko made up his first order. More catalogs arrived, and soon thereafter a parcel of books: Knaurr's *World Atlas*, which they examined together in great excitement. The ordering became, within the limits of Milinko's schoolboy budget, a constant occupation for them, an inexhaustible subject of plans and discussions.

But then, on Main Street, after large-scale renovation of an ironmonger's shop vacated by a Serb, there appeared display windows full of German books at very reasonable prices, and a sign over the entrance, in Gothic letters: DEUTSCHE BUCHHANDLUNG. Milinko could now browse, inspect, and buy on the spot anything he wanted, no longer needing the assistance of Kroner to cross the boundaries, albeit "erased," between countries. For Kroner, this meant a separation. If he went into the German bookshop with Milinko and was recognized as a Jew, they might throw him out, insult him. And he, insulted, might lose his temper. So he stayed at home, retreating into its rooms and furniture, into their lifelessness and silence.

For four hours in the morning and for as many in the afternoon, he was in the office, keeping the books, the inventory, listening to conversations, which ebbed and flowed, as in most places where people congregated, about what they felt, what they knew, and what they wanted to find out. Sometimes the words were addressed to him, sometimes to Count Armanyi, sometimes to Julia Nemethor, the cashier, or to Žarko, the porter. The words disturbed Kroner as much by their sound as by the monstrousness they carried. He had heared these things already from Sep Lehnart, in a dense, bloodstained mass, and could take no more; each new arrival, each new voice made his flesh crawl. Exhausted, he would return home and wrap himself in solitude like a man bandaging a wound. His family, too, troubled him, for their very existence meant the possibility of exposure to new harm.

Only Milinko did not disturb him, since Milinko's words were peaceful; they settled alongside the books like birds settling on their nests. Milinko, he knew, would arrive in the early evening, at the usual time for young lovers; the unimaginative young man had never thought to suggest anything else, and the time coincided with the hour Kroner withdrew after coming home from the office. Kroner sat in his room, the blinds lowered, separated from the dining room by a frosted-glass door that went from wall to wall, opening in the middle and folding back in double flaps. He did not switch on the lamp or turn on the radio, but sat slumped in his armchair, resting, his eyes closed. As soon as he heard the doorbell, however, he would take the book ready on his desk and open it at random. This was not hypocrisy—he liked to receive Milinko with a quotation from a book. It was a way of starting a peaceful conversation. He would look up from the book and see Milinko's outline approach across the dining room, stop to let the maid pass on her way to Vera, hesitate before the glass door, then lift his hand to knock. Kroner would shout "Come in!" and Milinko would enter. "What are you reading today?" Milinko would inquire and, without waiting for an answer, crane his neck to see. As a rule it was a book from Kroner's youthful Vienna days, stories or a novel by Arthur Schnitzler or Paul Heise, though he would sometimes select an older writer, Heine, Goethe, Schiller, from a series of collected works with titles printed in gold, or a biographical novel by Stefan Zweig or Lion Feuchtwanger. It had been a long time since he had read these books—some he had never read at all—but he looked at them now with nostalgia, turned them over, tapped them with a finger, as if they were made of the finest china.

"Goethe," he said, drawing out the name melodiously. "*There* was a phenomenon only the Age of Enlightenment could produce, that great century which celebrated light, clarity, and balance. We have no men and no writers like that today. Mysticism now rules the world, the cult of blood and violence, darkness, the longing for the past, nationalism. Do you think that anything great and noble, like this book, can come out of such chaos? No; you'll see, our time will be remembered for its barbarity and barrenness." At this point he felt that by generalizing he was rather dishonestly winning the young man over to a point of view rooted in his own downtrodden state, but he justified it with the thought that the enemy, fascism, without any such scruples, was corrupting not one person but thousands at a time. Kroner was attracted by the idea that although he himself could not take up arms, as Gerhard had suggested, he could at least prepare someone else to make that decision. This was also his answer to Gerhard, a justification of a kind, proof that he was not entirely incapable of action, that, though not a fighter, he could contribute in his own way to the fighting. Kroner, indeed, hoped, with the double egotism of a father and an ideological opponent, that Gerhard, his son, would fail as a fighter and that Milinko, his champion in the contest, would triumph through patience, reason, and determination.

Chapter 13

Street scenes. People strolling in twos and threes past shop windows displaying fabrics, wool, jersey, linen. Wishful faces; one leg at an angle in unconscious imitation of a posing mannequin. A little beggar, his short-cropped hair sticking up and eyes without pupils, sitting on the sidewalk against a wall, a black cap turned upside down between his bare feet. Bells ringing from the tower of the cathedral on Palm Sunday, children in new clothes, white knee socks, tiny bells on pink ribbons around their necks, clinging to the hands of grandmothers, who nod to each other in greeting. A column of soldiers with rifles, backpacks, rolled blankets across their packs, entrenching tools at their belts, and their boots crunching. Soldiers in 1940, in blue-gray uniforms with high collars and puttees; in 1942, in low boots and greenish uniforms, with the lightning bolt on their soft collars, caps low and angled to their faces; in 1956, in boots and olive-gray uniforms with gray ties. High-sided carts, a shovel planted at the top of a mound of coal. Carts with black rubber wheels, loaded with bottles of soda water, a chorus of a hundred voices, a hundred separate lakes gleaming through glass of different colors. Cabs with hoods in the shape of an open palm or a cabbage leaf. Streetcars swaying on sharp turns, their bells ringing. Buses taken by storm at lunchtime. Cars abandoned on the sidewalks of narrow streets, Baker Street, Furrier Street, Chandler Street, covered with dust, their windows gaping at the walls. Married couples with baby carriages on Sundays. A mob, their hands stuffed into their pockets, a threatening look in their eyes, released from movie houses. Seated in the sun on the wide sidewalk in front of the Queen Mary Hotel—formerly Queen Elizabeth, subsequently Erzsébet Királynő, still later Vojvodina—at marble tables inside a wrought-iron railing, over mugs of beer, glasses of slivovitz, cups of French coffee, merchants and tradesmen in bowler hats, officers of the Royal Army with their caps on the chairs beside them, actresses of the Serbian National Theater observing the scene through lorgnettes. A teen-agers' "row": a two-way battery of ardent glances and fixed smiles. The town's eccentrics: the seller of lottery tickets, hunchbacked, with a white goatee; the hairless idiot poking his flute in young girls' faces to play "Tamo daleko"; the woman in a long threadbare coat, gray hair hanging loose, wandering from shop to shop asking for empty boxes. Young girls in long skirts, like a shower in early summer washing the boredom off the dusty town. A woman in tight-fitting clothes, her legs the shape of upturned wine bottles, standing at the entrance to a department store. A woodcutter in a torn coat, two axes slung over his shoulder, a purple nose, a mustache white with frost, loitering on a winter morning in front of the Agricultural Bank. Two young teachers, one of history, the other of literature, the first straight-backed and balding, the second round-shouldered and with downcast, sad eyes, both gesticulating as they disappear into a restaurant. A truck with a bright-colored sign painted on its side and a loudspeaker in an inverted funnel on its roof, moving away as it announces that the circus has just arrived in town and is setting up at the fairground. Wreaths of multicolored lights, lanterns in the shop windows on New Year's Eve, confetti scattered over the sidewalk. The emptiness of a public holiday, solitary drunks with foreheads pressed against the advertisement kiosks, girls laden with bags hurrying off to visit their aunts. The muffled darkness of night, with its street cleaners, lovers returning from trysts, night-shift workers hastening to the factories. Peasant girls in wide, brightly embroidered skirts on market days, hanging around dairy bars and the stalls on wheels that sell scarves and bathing suits. Regiments of bathers at the bus stop, coming from the Danube, in shorts, cheerful tee shirts, loose dresses, and children sucking lollipops, cheeks red from the sun and legs heavy with fatigue. In front of the theater in the evening: two or three long skirts and high heels crossing the yellow circles cast by the street lamps and going up the steep steps. Lemonade vendors beside white iceboxes with bell-shaped glass covers; ice-cream vendors beside two-wheeled carts with shiny tin lids in the shape of a snail's shell and, on the top, a partitioned wooden box for the wafer cones; fruit-juice sellers with bottles lying flat on ice in the baskets of their bicycle carriers; bootblacks with little boxes and metal footrests between their legs. Street cleaners, each with a brush, a spade, and a tall cylindrical bin on wheels. The policeman on the corner, in his white peaked cap and long protective gloves of white canvas, stiffly and precisely indicating left, right, go, stop. Schoolchildren with their satchels plodding home, their dreamy eyes raised to the sky. A conversation at the corner: someone's wife and someone's husband, casting anxious looks around, afraid of being seen. Flower girls, baskets on their arms, making the rounds of the sidewalk cafés. Children selling almonds in little white bags. Flag-waving crowds on their way back from a soccer match, in lines of six or eight abreast, their open-necked shirts flapping, their faces dusty and covered with sweat. Draftees on their way to the station, arms around each other's waists, free hands holding half-empty green bottles, singing off-key in hoarse voices. A wedding in front of the Town Hall: cars, the bride in her white dress and veil, the sharp cries of the children as they run after the tossed coins rolling away. Around three or four in the afternoon, linked by an invisible thread, men and women walk toward the cemetery, the space between them diminishing as they approach their destination. Stray dogs, trotting along, sniffing the air, keeping well away from humans. Pigeons on the church porch and along the main square. The Austro-Hungarian colonel Kranjčević, retired these forty years, taking from the pocket of his heavy overcoat a little bag of bread crumbs, tossing the crumbs onto the snow. Above him, a leaden sky.

Chapter 14

Only Robert Kroner appreciated the aura of devotion that shone from Milinko, and it was questionable whether even his appreciation was sincere. It may have been the result only of the general decline of values around him. His wife interpreted the signs of the young man's respect in terms of his humble origins and modest circumstances. Here she forgot her own hatred, fed by poverty, for the well-to-do and the established, a hatred that had included the Kroners while they were her masters.

Reza Kroner had only the vaguest notion of events outside her own home, especially developments of international importance, and failed to see that the social status she had achieved through her marriage was inexorably disintegrating, that the name Kroner was no longer a guarantee of esteem, of prestige, and that the days of the family's material security and even physical safety were numbered. Since the birth of her son, who was to remain to the very end the apple of her eye, she saw those around her in terms of him and him alone. When Milinko first made his appearance at the house behind the Baptist church, there was nothing, in her eyes, that posed a threat to Gerhard's future. Gerhard had finished school a year before the war and that autumn had enrolled in the Technical Institute in Belgrade. Even though his studies were interrupted the following April as a result of the outbreak of war, she was not worried, for as soon as the Institute closed its doors, her son came home again, back under her protection. That protection meant little for his career, since during the Occupation he was prevented from continuing his studies, but her love, pleased at the proximity of its object, had no difficulty in postponing the righting of this injustice to an indefinite future. The more so since her son himself did not seem particularly disturbed by it.

Gerhard had no liking for school, for work, for anything that achieved its goal through long-term effort. He accepted almost with relief this change, though for him it was a reversal, and he looked with mocking eyes at the spectacle of humiliating falls and arrogant promotions, sucking noisily through his teeth whenever he spoke of them. Measures that affected him directly, such as the summons to forced labor for all those in his age group, he simply ignored. "If anyone asks, I'm still in Belgrade," he told his father, who tried to warn him, the day the notices were posted, of the dangers of failing to report. "But what if they see that you are here?" his father argued. "Tell them I just arrived and I'll report tomorrow." But that tomorrow never came, and while other young Jews pulled on their old clothes at the crack of dawn and hurried off, shivering, to the mustering points—to cart bricks, accompanied by blows and curses, all day long at the airport and to fill in craters made by German bombs—Gerhard stayed in bed, or loitered around the courtyard, or sat in the kitchen eating fruit from the basket the maid brought from the market, or vanished into the cellar with the neighbor's wife, or read Hungarian and German detective novels, with which the newspaper kiosks were flooded. Kroner thought this behavior provocative; everyone could see Gerhard, including Count Armanyi, the store official, who often stood at the office window watching. But Reza would not agree to Gerhard's remaining hidden in the house; the lack of sun and fresh air could harm his health. As for the regulations, announcements, and the threats they implied, she decided quite simply that they did not concern her son. She had agreed to let him accept the Jewish faith because at that time she believed that all Jews were wealthy, but now that the newspapers and the radio were accusing the Jews of being responsible for the war and the high prices, calling on Christians everywhere to help rid the land of them, she ceased considering him a Jew. Her own hatred of the Jews returned, especially after Sep's visit, which reminded her of her past servitude to that race, a race alien to both of them, and had she been asked to give her opinion, she would certainly have approved of their extermination. And her son would have, too.

The more brutally the Jews were persecuted and the greater the humiliations they suffered, the more bitterly Gerhard despised them. It was as if he had made all the Christian prejudices his own, while still belonging to the Jewish faith. He would leer mockingly when a dusty column of civilians passed in the street, driven on by two soldiers, forced sometimes to march at double time and sing some nationalist Hungarian song, often anti-Semitic. He would imitate their unmilitary stride, their cowed stance, would pout to make his lips full, like theirs, and flare his nostrils to enlarge his nose. As few dared, particularly now that taunting carried the threat of real danger, of the deprivation of all one's rights, he would say loudly, "Those Yids" or "Is he a Yid?" or "Are you a Yid?" to some unsuspecting fellow Jew, and the only reason he was not answered by a blow was that the butts of his mocking tongue were all too wretched, too frightened. It was this resignation that exasperated him.

He took a curious pleasure in studying the caricatures of Jews that appeared more and more frequently in the newspapers; the caricatures presented them as potbellied, hairy, thick-lipped, and having fleshy hooked noses, features that conjured up the vices of their race: greed and cunning. He could not stand the jokes that at that time the Jews were directing against themselves, for he was astute enough to understand that the purpose of that humor was to blunt the pain of reality. If anyone told him the kind of joke in which a Jew, in a situation of no escape, outwitted his enemy or found consolation in irony, Gerhard, instead of laughing, would say, in deadly earnest, "Yes, and then they grabbed hold of your Cohen and hung him on the nearest tree." And only then would he bare his regular, white teeth: "Ha-ha."

Gerhard became so unpleasant that Jewish circles in Novi Sad spoke of him in indignant whispers. Some thought him mad; others said that he had joined the Gestapo, making good use of his half-German origin, and had been given the special job of demoralizing the Jews. They began to regard even Gerhard's father with suspicion. Kroner's relatively favorable position in the requisitioned store and his friendly footing with Count

Armanyi suggested an accommodation with the Germans. And when it became known that Sep Lehnart was staying in the house, and when a bunch of old ladies on an afternoon visit to Grandmother Kroner came upon the young SS officer in the gateway, spick-and-span and about to go off into town, the disgust became total. Only the attempt on Sep's life, had it been made, could have dispelled this suspicion. But Gerhard's plans came to nought, and his associates, Franja Schlesinger and the Karaulić brothers, under the pressure of rumor and the disappointment of their failure, began to avoid him. This suited him well, because he did not have much confidence in them, particularly when their plan of escape by crossing over into Srem did not materialize. Now, left alone with his project, he could take action without having to worry about anyone else.

Like his uncle, he often went for long walks, but not in the center of town; instinctively, his wanderings took him to the remote streets on the outskirts. Those back streets, overgrown with grass and lined with squat, low houses, almost entirely inhabited by Serbian agricultural workers and small tradesmen, were scenes of the greatest cruelty when the Hungarian troops arrived. The soldiers, carrying out their raids, were not in the least restrained by the sight of such modest means, such neglect. There, among the houses with damp walls, faded flowers in the windows, the image of the killings still hovered, muted. The people who in the evenings came out to talk at their gates still pointed to the lampposts from which their neighbors had been hanged, and to the darkened windows of the homes from which a friend had been led away. For these people, there was no topic of conversation more lively. Gerhard enjoyed listening.

He knew almost no one there, but was helped by Milinko, who lived in the area and who, unaware that he was doing him a service, was flattered by the attentions of Vera's older brother. Milinko introduced him to his friends, his neighbors, and took him to the "promenade," the longest tree-shaded street in the neighborhood, where the young people, boycotting their haunt in the middle of town as a form of silent protest, now congregated. Gerhard's coarse ways were liked here; they went with the atmosphere.

After the tremendous shock caused by the senseless, wholesale killing, the young people, previously pacifists, slipped into the opposite extreme. The crimes committed against them and their like freed them from responsibility. Forgetting the ghastly gaping mouths of the people who had been hanged, they began to speak of them as simple fools who had not taken seriously enough the frenzied armored troops. It was as if this were no more than a soccer match, the first half of which had passed in blows and a confused passivity. But now that half time had arrived, they were preparing for a counterattack, rapidly hardening themselves to use the same means by which they had been beaten. Everyone now talked of rifles and revolvers, even couples holding each other close in doorways. So it was not difficult for the Communists who had managed to escape the first wave of arrests to find new recruits.

With the instinct of animal trainers, the Communists immediately chose Gerhard, because of his loud mouth, his arrogance, and his self-castigating outbursts against Jewish weakness, as the best of the lot and enlisted him in a shock group. Every day he walked a dozen kilometers, always taking a different route, to a small wood between Novi Sad and Kać, and there, with a whistle as a signal, met with three other comrades and a reserve lieutenant who taught them to fire a revolver and throw grenades, weapons that despite the regulations he had held onto. To avoid being discovered and to save ammunition, it was usually an empty revolver that they aimed and fired, and rocks instead of a bomb that they threw at a target. But Gerhard imagined, with every click of the hammer and every thud of a rock against a tree trunk, a mutilated body sprawled at his feet. His participation in the shock group filled an enormous void, and he stopped his insulting, his mocking. He became serious, precise, almost good-humored. He had no further use for Milinko, because now he knew the people in this neighborhood better than Milinko did, but he did not abandon them. Rather, he tried to convince him, in a few heart-to-heart chats, that he ought to dedicate himself to the destruction of the invader. But Milinko was too much an individualist to become part of a collective aim and will. His thoughts, spellbound by the quest for knowledge, kept him high above the ground he walked on, and his association with the elder Kroner and, through him, with the spiritual riches of Germany, dissipated any wish for vengeance. Milinko made excuses to Gerhard, who in turn shrugged him off. Also, while Gerhard spent more and more time away from the house because of his revolutionary activities, Milinko, as Vera's official boyfriend, spent much of his time there. Which was not to the liking of Vera herself.

Vera had had no fondness for her home, and when the steamroller of war passed over it, turning it into a house of people deprived of all rights, her feelings were given external justification. Now it was a trap for her. Sometimes she tiptoed from room to room, from windows facing the street to windows facing the courtyard. The building in the back, the storeroom, was a barrier to her possible retreat, and the windows on the street side were breaches in the defending wall. Sometimes she listened to people's voices—voices ordering merchandise, giving directions to the kitchen, greeting a guest—and they sounded to her like a strange ghostly jumble, confused echoes from another world. She asked herself what she was doing there and what bound her to the house. There were family ties, of course, ties, by her birth, to a father, a mother, a grandmother, and a brother. Yet when she searched their faces—she felt a need to look at them closely—she decided that her connection to them was a matter of chance, and harmful besides. Each one of them had his or her own idea of life, which was either different or else totally contrary to Vera's. Her mother, for example, considered life to mean serving Gerhard, which Vera thought was altogether lacking in taste, while Gerhard dreamed only of rebellion, of deeds that were clearly doomed to fail and dangerous for the whole family. When she learned from Milinko that Gerhard was consorting with the hotheads on the outskirts of town, she tried to explain to him where this would lead, but he, condescending to her as always, laughed: "You, young lady, take care of your own nice round little bottom and keep quiet."

But why should she keep quiet when it was her life that was being put at risk? In order to die quietly with the rest of the family? She had no stomach at all for such a family end, yet the house, remaining in the house, forced her toward death. Would leaving it bring salvation? But where to go, and with whom? She would not be able to escape by herself, not with this inexperienced, newly matured body of hers, so sensitive and vulnerable; she could see that clearly. With Milinko? But Milinko, coming to the house to see her, only stared wide-eyed at her father in the semidarkness of his room, and at his books, as if they contained clues to salvation, as if they could rescue one from being beaten, cursed, spat upon, killed. Several times she confided in him, told him of her terror, but in response received only moonstruck assurances of the inevitability of the victory of reason over the temporary forces of darkness, and in this she had no difficulty recognizing the self-absorbed delusions of the ineffectual father of the family, Robert Kroner. So she shut herself off from Milinko into a malicious silence, a silence broken only by a still more malicious, almost mocking encouragement, through which she pretended to be his pupil, the pupil's pupil, and watched him swell with pride as a result of the deception. She began to think that everyone was pretending, boasting of a power they did not have, while those who had the power did not talk but simply made use of it.

When her mother's brother, Sep, showed up unexpectedly at the house—she could just barely remember him as a boy from her rare childhood visits to Grandmother Lehnart's village—he was serious, dry, unresponsive, with a revolver at his side, the symbol of his power over life and death. For a while she hoped (as she had hoped about many others) that perhaps *he* could save her. She tried to approach him, but he sought only Gerhard's company; he even avoided her, for he was troubled by her youthful, sensual beauty, the alluring softness of her hips, the whiteness of her skin, her thick red hair, all of which, along with the knowledge that she was half-Jewish, even though his niece, aroused in him a secret lust.

Once, returning home late from his walk and supper, he could not find his key, and from the courtyard knocked on a window, thinking it was the maid's. But it was the window of Vera's room, and stretching out from it in her thin white nightgown with a deep opening between her swelling breasts, she handed him her key. That night he dreamed of a completely different redhead, much bigger than Vera, hovering above him, grazing his lips with huge, warm, milky breasts, but when he awoke, he knew that it was Vera. And Vera, too, dreamed. She dreamed of him as Saint George from a brightly colored picture she had seen in her childhood at Grandmother Lehnart's: on a horse, holding a lance that pierced a green dragon with a thin red darting tongue. Mounted on that horse, they galloped off together, his strong, muscular arm around her waist. Stone echoed beneath her, the Turkish cobblestones of her street behind the Baptist church; sparks flew from the horse's hooves; the wind sang, and it was a German song, in the voice of a male choir, "Der Erlkönig," which she once learned at Fräulein's, "Wer reitet so spät durch Nacht und Wind? Es ist der Vater mit seinem Kind," and she knew that the dragon was behind them, dead and crushed, that they were leaving the town and, with it, all dangers and ties. She saw a new, unknown region splitting open before her eyes, craggy and mountainous, uninhabited and therefore safe. Saint George with the face of Uncle Sep dismounted from the horse and helped her down, placing a firm hand beneath her foot. When she stepped on the ground, he disappeared, and all

120

around her, squatting on the soft grass, half hidden among luxuriant ferns, were a rabbit, a squirrel, a fox, a hen, a partridge, and a dozen other animals, all tame, whose shapes she recognized but whose names she did not know. Without interpreting her dream, in fact unaware that she was acting under its influence, she decided to tell her father that she wished to leave Novi Sad, to go to a place where she was not known, abroad if possible.

She found, to her surprise, that this was an idea that had been constantly on his mind, an idea that he was grateful for the opportunity to share with someone. He knew a great deal, it turned out, about the attitude of various governments toward the Jews, and of their treatment in countries in which they had already become the object of special measures. In Serbia, where the Germans ruled directly, without an intermediary government, from the very beginning the Jews had been placed outside the protection of the law; all their possessions were confiscated, they were driven from their houses, stripped of rank and profession, of the right to earn a living, used without payment as slaves for the most menial tasks, killed out of hand once they could no longer work. In Croatia, under the Ustaša government, there were no Jews at liberty; they were all in camps, and it was only a matter of time before they were exterminated. The Bačka, belonging to Hungary, which still clung to its bourgeois, even feudal traditions, was at the moment the best possible refuge among all the regions of dismembered Yugoslavia. In Hungary proper, said Kroner, the Jews still lived almost untouched, especially in the two-million-strong jungle of Budapest; the laws and regulations introduced against them had been subverted by the money and resourcefulness of the merchants, industrialists, and an active Jewish intelligentsia that had been absorbed into the public and cultural life of Hungary. To go to Budapest, to move there, would virtually mean returning to the old legal order, with just a few restrictions, but still with opportunities for work and earning a living, and for Vera and Gerhard it would mean a chance to study perhaps, and take part in the activities that were suitable for their age.

But when Vera expressed surprise that no steps had been taken yet for them to move there, her father suddenly became less definite, his lips quivered, his hands retreated into his coat pockets. He spoke of decades of work, his own and his father's before him, of the business, the house, the accumulation of furniture, the goods in the storeroom for which he had not been given a receipt; he reminded her how attached his mother was to Novi Sad and her few remaining acquaintances, without whom she would probably die of grief; he mentioned his wife's familiarity with the town's market, and—showing an obtuseness that disheartened Vera, as if he were not talking to her but to a third person—he mumbled something about her own attachment to the town in which she had been born and grown up. Vera replied sharply that all these reasons counted for nothing against the alternative—physical annihilation—which would make short work of both habits and possessions. The reference to this extreme danger caused Kroner to lose his head altogether; he began to stammer, to breathe heavily. Assertions became exclamations, impotent curses, revealing what lay behind the appearance of reasoned argument: the dispiritedness of old age.

So Vera went back to her original plan of saving

herself by making a break with her family. She told her father reassuringly that she had no intention of forcing anything upon him, but that she simply wanted to leave on her own, mentioning as a possible source of help her uncle Sep, who had, as an SS man, exceptional authority and power, which most probably included the ability to help someone secretly across the border to a country beyond the rule of Germany. What country? Kroner pricked up his ears. Switzerland, she answered, or another neutral country, like Turkey, Sweden; how should she know? Now it was Kroner's turn to be surprised at how well informed she was, because he had thought that she paid no attention to the discussions at the table or the talk on the radio. Pulling himself together, he promised to speak to Sep about it.

On several occasions he attempted to do just that, asking timidly, between his brother-in-law's ominous descriptions of massacres, if it was possible to escape them, to flee, under such close scrutiny, the wrath of the German forces. Many parents, he said, would gladly pay for their child to be exempted from the fate of their people and tribe, particularly if they didn't belong completely to that tribe, his own children being a case in point. But since he did not spell out his proposition, and Sep was not quick-witted enough to understand it in that form, such digressions from their conversation were met with silence, no response, quickly choked off by new episodes of SS heroism and terror. At first it seemed to Kroner that this was a stratagem to lure his fatherly concern to offer a greater and greater sum. By the time he discovered that this suspicion was unfounded and that Sep had simply not understood, it was too late. Sep was about to leave.

Part of Kroner, and he dared not acknowledge this even to himself, was thankful to Sep for keeping his daughter from embarking on such an adventure, to say nothing of the money. But the departure of her savior before that salvation was even brought up was a big disappointment for Vera. Only now did she see how mistaken she was not to have applied to her soldier uncle herself, to have let her father intercede for her when she knew how inadequate he was.

She would act on her own. As soon as she made this decision, she was amazed that she had not been led to it earlier by the personality of her newly designated helper. He had been there all along, constantly before her eyes, and yet she had not seen him. He caught her attention first simply as a man, then as the man who could deliver her from her terrible worries and difficult decisions. As she was mulling these over in her mind, she saw him walking across the courtyard, tall and powerful, full-blooded, with long, smooth brown hair and light, close-set sharp eyes that looked into hers with undisguised admiration. At lunch she heard plenty about him, for by now Kroner associated all the advantages and disadvantages of his business life with that same Miklós Armanyi, the official in charge of his business.

At first Kroner had feared that the foreigner might become his tormentor, for during the requisition of the store the man was cold and stern; he examined all the documents and looked into all the corners, and announced that from then on without his authorization nothing could be initiated, nothing changed. But it soon turned out that this strictness was an expression of inexperience, of fear of being drawn onto thin ice by deception. As soon as it became clear to him that Kroner's only desire was for himself and his family to survive, Count Armanyi abandoned these precautionary measures. He remained distant, but had no hesitation in telling, about himself, what he felt was essential to establish basic human contact. Soon, at the Kroner dinner table, it became known that Count Armanyi was unmarried and a barrister's clerk whom mobilization had thrust into this delicate position. A position he had no reason to complain of, since it brought with it a wage three times what he had previously earned, and a fine apartment in one of the commandeered buildings that had belonged to local civil servants, and the reputation of a government official entrusted with special responsibilities. But he did not seem to be able to make full use of this reputation in Novi Sad, where he felt half-exiled; among its mixed population, he did not know whether to be more suspicious of the noisy and wild Serbs or of his own Hungarians, who had fattened themselves on their neighbors' property and now wallowed in the euphoria of their oriental slovenliness and indifference.

He himself was from Pest, a civil servant's son who had been indoctrinated with the idea that the work and rank of a civil servant should be valued above all else. But here that conviction had been eroded, weakened under the dull pressure of the inefficiency, disorder, and uncertainties of wartime. In high school, Armanyi had learned that the whole nation wept when southern regions of Hungary were annexed by Yugoslavia, but now some of his neighbors told him firmly and openly, for they were Hungarians and not afraid to talk, that under the Yugoslav regime things had been in some ways better, that people had behaved with greater warmth and humanity. Looking at the dusty streets, at the cluttered, small bazaarlike shops, at the movie houses, where people pushed and shoved to reach the unnumbered seats, at the open squares in front of the churches where beggars stood in clusters, grimacing to arouse pity, Armanyi found in the dispossessed owner of the business he now managed, in the thin, dejected, peace-seeking and book-loving Robert Kroner, a spirit of industriousness most resembling his own.

He began to question Kroner about the world of Novi Sad, which he did not understand, and from the answers gathered that Kroner himself understood very little of that world but submitted to it in resignation; this brought them closer together. Did Armanyi feel exiled? Exiled was what Kroner had been here for these twenty-odd years, since the day he allowed himself to be lured back from Vienna to take over his father's store—temporarily, until a buyer was found, he thought, and until he could talk his mother into agreeing to the sale. But the few months he had expected became years; he was sidetracked by marriage and fatherhood. His way back to the centers of wisdom and civilization he had learned to respect in his youth was cut off: in fact, those centers were no longer there when he came to look for them. Would the same thing happen to Armanyi? Armanyi, too, had been transferred to the south for a short time, until the skirmish with the rebellious forces in the Balkans, which German and Hungarian cool-headedness would know how to subdue, was over. But then the war spread to the immeasurably vast fields of Russia, where battles were being waged whose outcome was by no means certain, while here, in the rear, the Bačka, which had been so easily captured, was a long way from submission. People seethed with expectation, and with scorn for the present situation.

That expectation was personified, for Armanyi, by Kroner's children, Gerhard and Vera, whom he could observe all day long from the window in their father's store. These grown-up children lived in idleness, and although he knew that this idleness had been imposed on them by the same state machine that had brought him here to watch them, he could not help but feel that it was part of their character. How could they walk around the courtyard with nothing to do, their hands behind their backs, their faces turned as early as the month of March toward the morning sun as it appeared over the store roof? How could they—with no apparent reason, such as reading a book or having a conversation—wander for hours in that confined space, which would have suffocated him had he not had his duties and his documents to occupy him?

At the end of May, deck chairs appeared on the grass that had come up between the house and the office, and the children sat in them and ate snacks. A few weeks later, Vera brought out a light, gray blanket, spread it on the grass, and, glistening with oil, in a two-piece bathing suit, lay in the sun. Every day, for hours, she lay patiently on the blanket, turning over, from back to front, from front to back, bending alternately her left, then her right knee, to be more comfortable and have every part of her body embraced by the sun. Now and then she would disappear into the house to shower, as one could tell from the droplets on her sunburned skin and the streaks on her bathing suit. Armanyi thought it sacrilege for her to bake her transparently white, smooth skin to a dirty pink and then a bright red. But once it took on a copper hue, it showed off still better the firm and gentle outlines of her young body, making it so alluring as to be almost unreal.

One afternoon, they met at the gate, and though she was fully dressed and wearing stockings and sandals, Armanyi could not resist telling her the impression she had made on him. "You really do not need to lie in the sun all the time." He removed his hat in greeting and held it in his hand. "I was going to speak about this to your esteemed father, but I restrained myself, and I am glad now, because it gives me the opportunity to address myself directly to you."

She expressed surprise. "You think the sun's not good for me?"

"Well, perhaps not good in such large doses," Armanyi replied, embarrassed at having failed to make himself understood. "But I really meant your appearance."

"My appearance? You don't like my appearance?"

Instead of making her blush, it was he who blushed. "On the contrary, your appearance . . . I find your appearance lovely. You're a beautiful girl, and watching you sunbathe every day is for me a privilege I never hoped for, especially here in a store, where in every other respect I am in despair, doing a job for which I am not equipped and for which I have not the slightest inclination. But still, it is a shame, because your white skin compliments your hair so exquisitely."

"You don't think a tan is becoming? It's fashionable, you know."

"Perhaps I am a little old-fashioned. Or old. That's really the trouble."

"How old is old?"

"Thirty-one. Much older than you and very much older than I would like to be now, talking to you."

"Why? That's a fine time of life. . . ."

"Perhaps. But not here. In Budapest it is. In a big, carefree city open to all pleasures and all ages. Have you ever been to Budapest?" Vera admitted she had never been. "Oh, you really should. Surely Mr. Kroner or Mrs. Kroner will take you someday to see our one and only capital."

"There's been talk of it, but no plans. We can't go there without a pass, you know, and one needs a special reason for a pass."

"Oh, if it's only a question of a pass," Armanyi said ardently, pressing his hat to his heart, "perhaps I can help. Besides"—he blushed again, realizing in which direction the conversation was headed—"you could come with me when I return to make my report. Traveling as my assistant, you would need no special authorization. What do you say? Would you like to?"

Vera shrugged hesitantly. "I don't know. . . . Yes, I would. But I would have to talk to my father first."

Armanyi coughed, uncomfortable. "Perhaps your father would not consider my offer entirely correct, at least not now. Perhaps it would be better to say nothing about this for the time being. But you and I, we are agreed, are we not? One day we will take off, escape from this boredom and have a taste of a fuller, more exciting life."

Saying good-bye, they left it there. But they were both a little frightened by this conversation. Armanyi asked himself whether it had not been underhanded of him to urge the daughter of the house, a house in which he represented the civilization of his country, to run away with him, and whether he had not greatly overstepped his authority and courage in promising to break the law. Vera was amazed that she had agreed to go off somewhere with a strange man, alone, without her parents' permission. But thinking it over as she lay in bed that night, she came to the surprising conclusion that she was not at all ashamed. She was sure of herself, convinced that Armanyi was in love with her. Recalling his misty-eyed look, the change of color in his face, the way his hand desperately pressed the soft hat to his chest, she almost laughed out loud. She was proud at having won such a big, strong, mature man, and was excited at the thought that she could, by her looks alone, by her body, which she was in a position to place in his way any time she wished, attach him to her still more strongly. She waited impatiently for the morning and the sun, when she could again show herself, almost naked, to his eyes, and with that thought she fell asleep.

And, indeed, the next day she lay on the blanket, in the sprouting grass as if in an embrace, her smile triumphant. For Armanyi, who feared that he had frightened her with his aggressive approach and that she might tell her parents everything, her reappearance on the grass was a clear sign that he had not made a mistake, that on the contrary his amorous advances had gone a long way to being reciprocated. He began to dream. He saw himself and the girl in a compartment of the Árpád express as it arrived, whistling, in Budapest's eastern railway station; he saw himself with her in a taxi taking them to his bachelor apartment; he saw himself handing her his pajamas from the wardrobe—for some reason he imagined her leaving home in a hurry, neglecting to take anything with her, and therefore lying next to him in bed in that too-large man's shirt, which emphasized the svelteness and vulnerability of her body. Crisply starched, the shirt crackled under his hand as he drew her toward him. The only thing he didn't know was what legal framework would surround that embrace. Would it be achieved with a promise of marriage, or was marriage impossible with a Jewess? Would she consent to become his secret mistress? Would this mean that he would have to resign his post in Kroner's store and make use of his connections and influence to be transferred back to Budapest? Or would their relationship receive the blessing of Vera's parents?

Vera, too, had her dreams. She saw herself on a busy street crowded with people, streetcars, cars, glittering window displays, where she would pass unnoticed, no longer Vera Kroner, daughter of merchant Robert Kroner, but a nameless creature, reduced to her own healthy, supple body, in which she had full confidence. No longer would there be obstacles to her traveling, to her changing towns and places of dwelling, escaping from the closing trap that was the house of her parents. In these images there was little room for Armanyi; he stood at the edge, head bent, hat pressed to his heart, looking at her with misty eyes. But her reason, which also played a part in these fantasies, was prepared to allow him to approach her, to be next to her, even to possess her if he kept his promise and delivered her from the trap. The two of them waited, observing each other through the windows and through the veil of grass as if across the sights of invisible rifles. Days passed.

Sometimes Vera's mother came out into the court-yard to caution her daughter (but absent-mindedly; her thoughts were on her son, who was away all day long) that she would get burned, or sometimes the maid brought out freshly washed fruit in a white dish, or sometimes Grandmother Kroner emerged, stooped and cautious, to heap muttered reproaches on her grand-daughter for exposing herself, a Jewess, to the eyes of Gentiles. Sometimes Gerhard, returning home from his training in firearms, scornfully indifferent to the pres-ence of his sister, wove his way lazily across the yard and, moving gracefully, like a panther, pulled himself up to the top of the fence in one movement and cast a swift glance toward the grass widow's house. She, wait-ing for him there, at that sign would change her dress and come over, to go down with him into the cellar. Milinko, too, came in the evening hours, after a day spent with his books, to chat with Kroner and then with Vera, who by then would be bathed, cool, dressed, ready to listen to him in boredom and to exchange an occa-sional kiss.

On one such evening there was a ring at the door, and when the maid opened it, three policemen burst into the house, ordered everyone to their feet, checked papers, searched the rooms, pulled clothing out of the closets and books off the shelves, including the note-book with the inscription "Poésie," which they leafed through but then tossed aside, because the dates in it were only prewar, and finally took Gerhard away. The reserve officer, arrested several hours earlier, under the very first blows had named him as one of the young men he taught how to fire a gun.

No one ever saw Gerhard again. He left behind him a yawning void, like an amputation, destroying the equilibrium that had been preserved, until then, with such great difficulty. Reza Kroner was stopped from hurling herself on the policemen by her husband, who restrained her physically. She demanded in her frenzy that the whole family immediately go and look for Gerhard, go from prison to prison and, if need be, tear him free with their bare nails. Kroner finally made her understand that her behavior was impossible, that it could even be harmful to Gerhard; he would intervene through a third person, and in a more effective manner, he assured her, without endangering the family. The only person of influence in whom he had any confidence, and the one he saw the next morning, was Count Armanyi. Armanyi was shocked by the news and readily promised to help. He went to see several lawyers of his acquaintance, who, like he, had been sent to work in Novi Sad from their native Hungary, but at posts closer to their profession, as judges and police officials. None, however, dared to intercede for a man arrested by the Gestapo, fearing that they themselves might come under suspicion. So their assistance was limited to information, arrived at second hand and unconfirmed: that the accusations against Gerhard were serious and that his fate depended on his confession and collaboration.

Knowing his son's pigheadedness, Kroner could not bring himself to tell his wife this. He assured her, instead, that Gerhard was alive and in good health, though for the moment his whereabouts were unknown (which was true), since he was being held in secret, which boded well for the outcome of the inquiry. Having taken the burden of this embellishment upon himself,

Kroner desperately tried to think of some way to persuade his son to give in and save himself. Through Armanyi he requested to be allowed to send his son a letter, but permission was denied. He then began to imagine their conversation in a cell, face to face, like their earlier discussions in the evening hours, when they listened to the radio, the radio for which now, alone, Kroner had neither the inclination nor the patience. But with the dank, solitary cell and barred windows as a setting, and with the sight of the bloodstained prisoner, his son's viewpoint always came out on top. Gerhard had been right, Kroner told himself in those one-sided conversations based on words spoken long ago. But now, in the new, grim light of prison, and of the suffering and misery he pictured, it was too late to admit this. In a cowardly way he was almost relieved that he had no access to his son. He continued every day begging Armanyi for help. Armanyi sometimes tried to do something, and sometimes only said that he had tried. Kroner compounded Armanyi's lie with his own, passing it on to his wife and daughter, and in time a dense and elaborate web of unreality was spun around the detainee.

Yet another person became entangled in this web, lured into it by Reza Kroner, who, not trusting the assurances of her husband, set about seeking help for her son in the quarter where she felt the most confidence: among her compatriots. Carrying a basket with food and clean clothing, she went to the German barracks, entered into conversation with the soldiers on guard, asked them to call the duty officer, and laid before the latter her petition. On one such occasion she came upon an

NCO of the Field Police, Hermann Arbeitsam, a forty-year-old from Mainz, who took pity on her and promised to try to find out where her son was. He, too, was unsuccessful (his rank not high enough), but their acquaintance, deepened by frequent meetings in the park near the barracks, by the woman's pleadings and the NCO's clumsy comfortings, grew into a friendship, and the friendship, for Arbeitsam, who had never married, into a true, late-life passion.

He would come and stand in front of the Kroner house on the pretext that he had new information, and Reza would run out and talk at great length, wiping away her tears and tolerating his friendly pats on the back and arms. Their meetings did not go unnoticed by the maid and later by Vera, whose own plans had become enmeshed in the activity following Gerhard's arrest, because the savior she had latched onto had now to be used for the purpose of saving her brother's life. But that savior was mortally afraid of being involved with a family that had brought down on itself the clanking of chains and the shadow of the gallows. He no longer came out to see Vera; he avoided her on the pretext of heavy new responsibilities. But Vera understood that he had cold feet and that the possibility of escaping with him was gone. She gave up entirely, fell back into the misfortune and shame of her home, tiptoeing around, listening for the front door, hoping for the arrival of a messenger, or even Gerhard, safe and sound, as they all did, but believing it less and less.

When the news came that he was dead, "killed attempting to escape," as the official communication was worded, she put on black, as did all the family, and wept with them, and tried to comfort them with her presence and gentleness, as she herself was comforted—but knowing, all the while, in the depths of her being, that she had been diverted from her own path, pushed against her will into that bloody and dark gutter that only she had clearly foreseen. Now she was slipping deeper into it, with the others, to destruction. She told Milinko, who came to express his condolences, that she could no longer see him, and the young man went away, agreeing that it would be sacrilege to continue with their courtship. So, too, the conversations about books in Kroner's study came to an end. The books the policemen had scattered during their search were put back on the shelves, and no one took them down again. What had happened during those last few months refuted them entirely, and they became what they were when not opened and interpreted with trust: objects of paper. With their fine bindings and titles, they looked out blankly at the people who still moved beneath them, who soon would be, under that blank gaze, taken away, torn from their resting place, and turned upside down, just as the books had been, but permanently.

Chapter 15

Natural deaths and violent deaths. Sarah Kroner, née Davidson, choking in an Auschwitz gas chamber disguised as a bathhouse. Stumbling, without Vera's arm to lean on, surrounded by shouts whose sense she cannot understand, her fingers too feeble to unbutton the front of her dress, the dress torn off her by someone else's hand, then her underclothes, down to her wrinkled skin. Her shame, her cry for protection, for her son, who was left behind somewhere, for Vera, who did not come with her, her prayers, no more than a meaningless mumbling, for she has nothing more to hold on to, nothing in the world but a chunk of soap pushed into her hand to fool her. She can see the faces around her turning green, eyes bulging; her own chest is racked by coughing, her mouth gasps for fresh air, but there is none.

In the Gestapo cellar, the shattering of Gerhard's skull under the blow of a wooden truncheon wielded by guard János Korong. "I didn't talk! Or did I?" The doubt echoes in his damaged brain. His gaping mouth turns toward his murderer's hand, his white, blood-stained teeth showing in a snarl at the thought that they may have let slip out names he can no longer remember but which he knows must be concealed by the silence of death.

Fräulein's struggle against her fever in Boranović's clinic. Her father's lame left leg, his limp, the movement with which he would drag his body out of immobility, out of deadness, into the green of the garden, the black silhouette of that leg, toward which she strains her every pulse, as if toward a high safe ledge, above the flames that are consuming her. Her arms have not the strength to raise themselves to touch that silhouette, that saving solidity that is moving away from her, limping, growing smaller, the uneven sound of its steps moving upward, becoming softer.

Robert Kroner lying on his black winter overcoat in the transit camp, his choking "No!" to Vera's imploring cries, that "No!" to a continuation of the journey, a continuation of the suffering, a continuation of responsibility, sinking into irresponsibility, eyes shut tight, ears refusing to hear, thoughts refusing to understand that he is letting them go, leaving them, being left behind by them, abandoned to the shouts, the blows, the rifle bullets that now, suddenly, hit him at close range, tearing open his chest, setting him free, at last setting him free.

Nemanja Lazukić's contempt for the roll call, for the lumbering prisoners tied to him, because he doesn't belong with them, hates them, would like to push them away, spurn the faces and names that intrude on his senses, the ropes that cut into his flesh, because the prisoners are dragged along by their own weight, their clumsiness, their jerking movements, their joints red and swollen, the stench from their sweating bodies. His attempts to catch the eye of one of the guards, whose faces, in the cold gray dawn, show neither interest nor pity. His shout of "Don't, brothers!," which is a lie, sour in his mouth, another lie among all the lies, lies from the beginning to this moment when truth is nothing more than contempt, the wish for exceptional treatment of which there is none, the revulsion that the shooting puts an end to, after which he is thrown onto a heap, on top of others, under others.

The amazement of Klara Lazukić at the rifles pointed at her in the same way, two years earlier, her dazed departure from her home (Have I dressed warmly enough? Did I lock the house?), her near-sighted eyes peering at the hail of killing on the other side of the street, which she can't understand, can't believe, her shudder at the detonations behind her, her scream, "Maybe they won't! I'm not guilty! I've got children!" Her old-maidish lips twisted indignantly, her eyes raised, askew, toward the blank wintry sky.

The quiet, somnolent last breath of Tereza Arbeit-sam, Kroner's widow, née Lehnart, in the hospital in Stuttgart, whiteness all around. Exhausted by her long illness, dimly aware of a face, the face of a nun framed by a stiff white headdress, the features as severe as a man's but the skin young and pink, a short, straight nose, red lips, that dear face to which she can no longer put a name or define its relationship to herself, and which swims away in the whiteness, in the cold mist.

Rastko Lazukić, crouched behind the boxes in a cart going at a full gallop, regretting that he didn't jump off when the firing began, hesitating whether to jump now, but the shaking is cut short by a blow to the back, which jerks him upright, like the horse rearing in front of him, its huge arched back and head high as he falls over the sharp edge of something. "Is that my suitcase?" he wonders, feeling his strength, his consciousness ebb away, pouring warm and sticky from his mouth.

Sep Lehnart moaning for water in the cellar beneath the ruins of the former kolkhoz building in the village of Starukho, deafened by the noise of guns and mortars, which have destroyed everything, burying him among groaning wounded men in a semidarkness filled with dust. He sees their terrified faces, hears their pleas for water, of which there has been none for days and nights, ever since his belly was torn open down there where his moist, numbed hands are holding it together, where it seeps out, where he would place his cracked mouth if he could move, if his innards didn't split apart at the very thought of moving. The wound pleads in vain for moisture, moisture to replace that flowing out, flowing out, which floods everything, the whine of the bombs, the dust and smoke, the cries that grow fainter, unreal.

Vera Kroner lying in the room overlooking the courtyard, the room that was once her grandmother's, covered to her armpits with three blankets, for she has heard that the body gradually goes cold. She swallowed the pills from the palm of her hand and washed them down with wine from a big round glass, purchased the day before for that very purpose. Her head falls back with relief, her eyes close. She opens them again to see once more: the table and chair, the empty shelf, the stand with the empty flowerpot—not to bid them farewell, but to make sure that she is leaving nothing important. She is leaving herself, she thinks. But what that self is she cannot define. Noises from the street, a car, the wind whistling among the scattered old crates and rusty hoops in the courtyard. There is nothing else. She feels sick, it must be the medicine. She hopes it won't get worse, it was only medicine, even though an overdose. Perhaps, instead, she should have lain down in a full tub and opened her veins, or have done that as soon as she swallowed the pills, as she first intended. It is probably too late for that now. Nausea shakes her body; she wants to vomit but knows she must not. With a great effort of will she stills the spasms in her stomach, forcing down the urge to vomit with all her pent-up fear, as with a fist, just once more, once more, she'll do it as many times as is necessary, it's like giving birth, but the opposite, she grits her teeth, this is the only way she can do it, and her child will be born.

Sredoje Lazukić, staggering, leaning on the boatman Steva Milovančev's firm young shoulder, leaving the tavern Stolac, next to the rowing club, his stomach swollen from too much brandy because he drank all the pension money he was just given. Flashes of light dance before his eyes, as has happened to him before, for a long time now, every evening, even when he doesn't drink. "I can't see," he mutters to Milovančev, who is dragging him on, but now his legs no longer answer to his will, they give way, he slips, and now lies on the grass of the embankment, with Steva shaking him and shouting. The flashes of light dance, violet and yellow, the ground is hurting him, there must be a sharp rock beneath him, if only he could move a little, to the left, but how can he tell Milovančev that when his tongue is stiff, his forehead, chest, and stomach are numb. The pressure of the rock in his side becomes unbearable, he pulls his arm out of its numbness and shoves it beneath him, but his fingers can feel nothing there but grass, the pain of the rock is inside him, it spreads through his chest, gripping him like an iron fist. Sredoje writhes. "Is it a rock?" he wonders and loses consciousness.

Around the bed of Milinko Božić, an unusually sharp current of air. Accustomed to sameness, to repetition, he senses danger, something above him, with his sharpened senses he can feel its size, a light breath on his face, male, not female, someone new, he concludes. The blanket is pulled back from his belly, fingers fall on his right thigh, pressing into his flesh, kneading it, looking for a spot to plunge the needle. Something is injected into him, although these last few days he has had no symptom of illness. Drowsiness. He is being anesthetized, then. Are they going to pull a tooth, he still has two or three, what else could it be? A new wound that opened up without his feeling it? The drowsiness enfolds him like feathers. How pleasant, he thinks, if they had kept me on that, I wouldn't have been trying to understand, but perhaps I would have anyway; a man is a man because he tries to understand, and now I understand almost nothing, and in a moment I'll understand nothing at all.

Chapter 16

Vera's regrets that she missed the chance to get away from Novi Sad were fed by more than the memories of her suffering in the concentration camp. That suffering, once over, was a part of her life, a part of herself, and she could not now imagine that it had never happened. It was her destiny, she decided, to return from the camp to her own town, her own because she had failed, before, to break free of it. Yet she experienced a warmth, a closeness, upon returning, both times, like a troubled attraction of gravity to a planet wreathed in vapors or a sun in mist, drawing her to it, or, rather, treacherously causing her to merge with it. Treacherously on both occasions, for by returning she found that she had gone away from it further than she could ever have imagined. After requesting transportation home from the liberated camp—from its cracked ground covered with bodies, from its torn-down fences from whose posts the corpses of the camp guards were still swinging—it was not home at which she arrived, though it was Novi Sad.

The official truck sent to meet the train from the camp deposited her in the street behind the Baptist church, but on the door of the house was the sign of a government office, a Supply Department, in the rooms a host of desks, and on the desks, chairs, with their legs up, because it was after hours. In what had once been her grandmother's wing of the house, the concierge came out in answer to her knock, a fat, pink woman, barefoot; she was waiting for her husband, a Hungarian, to come back from the front. Standing in the doorway on one leg, rubbing it with her other foot, she informed Vera indifferently that the last member of the Kroner family, the mother, had left with the Germans in the autumn.

Carrying her bundle tied to a long string over her shoulder, Vera could have turned around and left. But her weariness made her climb the steps past the woman, pushing her aside like a curtain, walk through the rooms, set down her bundle in the biggest, which overlooked the street and was virtually empty, and tell the Supply Department secretary, a middle-aged patriot in riding breeches and boots, who ran upstairs to challenge the intruder, that no one was ever going to drive her out from under her own roof again.

Now she was on her own ground. But where was her own ground? In Novi Sad, a low-lying plain in the middle of a swamp, by-passed by history, and to which the Germans, with their cruelty, their barked commands, their precision, uniformity in behavior and appearance, arrests, internment behind barbed wire, and even murder, had brought a terrible unity, turning the whole of Europe into one vast concentration camp that reeked with the fear of death. Of this unity, after its dissolution, there remained only the tatters of hatred. There remained the fat concierge, her hair unkempt and colorless, usually wearing slippers, always terrified, stranded as on a sandbank by her marriage to the door-man, a member of the "barbed crosses" from some god-forsaken village, to which, after a few days of Vera's uncomfortable proximity, she would return, in a hired cart, not daring even to take with her the few posses-sions that were strewn around the big room. And the secretary, sallow, balding, a survivor in the maelstrom of the Occupation only because it was over before he was completely choked by it—by forced labor (twice); by hunger, his own, his wife's, and his two children's; by his dismissal from a job in the brewery after it had been taken over and placed under the management of a Hungarian official; by the wounds sustained in the bombing of the textile factory where he had found tem-porary work; by the denunciations he did not make, for he had been too insignificant for denunciations to be demanded of him.

Living in close quarters with these two, Vera felt almost disappointed: Was *this* why they had won the war? Her gaunt body seemed hollow, a thing that strained to be filled: she had to obtain food and other necessities. As she made a round of the neighbors, she came upon Gerhard's former mistress, next door. The woman was frying potatoes in the kitchen, which opened onto the courtyard—it was the month of July, in 1945. At first she didn't recognize the visitor in her worn-out boots, yellow canvas skirt, and padded Russian tunic, but then she clapped her hands and gasped, as if a large bird had descended on her table. Vera could tell that her joy was not pretended. The woman called her husband from the room where he was reading a newspaper, and shared the surprise with him and then their little girl. The hus-band offered Vera a chair, and nodding now and then listened to the story of the Kroners' exile, which carefully left out her mother's betrayal of her religion and her marriage. It was here that Vera ate her first free meal.

Free? It seemed to her that she had the right to knock on any door and demand anything, simply by invoking her whole long year of deprivation. She felt a need to tell everyone of her terrible suffering, but the words that had not yet been said weighed her down with their truthfulness, and with their nontruthfulness, too, for some things remained stuck inside her, silent, like resin. Suddenly exhausted, sweating from the food, to which she was not accustomed, her stomach in a turmoil, she had to hurry home. There she collapsed on the floor and wept. The words she had spoken and not spoken choked her. The silence and nodding heads choked her. The cry she held back choked her: "And you, what did you do all that time?" She doubled up, a smell of dust reached her through the cracks in the floor, her stomach heaved, and she went into the kitchen to vomit. She looked sadly at the pile of half-digested food.

Tears came to her eyes as she realized how disgusting it all was, how unnatural. She would look for someone in authority, she thought, to report her neighbor. He should not be allowed, without anyone knowing, to hang around, in the shelter of his room, on top of his plump, red-faced wife, whom her brother, Gerhard, used to take to the cellar any time he wanted. She should go out into the street, to the main square, and shout to everyone all that she knew and they didn't know. She was about to spring to her feet. But she hadn't the right, because she couldn't tell everything. Instead, she cleaned up the vomit and dragged herself back to the big room. She sat in a chair, trembling. Where was she? Alone among empty people, strangers. They gave her food to eat and listened to her story, nodding, they walked in the courtyard of her house, from which her family had been removed, and none of them wanted to know what she knew.

Suddenly she felt that in leaving the camp she had left the one place where she was understood, where she was surrounded by real people. The wasteland covered with corpses rose before her, the twisted bodies of the camp guards hanging from fence posts. She almost felt sorry for them, wanted to kneel at their feet, help them down from the ropes, cry out: "Here I am. Beat me." Yes, she was still very much there, in that arena of oppression. She unbuttoned her blouse and read the black tattoo. Yes, that was she. Better to have stayed there, dead, like Magda and Lenzi, on her bed, riddled by the last of Handke's bullets, in the silent room of love adorned with red lights. She craved death as one might crave sleep. The nausea receded, the chair she sat in suddenly felt comfortable, and she dozed off.

Hunger roused her again. She must eat. She looked into the room adjoining; the concierge must be in the courtyard, or else had run off to see a friend, to recount the misfortune that had befallen her with the return of the house-owner's daughter, whom she had long since written off. "No, you won't! You won't!" she said aloud. She went into the larder, cut herself a piece of bread, tore off some sausage with her teeth, her eyes searching among the jars for something pickled to season it with. There was nothing. She heard a door bang and stiffened with fright. What was she doing? She had a right to all this; it was not stealing. With her teeth she straightened off the sausage where she had bitten it; the bread wouldn't be noticed. She walked back into her room, chewing slowly and with enjoyment.

Life. She must look out for herself. She returned to the kitchen and carefully washed herself, then dressed, meticulously smoothing out every crease. She walked into town. It was early evening. A man in rubber boots with a cap on his head was riding a bicycle with a bucket balanced carefully on the handlebars. Slops! It came back to her: peacetime. She was pleased with herself for being so clever, so composed. She smiled. She must buy a decent dress, shoes, she must get some money. She walked along streets that were the same as they had been a year earlier, but clear of Germans, of danger. There was occasional traffic. She reached a small square; Veličković's stationery shop was there, where she had often bought notebooks, pencils. She went in; the bell above the door tinkled as it always did. The shop was dark, no customers. Behind the counter stood Mr. Veličković, short, thickset, a graying toothbrush of a mustache beneath his flat nose. Vera remembered her father once telling her mother that the stationer didn't like being alone in the shop; he couldn't leave to relieve himself and as a result had bladder trouble.

"I am Vera Kroner," she said, coming to a stop in the middle of the shop, breathless from just those few words. "I don't know whether you remember me."

Veličković opened his small eyes wide; his mouth became rounded. "Oh, it's you, Miss. You haven't been around for a long time." And he stretched out both his short, fleshy hands across the counter toward her.

"I was in a camp," she told him, and tears came to

her eyes, because he seemed genuinely grieved. "I wanted to ask if you could lend me a little money."

"Of course," Veličković said quickly, and leaned over the counter to pat her on the shoulder. "The important thing is, you've come back alive." He looked around him. "If only I had someone to look after the shop, I'd take you home so we could have a talk." Vera wondered if he still had bladder trouble. "And your family?" he asked.

"I'm the only one who came back," said Vera, again making no mention of her mother. They stood silent for a moment. Then she stuffed the money into the pocket of her tunic and left.

In the next few days she made the rounds of the local offices, received certificates, ration cards. The Confiscated Goods Office she found in an unused mill; an NCO with a mustache showed her into a vast, cold room piled to the ceiling with wardrobes, beds, shelves, tables, and chairs. Spreading wide his arms, he said, "Take your pick, Comrade." She took her time searching for pieces that would suit her, secretly hoping to come across something of her own. For a moment she thought she recognized a settee from the maid's room, and she and the NCO clambered up to get it out from under other things. But the flowers on it were different. She took it all the same. She had to arrange for the carrying of the furniture herself, so she ran to the market and hired a porter; he loaded the pieces onto his handcart, and they started down the street. She felt ashamed; everyone was watching her, or so it seemed, but at the same time she had a feeling of triumph, that she had taken something, preserved it. She hurried needlessly, and several times had to wait for the porter to catch up with her. She unloaded the furniture in both rooms—the concierge had moved out the night before—and fell on the settee, exhausted. For days she did nothing. The furniture stood in disarray, and in the evenings she crawled under a bare quilt thrown over the settee. What were those possessions to her?

Yet hunger and discomfort drove her to continue with her petitioning. One office would give information out about another where she could obtain something she still needed. Finally she arrived at the Jewish Society, next door to the synagogue. She went in hesitantly, her heart beating fast, half expecting to find it ravaged, the floors spattered with blood. But when she opened the door, she saw two tidy, sparsely furnished offices; the front one was unoccupied, but in the one in back a dark, heavy-boned, big-nosed woman sat knitting behind a desk. She looked at Vera over her glasses, laid aside her knitting, picked up a pencil, and pulled a thin note pad toward her. She took down Vera's name and surname, address, inquired about her family. Vera told about her brother, her father, her grandmother, then stopped, undecided. The woman, as if guessing the reason for her hesitation, arched her neck and asked, "And your mother?" Vera explained that her mother was German and had not been deported, that she had gone to live somewhere else while Vera was in the camp. The woman sniffed doubtfully, went into the front office, opened the window, and shouted into the synagogue courtyard: "Deskauer! Deskauer!" or some such name. She shut the window again, and soon thereafter an elderly, round-bellied man appeared at the door. The two whispered, the man nodded from time to time, casting furtive morose looks at Vera, then the woman came back and placed two hundred dinars on the desk in exchange for Vera's signature. "We can't give you more," she said, putting aside the note pad. "We have a lot of people who are old and ill." Then reluctantly she added: "You can come back again on the first of the month." Vera went out past the old man, and in the corridor she ran into little wizened Mitzi, a Post Office employee whom she had known casually. Now Mitzi embraced her, pulled her head down onto her thin shoulder, and exclaimed in a hoarse voice, "Poor thing! Poor thing!" She asked Vera to wait, she had only to pick up her monthly allowance. Then they went off together, arm in arm, Mitzi full of questions about what had become of the Kroner family, and Vera replying reluctantly.

But Vera agreed to drop in at Mitzi's on the way home, and was surprised at the comfort of her room, which was on the second floor of an old mansion. There were armchairs, a couch covered by a blanket, a radio, stands with fresh flowers, even several framed embroideries. Vera asked how she had managed to keep them. But they were not hers, Mitzi explained, she had got them from the Confiscated Goods Office. Hadn't Vera been there yet? Who knows who they once belonged to—a Jew, or a German who had fled; it didn't matter. She wanted to make her little nook as cozy as possible in the present circumstances. She offered Vera tea, and soon the sound of water boiling came from the kitchen, cups appeared in whriling clouds of steam and on dainty porcelain saucers, and there were cakes, and even napkins, which Mitzi got from the Post Office, for she was already working. She had cut the thin office paper in squares and folded them diagonally. Her lively, volatile, tireless patter made Vera sleepy.

"Poor thing," she repeated, sipping tea and offering Vera cakes. "Now you're alone, and I know it's hard. But here we are, God wanted us to meet, and now we'll get together often, won't we? The few of us who survived that horror must be one big family, we must help one another." She enumerated the camp inmates who had returned—for Vera, they were familiar or not so familiar names, faces from the pages of an album. Many had already found jobs, and Mitzi knew where. Did Vera want to work? Mitzi could get her a job at the Post Office. Vera had finished high school, hadn't she? And they agreed that she should get in touch with Mitzi as soon as she was all settled. But to save time, Mitzi persuaded her there and then to fill out an application on the piece of white paper she pulled from a drawer. Mitzi would present it to the personnel officer the next day.

Vera went home in a fever of excitement, full of new discoveries and new decisions. She would arrange her furniture neatly, as she had seen it done at Mitzi's. But, tired, she stretched out on the settee and fell asleep. The next day, the meeting, her sudden and artificially fostered friendship, seemed faded to her, unreal. Had she dreamed it? She saw Mitzi's face before her, expressive with emotion, and then the faces of those she had mentioned, which swarmed around her, dancing a mad reel that wearied her. The room was silent, with the concierge gone, and the creaking of carts in the street and the cackling of hens in a neighbor's yard could be heard. Sounds of peace, in contrast to that rush of words, which took her back to the madness of killing, pillage, to death instead of the life that was here, warm and sleepy in her body.

Vera spent her days lying on the settee while time passed; she could tell it passed from the bands of light that moved across the floor under the curtained window. She would go out to buy food and cigarettes. She had started smoking on the journey home, and now could find no moderation in the habit, lighting cigarette after cigarette, and the butts piled up on the plates amid the leftover food.

One day, someone knocked at the door, then banged loudly. Mitzi came in, out of breath, her hair tousled, carrying two drooping pink carnations wrapped in thin office paper. She looked in the empty room that gave onto the courtyard, passed into the larger one facing the street, waved her free hand to disperse the smoke in the air, dropped the carnations on the table, went to the window, raised the curtain, and flung it open to the warm early-evening air. "You're letting yourself go, my dear, and that's no good!" she said reproachfully. Not limiting herself to words, she asked for water, a match, lit the iron kitchen range with a slip of wood she found in the pantry, and soon the dirty dishes disappeared into a bowl, from which they were resurrected, smooth and wet, to be laid out in perfect order on the top of a crate, which she had also found somewhere and placed on two chairs.

While she bent over the dishes, scrubbing, news came out of her in a stream: Vera's application had been accepted, she was to put in an appearance at the Post Office tomorrow, she would work in the accounts section, payroll, she would get eight hundred dinars a month, it wasn't a lot but would provide her with security and access to a good cheap dining room that the Post Office ran. Were those all her kitchen utensils? Mitzi looked around; the housework was finished. As soon as Vera got her first pay, she should buy some crockery, and first and foremost an electric hot plate; nowadays that was an essential part of every household. Why should Vera live primitively? There'd been enough of that during the war; that had been the Germans' aim, to make progress impossible; that's why they had it in for the Jews, because the Jews were the most progressive of all, the most resourceful. Now that there was only a handful left, they should not give the enemy the satisfaction of thinking that he had achieved his aim.

The next day, on the top, the fourth, floor of the Post Office, Vera was received by a hefty, slightly stooped woman with broad cheeks; she was kindly, talked in a loud voice, asked which camp Vera had been in, then told how she herself had been interned in Gradiška, in Croatia, until she escaped and joined the Partisans. She brought their talk to an end by banging her fist on the table and took Vera to the floor below, to a large room with six desks at which were seated a cluster of girls and one young man with flaxen hair, his left arm missing. No one seemed surprised when Vera walked in, not even Mara Brkić, a plump girl with a pouting mouth who had been her high-school classmate for a whole year. But they were all attentive; they gave the most comfortable chair to her, turned it to the light, cleaned the desk in front of her, smiled at her, and showed her how to transfer names and figures from small lined lists to a ledger that was half a meter wide. Then they forgot themselves, teased each other, laughed. A pretty, dark girl began to sing a marching song, which the others took up softly. They offered one another cigarettes, divided snacks, and Vera received her share on a piece of paper: bread and meat juice sprinkled with paprika, and water from a green liter bottle. At midday they all rushed off to lunch together, their wooden heels clattering down the corridor, down the stairs, and greeted the old mustachioed doorman as they emerged into the sunlit street and ran across to a dining room, in what had once been a tavern. They sat in two small airless rooms, waitresses brought them food, good-smelling, thick, greasy food, and they gobbled it up fast, because others out there were waiting their turn. Mara brought Vera a book of tickets with dates written on them and stamped with the words "Lunch" and "Supper," for which she would not pay until the first of the month.

So now Vera had another thing in her schedule: to go from her apartment to the dining room, and back, between seven and nine every evening. In the evening, she was no longer in the company she knew: the people at the table were strangers, but loud and eager to make friends. They asked no questions, they accepted her. Gradually she gained confidence in the group, adjusted to their ways. For these people were not only close to her in age but also like her in their vagabond independence: if they still had parents or relatives, even if they lived with them, they insisted on being separate from them, rejecting the norm in clothing and speech, competing for soldiers' trousers and jackets, neglecting face and hair, rushing to the dining room as if there was nowhere else to go for food and refuge. Several times, Mara said that she would be glad to visit Vera at home, and although Vera was reluctant to invite her, she couldn't avoid it the day they left the dining room together and were going in the same direction.

The emptiness and disorder of Vera's place delighted Mara; she clapped her hands as she turned around and around in the dim room, where clothing was piled high on the chairs and dirty dishes on the table and window sills. She threw herself on the settee, where the quilt and the pillow lay as Vera had left them, stretched her legs, stretched wide her arms. "Ah, what a life you have here!" She saw Vera's slovenliness as a protest against the bourgeoisie, and must have reported this to the others, for in the next few days Vera was surrounded with offers of friendship. But she shrank from this aggressive camaraderie. She felt that by opening her home to Mara she had exposed something private, secret, that her former isolation had been compromised, and at night she would lie down in disgust on the settee and pull the old quilt over her.

Vera continued to receive only Mitzi, who dropped in and, chattering on and on, washed the dishes and made tea for both of them on the electric hot plate she had finally bought for Vera and installed herself. Did Vera tolerate Mitzi because Mitzi was Jewish? No. Vera stayed away from the few Jews who had come back, and whom Mitzi wanted her to meet. Nor did Vera go again to the Jewish Society. She was afraid of questions that would probe too deep, a fear she did not feel with Mitzi, in whose curiosity she sensed an innocence, as of a spinster who never saw beyond the façade of married life, a façade of order, work, and family gatherings.

It was as if the hatred and distrust caused by inhuman cruelty had not touched Mitzi.

Yet Mitzi, too, had suffered: for four years she had worn on her chest and on her back the yellow star; had spent a year in a concentration camp; had been in the same transport as Vera and her family. Often they reminisced about the humiliations they had been subjected to, but in Mitzi's lively mouth those reminiscences were dry, clean, comprehensible. "You needed will power to survive" was her conclusion, as if she were talking about the treatment of an illness. "Anybody who gave up, who gave in, was done for. Me, I never did." Jutting her chin obstinately, she told how once, under the kapo's very nose, she grabbed a handful of potato peels from the rubbish heap and ran off through a fence gate that happened to have been left open, into a hut where she could not be recognized; and how, sent off to work in the salt mine, she had treated the chilblains on her feet with her own urine so the doctor would not send her to the crematorium.

"Your poor grandmother, of course, was too old to withstand all those ordeals," said Mitzi, allowing that exception to the rule. "But your papa, so proud and helpless, he had to break. It's better that they didn't suffer long. Think of it that way and you'll be able to console yourself." And as she listened, Vera felt that some higher, colder justice spoke through Mitzi, granting passports only to the strongest. Or to the most bestial. Mitzi's stories brought back images, and Vera saw a procession of shrunken, shaven heads on thin necks and emaciated bodies, like a field of sickly plants above which leered the ghastly faces of the kapos, masks from a madman's dream. She saw the Zimper sisters before they were taken out to be beaten, saw them sitting on the edge of a bed huddled close, their hands entwined, then saw their thin naked bodies tied to the wooden vaulting horses, heard the whistle of the blows. How was it that Vera was spared? Because of her faith in life? Or because of her lack of faith, her baseness, her submission to force? Having survived, she was numbered among the victors, and here she was with Mitzi, wielding wisdom over the mistakes of the dead. Ridiculous, vile. In the name of those who had died she ought to smash that cackling head. Instead, she was drinking tea, saying nothing, nibbling on cakes.

She went to work at the Post Office, to the dining room for lunch and supper, then home to rest. She filled out, her skin grew tauter, her hair became silky, flowing. "What do you wash your hair with?" her colleagues asked, touching enviously the thick red cascade. They envied her beauty, she could feel it. A circle of mistrust formed around her; the offers to visit ceased; Mara, who had invited her to see her place, stopped mentioning it. Only official invitations came to Vera, tossed from desk to desk, typed sheets of paper with spaces for signatures that were mandatory. These were meetings, called "conferences," of Youth, of the Popular Front, and were usually held in the early evening in the front hall of the Post Office. Stern new faces emerged in the light of the electric bulbs, among them the personnel officer, a hard, sharp woman, Comrade Jurković, who delivered a speech about lateness for work and the time wasted in talking. She read out a list of the names of the guilty parties, directing a glance at each one in the rows of chairs and benches. Roll call, it suddenly came back to Vera, and her throat tightened in fear. Would she be singled out, accused, ordered to take off her clothes, and tied to a pillar in the hall? Would each blow on her body be counted out loud? She broke into a sweat. She looked at the faces around her, terrified faces, like those of the girls in the house of pleasure when the Barrackenälteste passed between the beds, tapping the back of her boot with a whip. Vera had to be obedient, to hide any resistance. At the thought of how much easier it was here than in the camp, she almost cried out with happiness. She set her face in an expression of admiration and kept it that way until the end of the meeting.

She made a point of getting to work ahead of time; her colleagues would find her at her desk early in the morning, bent over papers. Several weeks later, Gordana Sekulić, a pale, unpleasant young woman, invited her for a walk after lunch. It was late autumn; a fierce wind blew right through them, and there was nowhere to take shelter. Gordana, shivering, became impatient. "Can we go to your place?" she asked Vera. Wary, Vera said no, and they went back to the Post Office. The cleaners were shuffling up and down the corridor; the room was being aired. Gordana shut the window, and they sat down on cold chairs opposite each other. Vera lit a cigarette. Gordana screwed up her face and, with her eyes fixed on the desk, spoke of the aims of socialism—humanitarianism and justice—aims certainly dear to Vera after what she had suffered. She, Gordana, had been entrusted, by the older comrades, with the task of inviting Vera to join the League of Young Communists. And Gordana raised her troubled, almost tearful eyes and asked tensely, "Will you?" To which Vera simply nodded. Gordana jumped up, hugged her, kissed her with cold lips, seized her hand, and the two ran down the stairs and out into the street, where the wind, whistling, drove dust and scraps of paper.

The next day, Gordana gave Vera a questionnaire and some sheets of blank paper to write her biography. "You mustn't leave anything out," Gordana said before placing the paper in Vera's hands, "particularly anything that concerns the Occupation. That's what Danica Jurković told me to tell you." Vera was supposed to return the papers within three days. That same afternoon, with some difficulty, for the questions were complicated, she filled out the questionnaire and at once set about writing her biography. She was surprised by how little there was to say once she had given the details of her family; so much of her suffering, she realized, was general, and the personal could not be recounted. But, remembering what Gordana had told her, she tried to put the unutterable on paper. The crucial events, it seemed to her, ought to be described in the minutest detail, but they were in disorder, unconnected, and connecting them in memory would cause immeasurable distress. She tried to generalize, but that didn't work, for her generalizations quickly degenerated into half-truths and therefore falsehoods. She threw the sheet of paper away, took another, and in a fury of decision hurled herself on that past which was suddenly demanded of her. But the words wouldn't come. She lay down, writhing in her impotence. She would have liked to rest, but her heart went on hammering, would have liked to run out into the street, but hadn't enough breath left to move. She was a prisoner of those blank sheets of paper, as she had been a prisoner in the camp.

This was camp, too, she realized, a continuation of camp, the camp in which she had been walled for a year and a half. The war had ended, but she had not escaped; her former captors, drowned in blood, even in death, stretched out their arms to her, to her captivity. She shouldn't have come back, she remembered, she should never have come back; she had made a mistake coming back, and now would pay for it. She tried to think of a way out. Go somewhere? But where? Apart from this house that everyone had abandoned, there was only one other: a wooden hut in a field fenced off with wire. There was no one there now, its inhabitants gone, a place of disgrace, a monument to its visitors—forced to visit it—full of judgments on the past. But she was part of that past and, although a victim, as guilty as the guilty.

She lit a cigarette, put on her coat, went to a nearby grocery, and bought a bottle of wine. She never drank, she never wanted to drink, but people said it numbed you. The wind was bitter and cold. She forced herself to gulp it down, but her stomach rebelled, and she ran out of her room to be sick. Broken, deprived of relief, she lay down and went to sleep. Heavy dreams, water, drowning, rain and snow in the square, on the roll call.

Morning found her listless. She went to work late, with dark circles under her eyes. She worked silently, angrily. The girl who sat next to her, Stasa Dimitrijević, a doctor's daughter, asked in a low voice what was wrong. Vera shrugged, barely able to hold in her hatred. Gordana, whose eyes she noticed looking at her worriedly, came up after work and asked if the application was ready. "It isn't and never will be," Vera replied with a decisiveness that surprised herself. "I'm sick of the whole thing!" Gordana recoiled as if bitten by a snake and hurried off. Vera felt delivered of a great weight. She went to the dining room, sat among strangers, then went home and lay down. After a short sleep, she drank what was left of the wine, drank it straight from the bottle, turned the bottle upside down and let the last few yellow drops fall on the papers scattered on the table.

Gordana, a few days later, was waiting for her in the corridor. "I told Danica you're not going to do your biography. Is that still true?" When Vera said it was, Gordana said, "Then it's as if we never had our talk. Return the questionnaire to me."

"It's already filled in."

Gordana thought a moment. "That doesn't matter. Return it anyway. It shouldn't be left lying around."

After lunch, at home, the first thing Vera did was clear the table of the papers, crumpling them up with disgust, with pleasure, and burning them in the kitchen stove, which had not seen fire for a long time. Then she sat down with the questionnaire and carefully crossed out, in thick ink, every word she had written. Now, following the questions was a row of black dashes, long and short. First name, last name: nothing. Father's name: nothing. Mother's name, maiden name: nothing. Day, month, year of birth: nothing. She was nothing, and she folded that nothing, put it in her coat pocket, and the next day placed it on the desk in front of Gordana. Soon thereafter the telephone rang, and she was summoned to Danica Jurković. She went up the stairs and found the personnel officer at her desk, her back bent almost double, her eyes tired, her face sagging and lined.

Jurković, not asking Vera to sit down, looked at the papers in front of her and in an expressionless voice read the dates Vera had been late to work. There seemed to be too many, but since Vera could prove nothing, she said that on those days she hadn't felt well. Jurković raised her tiny eyes, red around the rims, and explained that unless Vera had been to a doctor, her lateness was unexcused and that legally she could be dismissed from her job. Nevertheless, she, Jurković, for the time being did not intend to resort to that extremity, taking into consideration the fact that Vera came from a family that had given one martyr to the cause, Gerhard Kroner, and that Vera, too, in her own way must have suffered under fascism, though she had close relatives who were collaborators and it was not altogether clear how she had come back from the camp alive and in relatively good condition. For that reason, Vera's past would be looked into, and until then she should go back to work and had better guard against further infringements of the rules.

That afternoon, Mitzi arrived at Vera's apartment, out of breath, her face puckered with indignation. Jurković had called her in and expressed displeasure with Vera's work; she had also cast doubts on Mitzi's motives in recommending Vera. "What's happened, my dear? Everyone was so full of praise for you before!" Vera said nothing. She could not tell Mitzi what oppressed her, because the telling would lead to half-truths, not the final truth. "Well, say something. What is this all about? Is she lying now or was she lying before?" Vera's silence gradually exhausted her frightened curiosity, and the habit of always doing something diverted her attention. Mitzi picked up the dirty dishes that were lying around the room, began to wash them, and soon there were shining cups of freshly brewed tea between them, and a plate of cookies. "Aren't they good?" Mitzi asked brightly, and began to talk about old friends she had visited recently and the friends she had made. They were fine people, she assured Vera, inviting her to come the following Tuesday, because Mitzi decided that on Tuesdays she would hold a little "soiree" for her closest friends. But Vera would not go; the very thought of socializing scared her. She felt, now, as if a barbed-wire fence had been thrown up between her and the outside air, between her and the world, between her and words, between her and memories.

She withdrew into herself, this time consciously, since Vera was the only person left to Vera, being different and surrounded by hostility. She began to pity herself and to find consolation in taking care of herself. She bought better food, and sometimes skipped the dining room and cooked for herself at home a tasty supper of eggs, bacon, and onions, washing it down with a wine of better quality, for she had become more discerning. She bought some material that caught her eye in a poorly stocked, half-empty shop, found a dressmaker, and turned up at the office in a clingy new dress of artificial silk, blue with polka dots. Her hair she wore close to her face, with two bold curls turned toward her cheekbones. She tried to ignore everyone as she walked through the corridors of the Post Office and sat at her desk, with head down, but she was not ignored.

Voja, the young man whose desk was in the corner of the office, cast long, blushing glances in her direction. The men who worked on her floor brushed against her as they passed and greeted her pointedly in deep, admiring voices. This first provoked, then pleased her, as if she had opened a way through the enclosing wall of hostility, letting in the warm breath of existence. She was not beaten, downtrodden; she could still make an impression, accomplish something. Now she returned those passionate looks. She allowed Voja to meet her after work, on the way to the dining room, allowed him to find a table where they could sit alone, and laughed ambiguously at his awkward compliments.

So, she had broken down their wall, she decided as she lay on the settee, still dressed, stroking her thighs, which had become firm again, in a room warm with the approach of spring. She had divided them, she had revenged herself. And it became a pastime for her, those roving, hungry eyes—blue, brown, green—which rested on her, assaulted her, tried to slip under her dress, down her breasts, between her thighs, trapped as in a web. She recalled each male, as if they were strung out like trophies on a string, then made her selection, measuring one against another. She decided on several, like choosing decorations in a shop window: I'll take these. And, indeed, one of her choices accosted her on her way home, the Post Office secretary, a dark young former NCO recently discharged because of a wound in his leg. "Shall we go somewhere together?"

But, walking on the street, he soon tired, his bad leg stiffened, and beads of sweat broke out on his forehead. They stopped at a patisserie, a cool place, and empty except for the owner, a Macedonian in a short white coat and cap, who stood behind the counter. They ordered two cakes each and sherbet. The cakes were floury, the sherbet too sour, but the secretary didn't notice; he ate and drank quickly. Then, leaning over the table, pushing the crumbs around his plate with his stubby fingers, he told Vera how much he liked her, of the state he had got himself into because of her. He couldn't sleep at night, couldn't work during the day;

he had to study for his correspondence-school exam, but his thoughts kept turning to her; he would like to be with her all the time, look at her, talk to her. Would she be his girl?

Vera looked at him, at his excited, bashful eyes, the beads of sweat at the roots of his curly hair—everything about him was so soft and childlike that she had to laugh. And then she couldn't stop. She leaned back in her chair, shook with laughter. The secretary lowered his head gloomily, and the owner leaned over the counter in surprise and then went to the back of the room to watch from there. The secretary turned red, his lips quivered, he clenched his fist and hit the marble-topped table. The plates danced; a fork fell to the floor. "Stop!" he cried.

But Vera could not control her laughter. She was not afraid of him. Here was a person, for the first time in so long, of whom she was not afraid. She waved her hand to calm him down. "It's nothing," she said. "Don't worry, I'll stop in a minute!" And in fact, she slowly recovered, lit a cigarette, and suddenly felt distant again. This trembling, childish man irritated her. "Pay and let's go," she ordered.

His hand shook as he counted out the money and got up. "May I come with you?"

She looked at him. He was handsome, slim, quivering, like so many of those who had forced her to submit and then disappeared. They were now probably dead. "You couldn't if you wanted to. Your legs won't carry you." And, laughing in his face, she left him and turned the corner.

But her rudeness did not discourage him. He kept looking for her, popped up in unexpected places, but never again asked her to go out with him. Others did so in his stead: Voja, from her office, still saying nothing but looking at her plaintively, and several older Post Office workers, who confronted her in the corridors, waited for her at the dining room, stopped her at a street corner to breathe desire into her face. Even Alexa, the doorman, over forty, enticed her into his cubbyhole on the pretext that there was a letter waiting for her and tried to pinch her. Like a pack of wolves, who alerted one another that she was close by, or were alerted, perhaps, by the scent she gave off, they crowded around, baring their teeth and snapping, offering to prove their virility. The chase began to affect her. At night she was troubled by amorous dreams; in the afternoons, drowsy, she would get drunk and conjure up a man's words, a man's touch.

One evening—she had not yet switched on the light—she heard a soft knock at the door, almost a scratch, and when she opened it, she found herself face to face with the secretary. He looked haggard; his eyes were mournful. She kept him in suspense for several seconds, then stepped back and with a gesture of her hand invited him in. As soon as he shut the door, she pressed herself against him. Because his hands shook too much, she unbuttoned his trousers for him, and gave herself to him, right there in the kitchen, on the table, almost fully dressed, not letting him take her clothes off. Then she quickly refastened his buttons and pushed him outside. "That's it," she said sternly. "If you turn up again like that, uninvited, I'll call the police, and complain to Jurković to boot." She locked the door, drank some wine from the bottle, and lay down. The encounter had been too abrupt, it had come nowhere near satisfying her, but had shaken her up and left her moist. She vowed never again to give in to that kind of weakness. She ignored the secretary, who waited for her in the corridors of the Post Office with humble, imploring eyes, and turned an angry face to her other suitors.

But news of her indiscretion rippled through that swamp of collective lust. One evening, the dispatch clerk knocked on her door, a strong, mature man, and, without a second thought, she did with him exactly what she had done with the secretary. Then it was Voja's turn, who held her timidly, embracing her awkwardly with his one arm; then the handsome postman, tall and slim, with whom she happened to have shared a table at lunch; and finally her boss, with whom she had hardly ever exchanged a word, a clever man who had been a banker before the war. She was not worried about not knowing them better, but let them come in the evening, when drink and boredom had prepared her for weakness. All she asked was for them to keep silent, not to ask for an explanation or for the light to be turned on, or for her to show herself naked.

Afterward she felt remorse, disgust, but she was accustomed to that, and decided it was an inseparable part of sexual coupling. And again she would wait, sometimes in vain, if no one came. That made her happy, gave her the feeling that she had escaped something ugly; it was not unlike those days in the camp house of pleasure with no visits, when she pretended that she was free, in a town where no one knew her. But then someone would knock, and she came to terms with that, too. Men she didn't know swarmed around her now that they found out she lived alone and was available. They waited in the street near her house, approached her with a deep bow and flattering words, and if she so much as nodded in reply, they knocked on her door at twilight and begged her to let them in. Occasionally one of the strangers would bring a bottle of wine, or cigarettes, or a length of material for which one needed coupons as well as money to obtain. She accepted. She even took the money they placed on the table in the darkness after she had given herself to them, though they waved it in front of her eyes beforehand, so she would know who it came from. But these visits left her cold, disappointed, and she began to drink more and arrive at work late because of her hangover and the sense of futility.

On a few heavy, rainy days in autumn she didn't go to work at all. Jurković called her in for another talk, this time harsh. The absences of a person morally upright, Jurković said, could be pardoned, but she no longer intended to make allowances for Vera. The threat was carried out one December morning, the third in a row that Vera had lain around at home: the Post Office messenger, smiling as he surveyed the disorder in her kitchen, delivered a thin, folded paper on which were typed legal clauses, numbered, and, beneath the notice of her right to appeal within eight days, in large, widely spaced letters, her dismissal. Vera no more than ran her eyes over the document. She offered the messenger some slivovitz—she drank brandy now, liking it better than wine—and smoked a cigarette with him. The fingers of his right hand were missing, blown off by a mine, he said, in his Partisan days. They talked on, but his tongue ran away with him and she grew bored. Besides, it was too cold to sit in the unheated kitchen, so she stood up and saw him to the door.

She was out of work and surprised by how pleased that made her. The office, the inquisitive faces, the men's eyes glued to her body, openly desiring to undress her, to run their hands over her—all that repelled her. She was better off with these frankly sexual encounters, for which she answered to no one. She would not go to the dining room anymore, she decided, though she still had some unused vouchers; she would eat however she could, wherever she could. So she lived on gifts. As if knowing of her dismissal, no one came empty-handed anymore. The gifts sometimes were things of ridiculously little value—a pair of stockings, a half-dozen handkerchiefs wrapped in newspaper, or small change placed in a neat pile on the table. But, to make up for that, the man who came once a week in the early evening always left two hundred-dinar notes, practically enough for her needs.

He introduced himself as a local landowner, but his elegance and his fine-quality suits and shirts, although worn, told her that he was lying. No longer young, with thinning hair and glasses on his long, sharp nose, he was humble toward her and at the same time feverishly hungry at her touch. He reminded her of someone from the past, who, she didn't know; Count Armanyi, perhaps, but older. Was that why she felt drawn to him? Or was she pleased at his generosity? She couldn't make up her mind. She waited for him more eagerly than for the others, and her heart beat gladly when she recognized his careful knock at the door and saw, through the frosted glass, the silhouette of his wide-brimmed hat, always slanted to the left. After several meetings, in addition to the money he began to leave messages on the table, small scraps of paper typed out beforehand. They each contained a single sentence: "I love you," or "You're dear to me," or "It's wonderful to know you're mine." Later, more boldly, they referred to her body, her lovely derrière, her tiny, scented ear, her armpit with its little tuft of hair.

One evening, after he got dressed, he stayed longer than usual in the darkness of the room to recover his breath. Sitting in a chair, he asked for a glass of water and, at last, for the light to be turned on. Vera hesitated—it was against her rule—then did as she was asked. Her guest was reaching for his hat, which had rolled to the floor. He lowered his eyes, and suddenly they were filled with tears. "I'm not worthy of you," he stammered, wiping his eyes behind his glasses. "I'm a friend of your father's. I lost a daughter the same age as you." He turned his face toward her, his eyes half closed behind the glasses. "Don't you recognize me?"

Vera looked at him and thought hard: In the contours of his face she saw another, firmer, face, full cheeks free of glasses, strong teeth, thick brown hair that fluttered in the wind against a background of green hills, and in an instant the parchment of age was unrolled. "Is it you, Uncle Jacob?" He nodded and stifled a cry. "You knew all the time that it was me?" He nodded again, took off his glasses, reached for a handkerchief in his pocket, and wiped his eyes.

"Your mother wrote to me," he said awkwardly. "She asked me to find out what I could about you. I followed you. It was as if I were following my own daughter, our Erika. You remember Erika, how you all played together, you and she and Gerhard? But something in me went wrong, went crazy. You were alive and she was dead. I was alive and your father was dead, and your mother had left you, betrayed you. It seemed like such an injustice. Why didn't I have my daughter when those who were no more had theirs? An absurd thought, and I rejected it at once." He was silent for a moment, his mouth working. "But my sinful body," he shouted suddenly, beating his fist against his sunken chest, "it gave me no peace." He lowered his head. "I began to lust after you with the vicious lust of an old man. I could see the path you had taken, that you gave yourself wantonly to anyone. The first time I came here, I came to warn you, to try to turn you from that path. But your scent, your youth bewitched me in the darkness when you took me in, put your arms around me. Suddenly, after so many years, I felt that I was still a man, still alive, that I could be of use to someone. Forgive me." He shook his head in disbelief and closed his eyes.

Vera felt sorry for him. She picked up his hat—it had been cleaned many times, and the manufacturer's name was printed on its silk lining—and gave it to him. "Go now, Uncle Jacob."

It was as if he had not heard her, but after several minutes he got up from the chair, tilted his hat to his left ear, and wound his scarf around his neck. "I'll bring you your mother's letter," he mumbled without looking at Vera. "She lives in Frankfurt. She begs to be forgiven, wants you to go and live with her. She's all right. Married again. They keep a tavern."

For a second Vera felt a shock of amazement rise up inside her like a sob, but it subsided as suddenly as it had come, and in its place was the image of herself copulating with her mother's messenger, an act in which she had even found pleasure, and she was nauseated. "Go, go at once," she ordered, and opened the door.

172

She almost pushed him down the stairs, so she could lock the door as quickly as possible and forget him.

But no sooner had he gone than her disgust disappeared. She saw him again as he had been when he was younger, as in an old photograph, with other youthful faces around him: her father, mother, Gerhard, Erika. Gerhard and Erika had perhaps even been in love a little, in an innocent way; they would go off together into the hollows and woods when their families took excursions in cabs to the hills around Novi Sad. Her thoughts went back to the pleasure of that slow drive, the clatter of the wheels and the horse's hooves, the old driver's back bouncing up and down, his dark coat and tall black hat, the smell of the horse's sweat and droppings blending with the perfume of plants and the breeze from the Danube, which was a silver ribbon in the distance. Even so, Vera had not enjoyed those outings. She would sit opposite her father and mother, always aware of the tension between them, the fixed smiles, the words held back. She could hardly wait for the cab to stop. The adults would spread out the blanket in front of the cabs after the drivers unharnessed the horses and led them to the edge of the woods to graze, and on the blanket they would sit and play cards. Gerhard and Erika would go off, and she in turn would walk as far as possible, as far as she was allowed, enjoying her solitude among the weeds and bushes. But vegetation didn't inspire her; she couldn't lose herself in it, too conscious of the proximity of the group to which she reluctantly belonged, to which she would have to return, and in fact Vera waited impatiently for the time to pass, for teatime, when they went back.

Bernister, she remembered, used to visit them at

home, sometimes alone and sometimes with his wife. He had long discussions with her father in the study, nodding solemnly at her father's discourse, or correcting him on some point, for Bernister, a trade representative and agent for big foreign firms, was well informed about the movements of commodity prices in the world. Meanwhile, his plump wife chatted affectionately with Vera's mother about needlework and cooking. Afterward they would all sit at the freshly set table in the dining room, drink coffee, and eat kugelhopf, but Vera would feel distant and impatient, sensing the falseness of that friendly gathering. And she had been right; for the Bernisters, as soon as the trouble began between Germany and Yugoslavia, broke all ties with the Kroners. Vera saw Erika only once after that, in the white socks, shirt, and blouse of the Hitler Youth; she did not see the rest of the family again. But now that Bernister had reminded her of it, she suddenly wanted to return to that time of abundance, tense and false though it was, to the brightness and simplicity of those afternoons.

Also, she no longer thought of her mother with aversion. At her mother's side, she would rest, she would be cleansed of the murkiness that led to her shame and defilement. She remembered her mother's quick, light step, the energy with which she had brought her food and medicine when she was ill, or a dress just ironed. She must join her mother, she decided, and suddenly felt better.

During the next few days Vera waited for Bernister to arrive. She jumped up at every little noise in the hall. But Bernister did not put in an appearance. Having gone away ashamed the last time, perhaps he would never come back. Finally she dressed and went into town to find him. She tried several shops, asked the assistants and managers, all young men, but they looked at her blankly: trade representatives, as one floor manager explained to her, no longer existed. Desperate, she went in circles, but at last, in a newly opened "people's store," in a glass-partitioned area behind a row of counters, she caught sight of a stocky man with smooth graying hair and wearing a dark-blue suit. She stepped forward and knocked at his door. He raised a pale, bloated face from his papers, listened to her attentively, but after a moment's thought said that he didn't know Jacob Bernister. He got up to show Vera out, but she remained standing in front of his desk. He asked her why she was looking for the former trade representative. When he heard that Jacob Bernister had been a friend of her father and that her father was the late Robert Kroner, whom he had known personally—he said—and respected, he asked Vera to sit down, picked up the telephone, dialed some numbers, spoke to several people in Serbian and in Hungarian, then pushed a slip of paper with an address toward Vera.

The address took her along the main street past the Post Office, down the road to the station, into a narrow side street, and to a two-story house with a dingy staircase. On the second floor Vera found a door with the name she was looking for. She rang the bell, and the door was opened by Bernister, in a short, shabby dressing gown. He stepped back in dismay, was about to shut the door in her face, but in the dim light of the hallway Mrs. Bernister, now a gray, shrunken woman, appeared. Bernister pulled himself together and introduced Vera. "You remember, Robert and Reza's daughter, Erika's friend." He invited her into the living room.

A desk and a large typewriter with a black metal cover were all that was left of the trade representative's office; beyond them, a low, wide couch, armchairs, and cabinets crowded together. "Make us some coffee, will you," Bernister said to his wife, and as soon as she left the room, he leaned over to Vera and whispered anxiously, "You mustn't say anything about my coming to see you. Or about your mother's letter. My wife knows nothing." But he opened the desk drawer, took out a pencil and a piece of paper, and hurriedly wrote in printed letters: "Theresia Arbeitsam, Frankfurt a/M, Forellenstrasse 17." "Put that away. We'll talk as if you had found the address by yourself." And they did talk, first the two of them, and then in front of his wife, who brought in the two coffees and stood by the door listening. The former trade representative explained to Vera that she had to apply for a passport, told her where, promised to help her fill out the forms if she found that necessary, and, looking at his wife, timidly offered help with expenses Vera could not meet. The coffee was barely warm; they drank it quickly, and Vera got up. They were all victims, Bernister said in parting, though Vera had certainly suffered terribly. The truth was coming out now, things no one ever dreamed of. The Germans, too, had had their calvary; they had barely survived, and poor Erika had perished, so young. Every family had its pain, he concluded awkwardly as his wife wiped her eyes.

Vera went to the police station, filled out forms, handed them in at the counter with the fee. A young clerk told her she would be notified. When? He couldn't say. She was not pleased with this answer, for suddenly she was in a hurry. She felt she had wasted those long months since she had come back from the camp, trying to adapt to a life alien to her from the start. Then she received a letter from her mother, not in German, curiously, but in Serbian. It was difficult to read because the handwriting was poor and her mother had forgotten certain expressions.

"My dear Vera," said the letter, "I've written to Mr. Bernister twice, and have now heard from him that you are well and living in our house. I am sorry I was not there to welcome you, but fate decided otherwise. When they took you away, I had only Hermann left, and he had to escape from Novi Sad, though he did nothing bad. He was kind to all regardless of faith. Hermann is now my husband; he is forty-six, the same age as I am. We were in a camp in Karlsruhe and now live in Frankfurt am Main. We run a small tavern. Hermann says he would like you to come here. He will treat you like a daughter, for he has no children of his own, and he respects me because we manage our little tavern together. I am waiting for you. I wrote to Mr. Bernister also, to tell you to come and that I am expecting you. If you need money for the trip, I cannot send it to you because they told me I could not at the Post Office, but Mr. Bernister will give it to you, and we will pay it back to his brother in Hannover. So come quickly. Your mother, Tereza Arbeitsam, sends you greetings and kisses."

Vera placed the letter on one side of the kitchen cabinet, tucking its upper edge beneath the frame of the glass door, and the envelope with its brightly colored stamp on the other. Occasionally she would go up to it, look closely at her mother's slanted handwriting, read a word or two, or run a finger over the stamp, which depicted Johann Wolfgang von Goethe with a wide cravat under his aged, sagging chin. She now had a secret, a goal. When a man came and she gave herself to him in the darkness of the kitchen, her inner eye would go to the cabinet and her mother's letter, and she would not feel defeated, but somehow, because of her secret, triumphant. How she despised all those males who forced their seed, their unrest into her, quickly, violently, seed she could not germinate, for within her was an emptiness they did not suspect.

She waited for Bernister, sometimes resolved to refuse him, sometimes resigned to submit to him as before. But he did not come. Nor was there any communication from the police station regarding her passport. She went there, to the window where she had made her application, waited in a long line, inquired, and received from a different clerk the same noncommittal answer. Then she walked to the Bernisters. This time Mrs. Bernister opened the door; silently she stepped back into the dim hall, showed Vera to a tidy but unheated room, asked her to sit down, and went to make coffee. Mrs. Bernister herself drank no coffee; the doctor had forbidden it on account of her high blood pressure. Mr. Bernister was out of town; the year before, he had bought a vineyard in Fruška Gora, and since two of the rooms in their apartment had been taken over by a high-ranking officer, during the week her husband stayed in a hut he built at the vineyard, coming home only on Saturday and Sunday to wash his clothes. Inadvertently Vera was thus given the explanation for the regularity of his visits. Had Mr. Bernister been home in the last few weeks, she asked. Yes, said his wife, but he didn't go into town; he was tired and looked as though he had suddenly aged a great deal. That was said with a certain acerbity, with a meaning Vera could not quite unravel. Mrs. Bernister asked how Vera lived; did anyone do the cooking and shopping for her? And when Vera answered, the old woman nodded with a clouded, almost tearful look. Erika, too—she sighed—would have been an independent young woman by now, had she lived. Mrs. Bernister told Vera that Erika died on her way to visit her fiancé, a German airman stationed in Budapest, in the summer of 1943. American planes attacked the train, and a bomb destroyed the car in which Erika was sitting. Only her shoes were found, and that was how she was identified. Mrs. Bernister left the room; when she came back, she placed a pair of red shoes with wide cork heels, virtually new, in Vera's hands. Vera held them; they were light, like the last pair of prewar shoes her mother had ordered made for her by the shoemaker across the street.

The next time, Vera went on a Saturday, and found Bernister at home. Covered with dust, he was pulling sacks of fertilizer from a shed. He wiped his hands with a rag, inquired about the status of Vera's passport, and went into the house to type a letter requesting a quick response to her application. Vera signed the letter and put it in her handbag. Mrs. Bernister brought in two cups of coffee and stood, as usual, at a distance, watching them attentively. When Vera was ready to go, Mrs. Bernister accompanied her to the door and asked her to come again.

This Vera did on working days, when Mrs. Bernister was alone. She liked the semidarkness of the cluttered room, whose old bourgeois furniture so much resembled her family's. She missed those familiar surroundings, surroundings that had not been happy or free but soothed by virtue of their emptiness. Her own home was difficult for her, tense. Her mother's letter and envelope tucked between the glass and the frame of the cabinet now seemed to threaten rather than promise. They said that nothing changed, they pressed down on Vera like a stifling shroud, like mildew.

From time to time Mitzi showed up to reproach her for not having kept in touch, for not having put her life in order. Or some man would bring his desire and leave money. Vera dreaded both. She found it hard to sit still while Mitzi, chattering, went about the housework she felt it her duty to do in the unkempt rooms, or served tea and cakes, and when Mitzi left, Vera breathed freely again, as if she had escaped an attack on her life.

With the men, Vera truly feared an attack on her life, feared that one of them would strangle her in the middle of an embrace, or stab her in the stomach with a knife pulled out of nowhere. Why did she allow strange men into her locked room, allow their powerful hands to explore her body, even its most private places? She swore that she would never again let anyone in, that she would tell the next man who knocked to go away, acting tough, as she had done that time with the secretary, and if they didn't listen, she would rush to the window and call for help. But when a visit was actually announced by a catlike scratching on the door, her throat tightened, and her body, accustomed to its servitude, despite fear and common sense, began to inch toward that summons, her arms reached out, her fingers turned the key, and when the strange hands seized her, she melted and spread herself wide to accept the onslaught.

One day, after she had been tossing and turning

on her settee for hours, she jumped up, got dressed, and rushed off to see Mrs. Bernister. She rang, threw herself at the woman's feet, and poured out her anguish. The uncomprehending Mrs. Bernister helped her into the living room, sat her down on the couch, stroked her hair, mumbled words of comfort, and she, too, burst into tears, as if someone else's misfortune had broken down a barrier, and began hurling reproaches at her husband. All he had ever cared about were his indecent pleasures, the gratification of his urges. He had urged Erika on to her destruction by allowing her to become involved with a man in the middle of the war, who was thousands of kilometers away; Mrs. Bernister had begged him to act like a father, to make Erika come to her senses, but all in vain. And now he was running away from responsibility. Instead of finding work, like everyone else, he bought a vineyard to avoid being with her, to avoid sharing her grief and loneliness, the hardship of a divided apartment; he hid himself from her eyes, from her accusations, crawled into the ground like a mole, or else chased after peasant girls. "But I'll help you, my child," Mrs. Bernister assured Vera. Her subtenant, the officer, was a serious man, alone in the world, not well; she could see he was not unkind, and he certainly had influence; she understood nothing about those stars on his uniform, but a soldier delivered a newspaper to the house for him. She had never asked for any favors, though they had shared an apartment for three years. Every day she cleaned the bathroom they used in common and sometimes out of pity put a piece of his dirty laundry, left lying in a corner, in with her own, so that he wouldn't have to worry about it. Mrs. Bernister would invite him for coffee that evening, and Vera should join them. Now that they had a plan of action, the two women calmed down, and Vera left.

That evening Mrs. Bernister, neatly dressed, her hair brushed, opened the door to Vera at the first ring. Then, placing a finger to her lips, she went out and reentered through the bathroom door with a tall, angular, gray-haired man in officer's trousers and a worn officer's jacket with no badges. He looked Vera over and then offered her a large, firm hand. Mrs. Bernister brought in two coffees, prepared beforehand, and left them alone. Vera volunteered her story: the camp, the invitation to visit from her mother, the application for a passport to which she had received no answer. The words came easily; the man did not frighten her. His eyes were dull, his lined face like bark on a dead tree. It was as if he were not there, though when she stopped talking, she heard his hoarse breathing. She clasped her hands and waited for his reply. He looked at her thoughtfully, wearily, but said nothing. Suddenly, she slipped her dress off her left shoulder, pulled down the strap of her bra, and leaned over the table, so he could see the tattoo on her breast. The man merely picked up his coffee cup and sipped it slowly. Then he got up to leave, straightening himself to his full, awkward height, and, giving her his hand again, murmured good-bye and some excuse for having to hurry off. Mrs. Bernister came in at once, not hiding that she had heard everything, but she asked no questions. Vera felt drained, sapped of all her strength. On her way home, her thoughts went back and forth like a pendulum between hope and humiliation.

Five days later a messenger in a gray cap brought

her a stapled letter containing a permit to travel to West Germany. At once she threw herself into a frenzy of preparation. She went to get her passport, to be photographed, she filled in the forms for her visa and sent them off through a travel agency to Belgrade. She bought shoes, a dress, and because the shops were temporarily out of suitcases, borrowed one from Mitzi, who, thrilled at the news, gave her her blessing. On a rainy afternoon in October, Vera boarded a train that carried her into the impenetrable night air of a foreign land.

She had not taken a trip since she came back from the camp in a cattle car. Now she sat in a clean compartment with soft seats, sharing it with only one other person, a well-dressed older man, who occasionally went out into the corridor to smoke. At the frontier, the Customs officers saluted. Commands shouted in German ("Los! Los!" "Halt!") drifted in through the window and made her flesh crawl. But the men who had shouted wished her "Good morning" when they entered the compartment and smiled as they looked at her passport: law, authority were now on her side. She took it as a kind of reward for her suffering. The rattle and clatter of the wheels lulled her to sleep.

Daylight found her rushing across rich green countryside with neat houses here and there, passing towns with high, shining gables, which she remembered like a dream from the camp transport. In disbelief she read the familiar names of the stations, peered into the faces of the travelers—a stylish old lady, two young businessmen with briefcases—expecting to find some link to those uniforms and steel helmets. The tranquillity of the faces, the absence of guilt surprised her, all the more because she herself was so disconcerted. She didn't feel like eating, put off going to the toilet, kept her suitcase locked and under her watchful eye until she got to Frankfurt.

Her mother met her at the station, looking a little older, her hair still copper-colored, but she was half a head shorter than Vera remembered her (or Vera had grown), with an anxious expression on her smooth, round face. They kissed with less warmth than Vera had expected, and her mother pushed her toward a man with a nose like a duck's beak and small deep-set eyes, in whom she found it impossible to recognize the former field policeman (she had seen him before, but only a few times and from a distance). He now touched her hand warily and said "Hermann" in a hoarse voice, then bent to pick up her suitcase. They left the station, mother and daughter arm in arm and the mother's husband a step behind with the suitcase. In front of the station, ruins were being broken up by huge wrecking balls moved across the excavated ground by tractorlike machines. But at the very edge of that excavation was a wooden ramp with curving rails, and a group of people waiting. A streetcar came along, and they all climbed in. They rode through wide streets, between bombed-out houses and empty lots where the houses had been cleared away by noisy machines and men in overalls. They got off at a street corner and walked down a long avenue lined with single-story houses, passing small shops that sold furniture, woolens, vegetables. They stopped in front of a tavern whose shutters advertised beer in green Gothic letters. Inside, customers were sitting at a few tables; they paused in their conversation while Vera was introduced to them. Vera and her mother then proceeded up a spiral staircase of shining blond wood and entered a small, clean room with a bed and a wardrobe. "This is your room," said Reza Arbeitsam, nodding with pride. "The bathroom is at the end of the hall. Go wash and then lie down and get some sleep. I have to go downstairs and work."

Vera began a new existence. Her room was assailed from below by loud, beer-soaked German voices (as Fräulein's first hotel room in Novi Sad had been, but Vera did not know that). In the kitchen behind the counter, her mother, in a clean white apron, fried sausages, while a buxom girl by the name of Liese carried out tankards of beer. Hermann Arbeitsam brought the beer in kegs on his tricycle, or he went to the market or to the butcher's, or sat with the customers and listened, smiling obsequiously, to their talk. When there were a lot of customers, her mother would climb up to the second step and call: "Veraaa!" Then put a knife into her hands and place her in front of a table scrubbed spotless to slice cabbage and peel potatoes. Or ask her to take the food to the customers. "This is for Johann at table three, this for Lenz at table one." The tables were numbered even though there were only six. Vera carried out her orders obediently but reluctantly, for the customers were elderly people of little interest to her, and, feeling at home in the Beim vollen Tisch, they tried to start conversations, asked questions. The day after Vera arrived, her mother had warned her: "Don't bring up your father and Gerd, these people wouldn't understand. For them, you're simply my daughter who had trouble getting a passport to join me. Not a word about the rest."

But they were all refugees, like the two tavern own-
ers: from the Banat, from Slavonia, from Czechoslo-
vakia, and from the Hungarian Danube region. A blue-
eyed greengrocer spoke to Vera in Serbian, boasted of
having attended a school run by Franciscans in Bosnia,
and called her "my countrywoman." "How did you get
on under the Communists?" asked a tall, prematurely
gray railroadman with no right hand, from Silesia, and
everyone paused, beer mug in hand, to hear her reply.
"So-so. Neither good nor bad," said Vera, and their
faces registered disappointment. Reza called her daughter to task that evening. "You don't understand," she
hissed, turning red in the face. "These people are bitter,
they've lost everything, house, land, members of their
families. As far as they're concerned, anyone who doesn't
curse the Communists is a swine. Just remember that!"

This simple-minded warning from a tavern keeper's
wife echoed the prohibitions of Vera's girlhood. Everything in her rejected such mindless intolerance. Suddenly she remembered her father, his forever doubtful,
half-smiling shrug when confronted with intolerance of
any kind, such as Gerhard's in the last months he spent
under their roof. After all the killing, that attitude seemed
to her the only sane one. She noted with dismay how
much her mother's behavior had deteriorated since her
father's death; the vulgarity that as a child Vera had but
sensed and occasionally glimpsed now was obvious in
her mother's every word and action. She saw how coarse
and hard she had become, how carelessly she thrust out
her legs when she walked, how she stood, letting her
belly protrude, hands on hips, in front of the customers,
how wide she opened her mouth, with its row of gold

teeth, when she laughed raucously at their crude jokes. Vera felt a shiver of hostility toward her mother, and she withdrew to her room more and more often. But even there she was pursued by the crude voices, as if from an underground, invisible hell. On her bed with pillows over her ears, she tried not to listen, but she couldn't help but hear and picture, from the muffled snorting, what was going on downstairs: the drunken bragging of former policemen, SS men, camp guards.

She went out into the street, walked to the center of town. She saw shops full of brightly colored goods, saw restaurants and cafés in whose windows waiters moved quickly and elegantly, saw huge machines demolishing ruins and driving into the ground iron piles for future buildings. Streetcars, trucks, buses whizzed by, everything shaking, everyone hurrying, working, or relaxing in taverns that had childishly cheerful names, such as Beim vollen Tisch. Vera recognized that cheerfulness, the same cheerfulness that had produced the signs in the camp, the names for blocks, compounds, houses of pleasure, and that accompanied the marching of the guards or the training of the dogs to tear the flesh of insubordinate prisoners. All Germany, she felt, was an enormous madhouse, where thousands upon thousands of people, in total agreement with one another, spoke words, performed actions, carried out ideas that were beyond comprehension, cold, inhuman; construction that was insane but logical, like a bare concrete wall that served no purpose. And there was no escape from that merciless wall.

Despairing, she hurried home. Perhaps there she might find some voice of reason, some crack in the wall of madness. In the deserted tavern—Liese had lowered the blinds before leaving—Vera's mother, her head resting on her arms, sat next to Hermann Arbeitsam, he with a fixed smile, the two forming a grotesque tribunal. They scolded Vera for coming home late, asking themselves (eyes raised to the ceiling) why they worked so hard if Vera was unappreciative of their toil. The tavern, her mother went on, was very successful, and she planned to open another one soon, under the same name, in another part of town, a cosy, intimate place with a small selection of good, homemade dishes and a homey atmosphere. She had even chosen the location, an ironmonger's shop that was soon to close because of the competition from the big stores. All business in Germany was growing; the small shops were disappearing, crowded out. Tereza Arbeitsam warmed to her subject, pleased to be present in a revolution that was shaking the whole country, particularly since it spared the tavern business. In all other trades, she said, the trend was toward large-scale concerns and mass production, but here the consumer wanted something small and personal, where after the wearying crowd he could relax in the old, familiar way. She thought (here her blue eyes, made smaller by her fat cheeks, sparkled cunningly) that, with an increase in pay, Liese could take over the preparation of food in the old establishment, and the two of them, mother and daughter, provided Hermann kept them supplied, could work in the new premises. What did Vera think of that, she asked, but then exploded, because she could see, she said, that Vera was looking down her nose at the idea.

Why, then, did Vera think, was she feeding and keeping her? For the fun of it? When she was Vera's age, she worked and earned her living, she pulled herself out of poverty, acquired a family, a fortune. The war destroyed all that, it took her only son, her Gerd, who, had he lived—here she could no longer hold back two large tears, but wiped them away with the back of her hand and continued—would certainly have been worthy of her sacrifice. Yes, she was unhappy, in spite of everything. She dropped her head on her folded arms, her shoulders heaved; Hermann awkwardly moved a mug of beer toward her, pulled her head up, and urged her to take a few sips. "Don't let yourself go, Mamma! Think of your health!" he said to her, which may have been what he hoped Vera would say. But Vera had no thought of consoling her mother, of making promises; she had not even heard her mother's words, but merely watched the mouth as it opened, closed, twisted, making words and tears, tears and words, like a machine out of control. Vera was overcome by fear, gasped for air, felt the blood rushing to her head, swayed and almost fell. Hermann leaped toward her, attempted to help her to a chair opposite her mother, who looked surprised, but Vera, in a panic, asked to be allowed to go to her room.

Following this scene, Tereza and Hermann, evidently by mutual agreement, no longer spoke to Vera about working. They left her alone and when she came down for meals, discussed other, more remote, projects. Tereza began to question Vera about her expenses back home: how much lunch cost, how much an evening meal, how much dresses and shoes—in her mind converting the prices to marks. She was amazed to learn how cheap everything was there. She examined Vera's clothes closely, fingering the material, scraping the sole of a shoe with a fingernail, asking her daughter again if she had indeed bought it in Novi Sad and at the price quoted. She was interested in Vera's housing arrangement and was pleased to hear that she paid no rent. Couldn't Vera get the whole house back, or receive compensation for it? Vera knew nothing of such matters and shrugged the question off, but her mother threw a look at Hermann and suggested Jacob Bernister as a source of more reliable information. Bernister was an important factor in her calculations, anyway; through him, Vera could receive financial help, which could be paid back to his brother in Hannover. Five hundred dinars a month, for example, when reckoned in marks, would still be a lot less than her expenses in Germany. In any case, Vera didn't like it in Germany—wasn't that true, she asked, with no reproach in her voice, taking Vera's answer for granted. All that was left was to agree on the date for her departure; the middle of May would be just right, for the purchase of the new tavern would be completed by the first of June, at which time she and Hermann would have so much to do that it would be difficult for them to take care of her. Suddenly Tereza was generous; she left the tavern in Liese's and Hermann's charge for a morning and went out shopping with Vera. In a department store she bought her a coat, an umbrella, underwear, and as they were leaving, in the basement, at the last moment, a gold ring with a coral inset, to remind her now and then of her mother, she said. The packing was done. In addition to the suitcase she had brought with her, Vera was given a soft travel bag of waxed tartan canvas in which to put her newly acquired belongings. "Look, I dirtied it a little around the edges," her mother pointed out. "You mustn't tell Customs that you have anything new, otherwise they'll skin you alive."

The three of them took the streetcar to the station, the same one they took when she arrived half a year earlier. The tall buildings with shops on the ground floor and the empty lots between them went by. At the station Hermann carried her luggage into the train and placed it in an empty compartment; they now waited for the train to leave. "Do you ever see any of Gerhard's friends?" Tereza Arbeitsam asked unexpectedly as her lips twisted tearfully. Vera thought for a moment, mentioned two or three names, but there was no more time to talk; the conductor told the passengers to board the train, mother and daughter kissed quickly, and Hermann shook Vera's hand and bowed abruptly. Vera went into the compartment, stood by the window waving to her mother and Hermann as they walked along the platform, until the train picked up speed and they disappeared from sight.

Alone at last, Vera threw herself on the seat with a sigh of relief. As the train rolled on, she felt as if she were withdrawing backstage after an exhausting performance, which she felt her stay with her mother had been. Towns with tightly packed buildings passed, factories, orderly farms, everything spick-and-span, but, to her, impersonal. And unfamiliar, as if she had not traveled along that same route in the opposite direction with her heart thumping. She dozed off while it was still light, and was awakened by the conductor, a red-faced, rotund man who, businesslike and polite, asked for her ticket. Then she closed her eyes, shading them with the curtain, and went back to sleep. The train stopped from time to time at deserted stations. Occasionally someone peeked into the compartment, only to continue along the corridor looking for one that was empty. The Customs officers knocked on the door, checked her passport, whispered something to each other, asked what she had in her luggage, but did not search it. The night was cool; she wrapped herself in her new coat. They were now riding through tall mountains, the trees swaying nervously in the wind. The train stopped at a station with a large, brightly lit yellow building; railroadmen ran around waving little flags and blowing whistles. New Customs officers came on board, Austrians, quieter, slower. They greeted her pleasantly, left, came back again, this time with several Yugoslavs, all of them tall, hardy men who moved like people unaccustomed to being indoors. They called her Comrade and all but clapped her on the back. "Have a good time in Germany?" asked one, showing healthy white teeth. He wished her a pleasant journey, as if congratulating her on going home.

Men and women crowded into the compartment, carrying bundles and baskets, which they pushed under the seats; sitting, they took out bread, bacon, and bottles of slivovitz and water, offered food to Vera, who refused, even though she was hungry. They chomped and slurped, lit cigarettes, their bodies exuding the smell of sweat. It was a familiar smell, one that had surrounded her all her life but had been conspicuously absent on her mother's premises. Frequent baths, Vera concluded simply, and saw her mother in the room above the Beim vollen Tisch telling her to wash after the journey, and that vision melted into the face of the Blockälteste, her arm pointing imperiously, sending prisoners to the showers. Was bathing part of the mania of cheerfulness? The air in the compartment grew thick with the smell

192

of greasy food, exhaled by the gaping mouths of those who fell asleep. The sleepers: faces bony and swarthy, hands big and dark, bodies sprawled, legs stretched out in an unfinished movement, clumsy and uncomfortable. Their clothes were rumpled and not particularly clean, either. Poverty. Vera was slowly sinking into poverty, dropping on the social scale. The train passed through empty fields; barking dogs could be heard; at the stations shouts and curses echoed; faces glistening with dew or sweat appeared in the doorway, took a long look at the sleeping passengers, though it was clear from the start that there was no room.

At Stara Pazova, Vera got out to wait for her connection. It was early morning. The restaurant was closed, the waiting room full of scaffolding and buckets of whitewash. No shelter there. Shivering people were grouped around a heap of suitcases tied up with string. Then they all boarded a rattling, filthy old train that was saturated with the smell of urine. Chugging, wheezing, whistling desperately, it struggled over the bridge across the Danube. Novi Sad was her station: familiar porters, railroadmen, drawled speech. She took a streetcar home, entered the apartment, in which everything was just as she had left it. Disorder, neglect. Opening the windows wide onto the empty, quiet, barely awakened street, she had a sense of teetering over a pit of darkness and mud.

She had no regrets about the life she had left behind, but much regret about the life she now had chosen. Regret about everything: the quiet streets, the exhausted passers-by, the unsightly grass that pushed up between the worn Turkish cobblestones, the houses that seemed a shade darker since she last saw them. She went to the Bernisters' to pick up her first allowance;

it was a working day, but the trade representative was at home, as if expecting her. He gave her the money; his wife brought in coffee and stood in the doorway. They asked about Germany, Frankfurt, her mother, about Bernister's brother, whom Vera had seen only once and who had asked similar questions about his relatives in Novi Sad.

She went to see Mitzi, but found someone else's name on the door. She rang the bell, and an elderly woman, the new tenant, informed her that Mitzi had passed away two months ago. Mitzi had retired from her job, was about to move into an old-age home in Zagreb, had made all the arrangements, paid the first installment, chosen the room, and on her last day said good-bye to her neighbors, packed her belongings, sold or gave away what she didn't need, and in the evening dashed off to the hairdresser's to have her hair done. She came home, got undressed, went to bed, and the next morning, when the taxi driver she had ordered to take her to the station arrived and the neighbors broke down the door, they found her in bed, neatly covered, her freshly waved gray hair held in position by a hairnet, dead of a heart attack.

Vera went to the cemetery, found the mound with a polished wooden board at its head giving Mitzi's name and years of birth and death. She looked around and left, visiting no one there but Mitzi, because they had all gone unmarked—her father, grandmother, brother— and it was hard enough to see the grave in which Mitzi lay, with her wrinkled face and waved hair, slowly de-composing. Whom should Vera mourn the most? She mourned them all. She remembered the old ladies, her grandmother and her friends, who, along with Mitzi, only a few years earlier, had left their houses in a column escorted by soldiers with bayonets fixed. How they had wept, turning back to look at this dusty town, which, indifferent, continued to live without them.

She walked home, and as she approached it from the corner, the house looked the same as always, its foundations deep in the ground, its walls scarred by rain and wind, and its roof blackened, with the apartment that had once been her family's turned into an office, and her father's shed transformed into a storehouse for lentils and beans. She had the feeling that she was entering yet another cemetery. Here, at the gateway, she had usually met someone, her father, her brother, the maid; and from there her grandmother, absurdly dolled up in her black dress with white polka dots and black straw hat, used to go off on her visits; and there Count Armanyi had stopped her and, clutching his hat to the breast of his expensive gray suit, spoke of his longing for her. She mourned him, too, now, that man in whom she had once placed her hopes even though she had seen through his selfish intentions from the start. Even his selfishness, male and petty, she mourned, wondering what it had become, what the man had become. Was he alive, or dead like Mitzi, under a mound in Hungary or somewhere else?

Vera mourned everyone who had ever spoken to her, who had longed for her, whether out of love or out of lust, even the German soldiers whose convulsive spasms on top of her before they left for the front were the last expression of their will to live. They were all shadows now, voices from the past. Was there anything solid on this earth, anything that stood firm, so one would not need to say of it: That, too, has passed? It seemed to her that there was nothing. Desires, plans, people sending their calls of love and screams of pain into the air, and ultimately all this dissolved into a fog that floated aimlessly. And she herself was a wisp in that fog, lost among strange shadows and voices. Did she exist, or was she just another of those shadows and voices? She didn't feel like going in, didn't feel like eating or drinking. She had no need of anyone's company.

A person from the past found out that she had come back and, in the early evening, day after day, knocked at her door. She saw his silhouette in the frosted glass. It was not Bernister, it was a young outline, with a lock of unruly hair combed to one side. Unable to remember anyone like that and not wanting to, she simply waited for the man to go away.

And out there the seasons changed. It was autumn again, early autumn, still warm; the earth swelled; the trees in the courtyard bent low with dusty leaves; flies and bumblebees buzzed their way in through the window but could not find their way out. Vera got dressed and went out to buy food. (She went out only in the evening.) The windows were lighted; she could see women getting beds ready for the night, she could hear music blasting from a radio and a child's voice shouting "Mammaaa! Mammaaa!" in despair that there was no response. The cry grew softer as Vera moved down the street. Perhaps Mama was lying beneath Papa, or was out in the yard hanging up the wash, or had not come back from her afternoon visit. Who could tell? Not that it mattered—the misunderstanding remained, the child's vain call determined by some remote, unknown inevitability. Vera's eyes were moist: she knew that she would never be the cause of such a misunderstanding, because that possibility had been torn out of her. The sense of futility grew unbearable; she felt that she was ill, ill in her mind and heart, as if some germ had found its way into the coils of her brain and was digging, digging, and she could do nothing about it. And when it dug to the center, she would collapse or go mad. Then she heard her name repeated several times and saw a man of medium height hurrying toward her; his teeth gleamed in the light of a street lamp as powerful arms folded around her in a familiar embrace. When the arms released her, she looked closely at the man's face and saw that it was Sredoje Lazukić. She dropped her head on his shoulder and sobbed.

Chapter 17

Sredoje's meeting with Vera Kroner concluded a long, roundabout chain of events that began with his acceptance of the role of obedient son.

Six days after the outbreak of war, he left Novi Sad with his father, who dared not await the German and Hungarian forces under his own roof, having no desire to leave his male offspring as hostages to the enemy. Always loud in his public denunciations of Germany, as well as of the other nations who could play the aggressor on their own and threatened to do so, Nemanja Lazukić greeted the tearing up of the pact with Germany by making a speech from the balcony of the Town Hall, immediately after Dr. Marko Stanivuk, the leader of his party. He did not believe that he would actually have to make the sacrifices he vowed to make as he shook his fist above the heads of the assembled citizens; quite the contrary, he believed that his pronouncements would discourage the enemies in Berlin, Budapest, and Sofia. It was with this sentiment that he calmed his wife on returning home from the banquet that evening. And even when the sirens wailed and the silver German aircraft passed slowly across the sky in neat formations, he was troubled only for a moment. In the quiet of the dry cellar to which he had led his family, he declared, eyes raised prophetically to the ceiling, "This will cost them dear. They will have to subdue the entire country, and the Serbian soldier will stand firm."

After the alert was over, he went into town and returned with the news that Belgrade had been bombed. "Good. Everybody will hate them now." He packed his shaving kit and a towel into a small bag, because he had volunteered, being a captain in the reserve, for the post of deputy commander at the civil-defense headquarters. He remained on duty day and night, telephoning his family only once, to announce that the Yugoslav army had advanced deep into Bulgaria. Yet the town streets were filling up with retreating troops; hungry and tired, they sat on the sidewalks and knocked on doors asking for water. It was through their disordered ranks that he finally reached home, almost as crushed as they were. "Treason," he said. "We have to get away. Only temporarily, of course, for we'll win in the end, just as we did in the last war." He went into the spare room and took the suitcases from the closet, and asked his wife to pack everything he and his sons would need for a long trip. "You, my dear, will have to stay," he told her, placing his hand on her shoulder and looking her straight in the eye. "You'll take care of the house until our return, which won't be long." He went into town to look for transportation, and after many hours finally came back with Jovan, the elderly, broad-shouldered taxi driver who used to drive him to hearings in the neighboring towns, and, pointing to the suitcases lined up in the entrance hall, went to his room to change. His sons were already sitting in the low-slung blue car, and his wife stood by the windshield, wiping the tears from her eyes, when he appeared in the sports suit—plus fours and woolen knee socks—he wore for country outings. "Let's go." He gave the sign, then kissed his wife on both cheeks. "Don't you be afraid! You're a woman, so no one will do you any harm." Klara Lazukić stammered, "But where are you going, where are you taking my children?" Seated next to the driver, he stuck his head out of the window and said in a low voice, "Perhaps to Albania, perhaps farther. Until the fortunes of war bring us back to you." The taxi moved off.

At the first corner it had to slow down for the soldiers, who, pouring in from all directions, jammed the streets. The taxi edged its way through the ragged army lines and advanced along with them at a walking pace as far as the bridge across the Danube. Lazukić and his sons sat in soft, well-padded seats; through the glass they saw the faces of the grimy soldiers and felt like averting their eyes. "Fight on, you brave fellows!" Lazukić mumbled, unheard by the objects of his encouragement. Then he grew preoccupied with the car's slow progress and, leaning forward, urged Jovan to speed up. Jovan was silent, morose, uncomfortable with the assignment he had taken on. At the bridge they had to come to a stop before they could get their wheels aligned on the narrow causeway. The blue of the river stretched to the left and to the right and far into the distance. They turned to look back at the houses of Novi Sad, which stood still, as if expecting something.

On the main road they were swallowed up by the traffic. Columns of soldiers, horse-drawn guns on carriages, an occasional truck, field kitchens on high wheels, wagons carrying ammunition bumped against each other, all in a rush but powerless to widen the asphalt highway, on either side of which, in the ditches, lay burned overturned vehicles and equipment. They crept along, to the shouts and curses of the officers desperately urging on the soldiers and horses. Jovan clenched the steering wheel and changed gear constantly, while Nemanja Lazukić fidgeted in his seat and offered pointless advice. Rastko withdrew into his own thoughts, and Sredoje observed the scene with a mixture of shame and curiosity, as an unwelcome but exciting novelty.

At dusk they reached Indjija. Although Lazukić swore to God that the troops would stop there—he was reliably informed that a defensive front would be established on the slopes of Fruška Gora—the column continued to move in a dense, nervous mass. It was well into the night when they arrived at Stara Pazova. Worn out, they turned into a side street and stopped. Lazukić went off on foot to look for a place to stay. He was unsuccessful but decided to drive no farther; they would make do with the courtyard of a nearby inn, which could provide, if no room, at least the comfort of a hot meal. They took out their luggage, relieved their swollen bladders, washed their hands at a well, and, by the light of a kerosene lamp—for some reason there was no electricity—sat down at a round table in the downstairs room to a supper of goulash and pickled peppers. Lazukić engaged the innkeeper in conversation, told him what they had seen on the way, evaluated with him the chances for defense, and examined the possibility of asking a Slovak woman, who lived nearby but worked at the inn, for a room. Following the innkeeper, or, rather, his barely visible outline in the darkness, which echoed with the rumble of vehicles and the shouts of men from the main road, they walked through a garden, opened a creaking gate in a plank fence, woke sleeping dogs, listened to a hushed conversation, and heard a door bang open. Finally they were let into a large room with a low ceiling, rag rugs, and two immense beds pushed against the far wall. A buxom peasant woman wearing a head scarf and wide skirts prepared the beds for them, unfolded layer after layer of quilts, gave them a candle, accepted a tip, and left. They, in turn, undressed, climbed into the beds, covered themselves with the quilts, and, muttering about the cramped space and lack of air, fell asleep and slept through their first night as refugees.

The following morning, after breakfast at the inn, which took longer than they had intended, their plan to continue the journey was unexpectedly threatened by their driver's decision to return home at once. Lazukić pleaded with Jovan, reminded him of the many lucrative trips they had taken together, though he could not deny that he had hired the taxi for one day only; one day, he had thought, would be enough for them to reach Belgrade. The innkeeper, who was listening to the dispute with considerable interest, now interrupted to say that, according to what he heard that morning from a soldier, it was impossible to get to Belgrade now, because the bridges had been destroyed and the troops were moving in the direction of Obrenovac. This information silenced them for a moment, then served as a basis for new negotiation. Lazukić offered Jovan more money, for which Jovan agreed to take them to the ferry on the Sava right across from Obrenovac, but, as he said, not a step farther. They got into the taxi and pulled out onto the main road.

The column was still inching along in the same thick confusion of people and objects. Jovan had to wait for an opening in the stream, and as a horse harnessed to a cart lost its footing, he quickly moved in among the pedestrians and the vehicles. But they went even more slowly than the day before, because exasperation had made the men irritable, stubborn, and no one would give way to anyone else. The faces that peered in the car windows were no longer indifferent or curious, but hostile; their eyes, narrowed from lack of sleep, glared at the passengers with suspicion and hatred. Oppressed by this hatred, they drove on, almost holding their breath, and passed through occasional villages until dusk, when they finally reached the embankment, which teemed like a fairground with unharnessed, agitated horses, loaded carts, and milling hordes of people in uniform and in civilian clothes. As soon as he was paid, Jovan took his leave curtly, unpleasantly; restarting the engine, he turned the taxi around and disappeared in the dust made rosy by the twilight.

The three Lazukić men picked up their suitcases and clambered onto the embankment. In front of them were woods swarming with human figures, and beyond, wide and dark, the glistening surface of the river. They walked down the embankment and through the woods, stumbling over roots and the legs of people stretched out on the ground, and emerged at the water's edge, where they stopped to wait. On the other side of the gently flowing river, the far bank could be made out, black with vegetation under the pink vault of the sky. Nemanja Lazukić turned to the man next to him and asked about the ferry. With a listless hand the man pointed to a small dark shape that was in the process of detaching itself from the opposite shore. As if responding to a signal, the people around them got to their feet and, jostling for position, moved. Carried by this human current, Lazukić and his sons came up against an impenetrable wall of backs. Anxiously they watched the ferry approach slowly and finally, fifty paces to the right, touch ground. The crowd swung forward, which brought them ten paces closer to the place of embarkation. But the forty remaining paces were an impassable barrier. Worn out, they put down their suitcases and sat on them.

It took six crossings—three quarters of an hour each—before they reached the wooden landing, where with great effort they managed to elbow their way up the gangplank and onto the ferry. Greatly relieved, as if they had escaped a fire, they glided over the water, propelled by the boatman's long oars, to the Serbian side. There they found no smaller a crowd; pushed, shoved, and cursed at, tripping in the darkness, they proceeded slowly along a muddy road until they reached the town. They had hoped to find a place to stay the night, but everyone else had the same idea, and at the few lighted houses there was a departing stream of people who had already been turned away. Only the spacious railroad station was open to them, and there they collapsed, keeping close together, on the stone floor of the waiting room. Through the night they were wakened by newcomers, who stepped on them and pushed them closer to the wall. They dozed fitfully until the cold April dawn.

Hungry, they set out to look for food, but could not get near the inns, all besieged by crowds. They saw people carrying bread, and following the trail of this shining brown burden under so many arms, they found a bakery, which by some miracle was ignoring the war. In front of it, a mob pushing and fighting. While Rastko took care of the suitcases, sitting on them with his head bowed, Nemanja and Sredoje plunged into the battle for bread. They were the last to be served, and emerged with two loaves. They devoured them right there on the street, quenching their thirst with water from a fountain in a deserted marketplace, then picked up their suitcases and continued on their way. They came to a field not far from the town and paused to regain their breath. Nearby was a peasant cart with horses harnessed to it, and next to it a fire crackled; a mustachioed NCO was burning papers that two soldiers handed him from a chest.

Nemanja Lazukić walked over and started a conversation. The NCO, the orderly of a battalion in retreat, had just been told to destroy all confidential papers and was burning what he could before moving on. Lazukić asked if he could load their suitcases on the cart; the NCO hesitated but finally agreed. The cart rolled onto the road, and Lazukić and his sons walked in step behind it, staring at their suitcases; they identified now with the soldiers who the day before had glared at them as they sat uneasily in Jovan's taxi. Now they, too, were preoccupied with the road on which they trod, its bumps, holes, dust, and piles of horse droppings.

They were tired; Rastko began to limp. Stopping at the side of the road, they hurriedly removed his left shoe and sock and found that he had a large red blister on his heel. The father scolded his son for carelessness in the choice of shoes, mentioned the mother's negligence and the family's failure to understand the harsh realities of war. But Rastko limped no less after these reproaches than before and began to drop behind. Lazukić was obliged to negotiate once again with the NCO, who glanced at the youngster and motioned to him indifferently to climb onto the cart. Now Rastko's legs dangled over the side, between the slats, his eyes penitently glued to the road.

There was a rumbling of engines in the air, and as heads turned up to look for the source of the noise, aircraft appeared in the cloudless sky like huge birds and cast their shadows across the road. A rain of bullets ripped into things and people. The column scattered into the fields on either side of the road; the horses, frightened, began to trot. Sredoje jumped over a ditch into a plowed field and ran, and when the roaring of the planes grew louder, he lay on his stomach pressing against the warm, soft, freshly turned earth. In dismay he watched as the bullets approached; he was sure they were coming straight for him, and his heart missed a beat, but the shooting quickly subsided and he was unhurt. He raised his head and saw the road empty all the way to the next bend, where a white horse, free of its harness, was dragging behind it a purplish braid suspended from its torn belly.

A second wave of planes came over, a third; then there was silence. Not at all sure that the danger had passed, people rose from the field slowly, hesitantly, like animals awakening. Sredoje, too, got to his feet, listened for a while, heard nothing, and walked back to the road. He saw his father emerging from the ditch, looking at his feet. "Are you all right?" Sredoje asked. "Yes, I think so," answered the lawyer, "but my feet are wet through." He climbed onto the road, took several steps—with each step water squished from his low shoes—then sat on a milestone, unlaced his shoes, removed them, peeled off his socks, and wriggled his white toes. "Where are the suitcases?" But the road was deserted, the cart with the suitcases and Rastko long since gone. Lazukić thought for a moment, then felt in his pockets, took one white handkerchief from his coat and another from his trousers, wrapped them around his feet, turned his shoes upside down to drain the water out, and put them on again. "Like socks!" he said, almost with satisfaction, and walked, at first with an uncertain step, then more confidently, his calves bared and the white handkerchiefs flapping, their corners dragging on the ground and rapidly turning gray. "Hurry! We must catch up with Rastko."

They continued along the road, and only there, from a higher vantage point, noticed the destruction that the machine guns had left behind. At the edge of the road, next to a knapsack, an officer in an overcoat, bareheaded, was lying on his back, his arms and legs spread out as if he were asleep. Farther down the road, a white horse was dying, rolled to one side, its head jerking convulsively, its powerful hindquarters, caught in the coils of its entrails, kicking. A cart with a field kitchen was on fire; behind it two soldiers were kneeling, bent over a third, who lay groaning on the ground.

They were alone on the road as far as the eye could see, but when they turned around, they saw groups of soldiers and civilians moving away from the road and scattering in the direction of peasant houses. Again they heard the roar of engines and, without a word to each other, threw themselves into the field. Instinctively they ran toward the nearest house, but when they approached it, they saw men and women rushing out, taking cover in the bushes. "Over there!" Lazukić shouted to his son, running to a barn perched on posts, to the shelter of the knee-high space beneath it. In an instant they slid inside, and from there, panting, watched the road.

The noise came from beyond the hill in the road; then, at the top, something huge stood silhouetted against the sky, and when it came rolling down, they saw it was a tank, its front covered by a red flag bearing a crooked black cross. As they stared at that fluttering, miraculously clean red-and-black fabric, the tank slowly and steadily came so close that they could make out the face of the helmeted soldier standing in the turret. Another, smaller, vehicle appeared at the top of the hill, a motorcycle, its driver sitting tall in his seat, and next to him a second soldier, almost prone in the sidecar, his finger on the trigger of his machine gun. The tank rumbled ponderously along the road, followed by the motorcycle. "God, it's the Germans!" a high-pitched woman's voice cried out, and then a man's voice said, as if in answer, "Yugoslavia's done for."

They crawled out from under the barn, shook the dust off their clothing, and walked over to the peasant house, which drew those same people who had minutes earlier abandoned it. A woman, probably the one whom Lazukić and his son had heard, sank on a bench by the wall and covered her face with her hands; a group of peasants and two soldiers gathered in front of her, watched her with curiosity. "What'll we do with these?" One of the soldiers picked a rifle off the ground and held it by the barrel like a staff. The other continued to stare at the woman. The first soldier now turned to the peasants: "Is this your house? Can we bury the rifles here?" The second soldier gave a start. "Shut up, you fool!" he said, grabbed the rifle from his comrade, picked up his own, and carried them off behind the house. He disappeared among the fruit trees there, and when he returned, he no longer had the guns. "Come on," he said to his comrade, tugging at his sleeve, and they were off, past the back yard and into the field, walking briskly, heads forward. They disappeared from sight at the first dip in the ground.

Lazukić and Sredoje also decided to leave. But as soon as they started walking, they found themselves at a loss as to which direction to take: trudging through the fields along unfamiliar paths made no sense to them, and going back on the road seemed too dangerous. They felt hungry and tired, and at the same time realized, to their surprise, that it was growing dark. They looked at their watches: it was almost six. The day had seemed endlessly long, yet was over quickly. They decided not to journey at night and returned to the yard in front of the house. They discovered that the peasants gathered there were also refugees and that the owner was hiding inside. They knocked on the door, went in, and found an elderly peasant with a large red mole on his cheek, who was lighting a fire. The smoke sharpened their hunger and they asked for food.

The peasant, turning his eyes away as if to protect them from the smoke, was silent for a moment, then said, "All I have is eggs, but they're two dinars each now." After Lazukić agreed to that astonishing price, the old man let them sit at the table and called in a woman. She was much younger, perhaps his daughter or servant, and silently prepared scrambled eggs and then cut two large slices of bread on the rough, bare table. Immediately after supper the peasant took them to a barn in back of the house, with barrels stored in one corner; he put down some clean straw for them and spread two worn blankets over it. They asked for water to wash their faces and feet. Lazukić hung his socks to dry by the window. Groaning, the two of them stretched out on the straw and covered themselves. They felt like kings: a fresh breeze drifted in through an open window; their numbed legs were at rest; from the road came the rumble of threatening vehicles, but here, within the walls of the barn, they felt temporarily safe. "Where is Rastko now?" Sredoje wondered out loud, drifting off to sleep. "In German-occupied territory," his father answered. "You see how fast those devils move. We'll find him tomorrow." They fell asleep.

The next morning the cold roused them early, but their hosts were already up and about. They had breakfast, scrambled eggs again, and set off at once. The road was full, crowded with people moving in both directions: refugees and soldiers with no rifles. Abandoned cartridge belts lay in large piles on the roadside. Lazukić and Sredoje paused to get their bearings. "We must continue in the direction we were heading yesterday," Lazukić said, "until we find Rastko and hear what's going on in Belgrade."

They had to pick their way through a mass of objects left lying on the road after the attack of the day before: crates, sacks, overturned carts, and here and there the corpse of a soldier pulled to one side, hands crossed on his chest. From the winding ribbed tracks, it was clear that the tanks, too, had circled the debris. Now the tanks were nowhere to be seen; it was as if they had simply traveled through and disappeared into the distance, but motorcycles spluttered by every few minutes, always with a sidecar and a crew of two Germans. The drivers no longer wore helmets, but tight, lightweight caps, and they passed the refugees and unarmed soldiers without so much as looking at them, focused instead on a task that had evidently been assigned them. The people on the road moved warily out of their way, lowered their voices, squinted at them uncertainly, and now and then a hand waved abashedly, an expression of gratitude and relief that no one was being harmed. The nearer Lazukić and Sredoje got to a town, the more Germans there were, and on the outskirts of Ub a whole column of German trucks was lined up along the edge of the road. Their crews, sprawled on the grass, eyes half-closed against the sun, were breakfasting on canned food and beer. The people passing looked in amazement at these enemies comfortably installed and enjoying themselves, as if disbelieving this evidence of their humanity; a crowd of children stood staring at them, sucking their thumbs. Lazukić looked at them too and remarked, "They don't go hungry, like our men."

The town of Ub seethed with people; now that the danger was over and they were out of hiding, everyone was eager to stretch his legs and size up the new situation. The shops were closed. The first inn Lazukić and Sredoje came across was full to bursting. Lazukić fought his way to the counter behind which the hefty, bare-chested proprietor, with eyebrows thick as mustaches, was serving slivovitz.

"Good morning," Lazukić shouted above the noise of the customers. "I'm looking for my son. A student. He must have passed through here yesterday afternoon."

The proprietor put down the bottle of slivovitz. "Where are you from?"

"Novi Sad. We were separated from my elder son en route."

"A student, you say?"

"Yes, a student."

"They say there's a student lying in the church. A schoolboy, more like."

"How do you mean, lying in the church?" Lazukić stammered, clutching the counter, because his legs were giving way.

"How? The planes killed him, the soldiers carried him into the church."

Lazukić stared with a completely blank expression, then turned and, without looking left or right, rushed out. Sredoje, who had only half heard the proprietor's answer amid the clamor, followed. But he couldn't catch up with his father in the crowded street. He bumped into people just as his father did a few steps ahead, lost sight of him, spotted him talking to someone; then his father disappeared again, diving headlong into the crowd. Sredoje reached a square and saw the broad façade of a freshly whitewashed church and, in front, his father alone, arms spread wide, rushing in through the open doorway.

No longer hurrying, a premonition of disaster making his step heavy and hesitant, Sredoje went in, too. After the bright sun, in the dark interior of the church, he could not at once make out his father. He went past a row of lighted candles, headed toward the pulpit, before which, on trestles, stood a freshly constructed, unpainted coffin, and inside it a sharp, thin face propped up on a cushion. It was not until he looked closely that he recognized his brother. Without glasses, Rastko looked younger, childlike. Then Sredoje felt a shapeless mass of clothing and limbs at his feet. He bent down to look: it was, indeed, his father. From the depths of the church, people came forward, a hand sprinkled water from an earthenware vessel over his father's face. His father opened his eyes, groaned, tried to get up, and again collapsed, sobbing, on the floor. Sredoje tried to catch him under the arms; other hands helped; and as they got his father back on his feet, a dark-skinned priest with a short trimmed beard hurried up to them and beckoned them to a side door. They took Lazukić out into the open air, through a porch entrance to the priest's lodging next door, and sat him on a couch.

The priest's wife ran up, dark, pretty, with down above her upper lip, in a black dress that had grown too tight for her and molded her small, protruding stomach. She bustled about, opened a cupboard the width of a whole wall, and took out a bottle of brandy. Together they forced several drops of the liquid between Lazukić's lips. He sucked the brandy in, came to his senses, and looked around. "Out, everybody, out," the priest urged them all impatiently, and one by one, though reluctantly, Sredoje's helpers left.

"Are you with him?" asked the priest, looking sharply at Sredoje, who had not left.

"Yes. I'm the brother—I mean, his other son."

The priest nodded. "My condolences. I've made arrangements to bury the boy today." He stood there as if expecting an answer, but since Sredoje said nothing, he left the room.

Sredoje was now alone with his father, who fell into a half-sleep from which he occasionally started with

213

a sob. Outside, the sun emerged from the clouds, brightening the room; a yellow ray illuminated the bottom corner of the couch and Lazukić's feet in their mud-encrusted shoes. A rhythmic banging was heard, and Sredoje realized that someone was nailing down the coffin.

His brother's death, because it was so unexpected, was a shock to him. He recalled exactly the details that led up to it, starting with the blister on Rastko's foot and his father asking the NCO to find a place for Rastko on the cart. What would have happened if it had been he, Sredoje, and not Rastko, who got the blister and was put on the cart? In that case, the cart would have bolted with him, the bullets would have torn into him, and *he* would now be lying in the coffin dead, with no more blood in his body, oblivious of the warm day, of the morose priest and his pretty, energetic wife. That not only could have happened, but that would have happened, and the thought sent a shudder of the unknown through Sredoje.

Impatient, tired of staying where nothing was going on, he went out to the porch. There, the people who had helped him carry his father into the priest's house were standing in a circle. They must have known by now who Sredoje was, because they fell silent when he appeared and stared at his face. He felt uncomfortable that in that face they did not find the despair they were expecting; in self-defense he went up to them and asked the first thing that came to mind: "Where is the priest?" No one answered; they went on looking at him with intense curiosity. Then the priest appeared and shouted, as if giving an order, "Let's go!" He went into the room, and Sredoje followed. Lazukić was sitting on the edge of the couch, head in his hands. The priest donned his vestments and approached them. "What was the young man's name?"

Sredoje looked at his father and saw that his chin was trembling. "Rastko Lazukić," Sredoje answered.

"Profession?"

"Law student."

At that, Nemanja Lazukić raised his weary face. "My son! My firstborn!" And he began to weep uncontrollably.

Sredoje sat down beside him and put an arm around his shoulders, surprised at how small and frail his father's body had become. He said, "You stay here. I'll go alone."

His father shuddered at the suggestion, jumped to his feet in fear, swaying slightly. "No, no. How could you think of it? I'm coming!"

They walked out arm in arm. On the porch the funeral procession was already lined up: the coffin, nailed down, covered with black cloth, stood on a cart, followed by the priest and the same cluster of people, though now fewer in number. Sredoje cast a glance at the house, hoping that the priest's wife would put in an appearance, perhaps even join the procession, but she didn't even peep through the door. Two men from the group pulled the cart, and the procession moved from the porch, down a passageway behind the church, and into a narrow, crooked street. Supporting his stumbling father, Sredoje looked at the houses and the men and women lined up in front, their eyes fixed on the procession; he still felt uncomfortable because he was not properly devastated by his loss, though less so as he grew used to it. Slowly, very slowly, they wound their way out of the town between run-down houses with gypsies perched in front, reached the cemetery, crisscrossed with bushes and trees, and stopped next to an open grave, where two men in worn, ragged clothes were sitting on a heap of fresh earth.

The priest cleared his throat, read a prayer that incorporated Rastko's name and profession, in a clear, sharp voice intoned the psalm for the dead, and, making the sign of the cross over the grave, signaled to the two gravediggers with his eyes. They set to work, lowering the coffin on ropes and shoveling earth over it. Nemanja Lazukić moved toward the grave, but Sredoje held him back until he realized that his father wanted only to throw a handful of earth on the coffin. He helped him to do this, and repeated the gesture himself. When the grave was filled and the earth shaped into a mound with light blows of the shovels, Sredoje gently urged his father to move away, to leave.

The priest fell in step beside them and asked, "Where will you go now? Do you have a place to stay?" When they said no, he nodded as if that was what he had expected. "I'll go with you to the inn and we'll make arrangements with the landlord." They quickened their pace back into town, taking the same streets. The priest asked briefly how Rastko had met his end, wrinkling his nose at their answer. Lazukić stammered out a question about the funeral expense, but the priest with a wave of the hand murmured that there was plenty of time for that. "Now we will have to help one another more," he added after a pause, lowering his voice confidentially and casting a glance at the two of them.

It was dusk now, and there were fewer people on the streets, but the inn, the same inn they had entered upon their arrival in Ub, was if anything more crowded, and at a table in the center two German soldiers sat with glasses in front of them. The priest motioned to the proprietor to come out from behind the counter and talked with him for some time; then the proprietor came up to Lazukić and told him that he had one guest room upstairs and would prepare it for him. The priest said good-bye to them and left.

"Would you like a bite to eat?" asked the proprietor.

Lazukić shook his head indifferently and asked where the room was. But at the mention of food, Sredoje felt a hunger as violent as a blow in the stomach. "I don't mind waiting for something to eat," he said.

While the proprietor took his father upstairs, Sredoje found an empty chair at a corner table next to a man who was half asleep. It wasn't until he sat down and leaned against the back of the chair that he felt how tired he was; his whole body throbbed. The proprietor came back, looked for Sredoje, and walked over to him. "I only have beans, but they're good." Sredoje nodded. The food arrived, and he threw himself at it, savoring the warmth and flavor of each spoonful he swallowed. After polishing his plate and drinking his fill of water, he slumped back in his chair, covered with sweat. The proprietor lit a kerosene lamp behind the counter (evidently there was no power), and the customers, as if at a prearranged sign, began to leave. Even the man at Sredoje's table came to life, got up, and hobbled off.

But several guests stayed on at the middle table, gathered around the two German soldiers. The soldier who sat facing Sredoje, a fair-haired, middle-aged man, took out of his jacket pocket letters, photographs, cigarettes, and a penknife, and displayed them to those assembled, precisely pronouncing the German words for each—*meine Frau, mein Sohn, meine Tochter, Deutsche Zigaretten, Taschenmesser*—as if introducing them to parts of himself in order to become closer to them, to be better understood. The locals—one a dark, stout, older man in a worn suit, another bony, with close-cropped hair, and another wearing a hat, his mustache drooping— obediently observed these objects, nodding, and with smiles described to each other in Serbian what they saw, as if it were something of great value and importance. Then they in turn, poking their thumbs at their chests, gave their own names and professions. The stout man was a barber, and as proof he produced a razor from the top pocket of his coat; the man with the close-cropped hair was a leather worker; and the one with the hat and the drooping mustache was a cobbler. All had their businesses on the main street, they informed the German, calling him over to the door and pointing, after a few misunderstandings, to their shops.

When it seemed that subject was exhausted, the German beckoned them to the table; the proprietor, too, approached. Then the German took out a pack of cards and, grinning at his own cleverness, started to cut and shuffle with the fingers of one hand. He laughed, showing a row of metal teeth; everybody else laughed, too, except for Sredoje, whose eyes were too tired to watch the lightning movement of the brightly colored, smooth surfaces of the cards. His head ached, so he got up, left the laughter and exclamations of approval, and went up the stairs. At the top he found a half-open door to a little room and in the dimness recognized his father on the only bed. Sredoje undressed and lay down next to him. His father sighed, "My Rastko, my Rastko," let out a moan, then continued snoring fitfully. For a long time Sredoje was kept awake by his headache and the laughter from the room below, which now and then exploded into roars of mirth.

The following morning he was again awakened by shouts from below. He opened his eyes and saw his father sitting on the bed, barefoot, staring into space, fingering his three-day growth of graying beard. "Poor wretches that we are, my son," he muttered, shaking his head. They got up, dressed, and went downstairs.

Sredoje saw the same faces he had left the night before: the barber, the proprietor, the leather worker. Only the Germans and the cobbler were gone. He said to his father, "That dark-haired man is a barber. We'll ask him to shave you." But the proprietor, who had overheard, laughed loudly. "Shave you! Don't you know? They cleaned us out!" That started the rest of them talking, interrupting each other: their shops had been broken into and looted; everything that could be taken had been taken, everything.

"Even our razors and scissors," said the barber in disgust. "Our needles, too," said the leather worker. "All the bottles, glasses, all the money from the till," said the proprietor in despair. But the thief was not named.

Nemanja Lazukić, unaware of the Germans the night before, asked what had happened, but the only answer was a dismissive wave of the hand. The talk of possessions disappearing prompted him to inquire about the suitcases Rastko had with him in the military cart: Had anyone seen them? Had the soldiers who brought in the body? But no one knew anything about the suitcases or the soldiers.

"There's no hope at all," the proprietor told him. "Since this morning they've been taking the soldiers away, and your men are probably among them." For breakfast, all the proprietor could serve was sherbet and bread. "I couldn't give you anything else if you killed me," he growled. "They even took my coffee. I don't know how I'm going to feed my family." But after breakfast he invited Lazukić and Sredoje into the cold kitchen, where he let Lazukić shave with his razor.

Once in the street, Lazukić and Sredoje saw a group of Yugoslav soldiers, without rifles, walking two by two, escorted by armed Germans. The local people stood on the sidewalk, watching this silently, solemnly, but with no sign of life in their eyes. No one paid attention to Lazukić and his son anymore; it was as if they had been absorbed into the occupied and looted town of Ub. They went to see the priest.

They found him in front of his house, without his surplice, in trousers and an old coat, feeding the chickens. They barely recognized him. He did not put down the basket filled with maize or ask them into the house; he simply accepted the money that the lawyer put into his free hand and nodded.

"Will you look after the grave, please, until I am able to do so myself?"

"I will, I will," replied the priest, turning to the chickens, who were piping impatiently around him.

They went out to the cemetery and found it deserted, not a single visitor. Lazukić wept before the fresh mound, caressed the cross, which bore no inscription. "We'll come back soon, we will," he whispered. Then they walked back into the town.

At the inn they asked the proprietor over to an empty table to consult him on how to proceed with their journey. Confidentially, as if they were his own family, he told them all he knew: the roads were jammed, the Germans were looting and capturing Yugoslav soldiers stranded on the roadsides, and prices were astronomical.

"Any news about Belgrade?" asked Lazukić.

"They say Belgrade's been razed."

The lawyer flinched. "But where can we go to, other than Belgrade? I have a good friend there who will take us in."

"Why don't you go home?" the proprietor suggested, blinking at them from beneath his impressive eyebrows.

"Home? Never!" Then Lazukić qualified the refusal: "At least for the time being, until we hear what's going on there. But help us find a cart to take us to Belgrade. I feel so weak after all that has hit me that I can't go on foot."

The proprietor promised to do his best. He gave them lunch, despite what he had said earlier about having nothing: beans, perhaps from the same pot from which Sredoje had been served the night before. They spent the afternoon in the inn, listening to idle talk, until they were bored to tears, and to bickering, to rumors of looting and battles "down south," where it was said that the main force of the army had remained intact. In the late afternoon the proprietor brought a well-fed young man to their table, who downed two brandies at Lazukić's expense before agreeing to come with his cart the next morning. They went to bed.

In the morning, when they looked out the window of their room, they saw a fine, light sleet falling on roofs and streets. They went downstairs, drank some sherbet, and waited. Their driver was not to be seen. Lazukić paced impatiently to the door and back, asking the proprietor question after question, while the latter tried to calm him: Yes, the man would come; for the money he was promised, he would not let them down. And indeed, suddenly the driver appeared at the door in rubber boots, holding a whip. "Where are those people bound for Belgrade?" he shouted. "Let's go, we must hurry!"

Taking their leave of the proprietor, they went out into the street, into snow, and saw a peasant cart with a small horse, its head lowered. In the cart were two elderly peasants and a fat woman wrapped in a black shawl with a child on her knees.

"You didn't say there would be other passengers," protested the lawyer.

"That's the way it is, sir," retorted the driver with an impudent grin, tightening the horse's harness. "Take it or leave it."

They climbed into the cart, squeezed past the other passengers, and found a place for themselves on a thin layer of straw. The driver jumped on in front (there was no seat for him, either), sat on the floor of the cart with his legs hanging over the side, and cracked the whip. The little horse set off at a canter, slowed down at once, and continued at an even walking pace. Under the heavy sky, along the slushy road, side by side with columns of soldiers marching into captivity, they covered, just barely, the distance to Obrenovac by evening. The driver unloaded them at the marketplace and announced that he was returning to Ub.

"We agreed that you would take us to Belgrade! That's why I gave you a thousand dinars." Lazukić was the only one to object.

"I don't know anything about that! There's a war on!" replied the driver gruffly. He whipped the horse. Yet as he was turning the cart around, he shouted over his shoulder, "Go see if there's a train."

This they did at once, and at the railroad station found out that there would be a train for Belgrade the next morning. They spent the night in the waiting room, and the next day, just before noon, the train was ready. Without tickets—the ticket office was closed—they jumped into a car, along with hundreds of people carrying suitcases and bundles. The train lurched and rattled along for four hours, until it reached Belgrade.

Lazukić and Sredoje set off on foot. Directly opposite the station, they saw the first heavily damaged building, around which a group of men were digging, supervised by armed Germans. There were ruins on every street, mansions and shacks reduced to the equality of rubble. Bricks and mortar lay everywhere. They had to make their way around them or, in places, climb over. Closer to the center, there was less destruction, but at one corner they came across a corpse: a man stretched out, feet in low shoes, legs spread wide, body and head covered with wrapping paper held down by half a brick, which someone had placed there to keep it from blowing away. From beneath the corpse had come a dark pool of blood, now coagulated, like jelly. Down the street a German soldier in a steel helmet with a machine gun across his chest, guarding a gate, looked at them hard. "They mean business," Lazukić whispered to Sredoje after they passed the soldier, and he quickened his pace. "As long as we find my good friend at home. Where else could we go tonight?"

At Terazije they entered a multistoried building, climbed to the third floor, walked all the way down a corridor open to a courtyard, knocked on a door. Nemanja Lazukić threw his arms around the heavy man with a mane of black hair and a neatly trimmed mustache who came out in his shirtsleeves, squinting suspiciously. "Spaso, brother, it's an evil hour that brings us together."

Chapter 18

Other departures from home.

Sep Lehnart's, on an early morning in May 1941, in blue trousers too short for him, in a white shirt and canvas shoes with worn rubber soles that let through the cold of the earth. Bareheaded, his hair newly cut, and carrying a small parcel of food his mother had prepared for him and silently, tearfully pushed into his unwilling embrace before letting him go and awkwardly walking after him as far as the gate to wave farewell. Pride and shame. Straightening his shoulders, so everyone can see how grown-up and determined he has become, but pressing the parcel against his thigh so no one will notice it. Just trying to get through the streets as quickly as he can. But no, let it last as long as possible, let everyone watch him from behind the curtains secretly drawn in front of their thumping cowards' hearts. Girls still asleep in their high beds, in white linen nightgowns, with the scent of their bodies beneath the eiderdown, while here, a mere two meters away, strides tomorrow's soldier, hard, pitiless, ready for the ordeals of battle. Degenerate Germans, those neighbors of his, fat-bottomed, dull-witted, greedy for a mother's chicken *paprikash* and a new motorcycle. Rich, they don't understand that wealth is uncertain if not backed by force, here in a foreign land where the people would happily drive them out with jeering whistles and stones. Wealth-weakness, wealth-sin. Only the wealth of an entire nation is justified: as a means for it to spread worldwide, in the cause of power everlasting.

At the cross-street he passes Heim's house—where he used to roll barrels, suffer blows—the house pretending to be padlocked, with shutters lowered on its dozen windows: We're not here, we don't exist. To smash that silence, that sniveling, that false humility, to break the gate, the windows, and drag them, the bloodsuckers, out by their fleshy bat ears—the bearded old man, his bald, weak-eyed wife, and his repressed son—onto the dirty street, to wipe it with their faces in atonement for having lifted their hands against a German. His muscles are quivering; it's he who has to be silent now. Restraint, denial of vengeance, not being allowed the pleasure of a personal settling of scores. Everyone will settle scores with everyone, but impersonally, coldly, when the order is given, when the time comes.

Down there on Dudarska Street the truck is revving up. Could he be late? He breaks out in a sweat; he has no watch, but he knows that he started well ahead of time. But here comes one of his companions, along the opposite side of the street, not hurrying. His friend at least has a bag, old and shapeless, it's true, his father's locksmith's bag, but not a bundle deprived of any sign of profession. Perhaps Sep could ask him to take the parcel and put it in the bag. But that would draw attention, it's better to say nothing, and anyway, why not be proud of his poverty, the fact that all his provisions are wrapped in a sheet of paper and held in one hand? Is it not a state that already belongs to the past? The boys on the truck are humming, two of them are jostling, to get warm. But Sep is no longer cold, he is warmed up from walking and also at the thought of leaving.

Here's the driver, a real soldier, in uniform, hands in his pockets, cigarette hanging out of his mouth. Is it far? No one knows, it's a military secret. Good. As far as Sep is concerned, they can go to the ends of the earth and never again set eyes on this selfish village and its people with no honor and no backbone. He puts his hand on the truck's cold metal side, to climb on, but his parcel is in the way. He drops it, the paper comes open, two pork chops roll into the grass. He sweats again. Did anyone notice? They're laughing, but fortunately not at him; one of his comrades slipped in the scramble and fell into the truck. Sep clambers over the side. From now on, if anyone asks, the package is not his. If only they would get moving as quickly as possible.

Reza Kroner's departure in the autumn of 1944. Flight. Shaken by the uncertainty of whether they will leave or not, uncertain night after night next to Hermann in bed, often with no embrace, for he is exhausted, having to run around all day long with messages; there are too few men left, what with all the larger units withdrawn. Rumors. Snoring, waking, listening to the distant rumble, it's the guns, she knows, though it's the first time she's heard them. But he denies it. No, the Russians aren't coming, he knows for sure, he's been told, they'll be stopped by a counterattack from the flank, near Belgrade and in Hungary. You're crazy, Hermann, she tells him, you're blind, the last faithful dog, can't you see that everyone is running, even the captain has left, and that lieutenant will, too, we'll be the last two left, they'll shoot us, I don't want to be shot, I've suffered enough, you killed my son, I can't go on. She keeps on at him until he shuts her up with "Jewish whore!" Silence. In the morning her eyes are burning, as soon as he leaves she falls into a deep sleep and dreams of water.

She gets up, goes shopping, the streets are full of movement, the army is packing up, German citizens are climbing into carts, just as the Jews climbed into carts half a year ago, her Vera and Robert. She sees people she knows, approaches them, asks where they're going, but they answer through clenched teeth. To them, she's Kroner's wife and they're angry, as if it's her fault they're losing the war. If she asks a Serb, she doesn't get a straight answer either, because they know about Hermann and hate her or are afraid of her. Here Hermann comes at last, sweating, his cap pushed onto the back of his head, his eyes bulging, and his face gray. His long nose quivers.

"The Russians are outside the town. We must leave."

"What about the lieutenant?"

"They all left this morning. I only just managed to stay, for your sake."

She's moved by that. With him, then, in life or in death. To redeem her dead son. "When?"

"Now, right away. The truck is waiting on the road to Futog."

"Won't they come and fetch us?"

"How can they? All fifty of them?"

She looks at him. Before her eyes appear the possessions she has been jotting down for weeks as the most important to take: winter suit, fur coat, quilts, Persian carpet from Robert's room, leather armchair, German books with their gilt embossed titles, icebox, almost new. "Are you mad? How can we leave empty-handed?"

"Take what you can carry," he yells, "or the truck will leave without us."

Like a sleepwalker she obeys, grabs her bag with her money and jewelry, yanks her fur coat from the closet, picks up the cut-glass vase from the table, and he's already pushing her out the door. "On foot? Like this?"

He clutches his head, tortured by her pleading tone, her woebegone face. "There's a bicycle in the hall."

"Gerd's bicycle?"

They climb on it, she on the crossbar, hugging the bag and the fur coat and the vase, he perched on the saddle behind her, his jacket half-unbuttoned, like two young lovers going to the river for a swim. Hermann pedaling, out of breath, sweating, she cramped by the crossbar, which cuts into her flesh, they go through the town, past hidden, mocking eyes, not looking back, afraid that someone will run up to them and knock them down on the main road.

Gerhard dragged away, a year and a half earlier. Between two policemen, handcuffs on his wrists, through the entrance hall, past the bicycle, which has been standing there ever since the official took over his father's business. What if he jumped onto the saddle, threw off the policemen on either side, rode through the open door and out into the street? He could steer even with his hands tied. But they would catch him before he could pick up speed, would knock him down or shoot him. It wouldn't matter if they killed him, but if they wounded him, that could weaken his resistance to interrogation.

He should have defended himself the moment they entered, should have made a dive for the kitchen table and stabbed at least one of them with a knife. Selling his life dearly. But even that could be a mistake, a hasty assumption, because he didn't know the charge; there was always a chance, one in a hundred, that this might be a mistake, against which he could defend himself.

They manhandle him through the gateway to the street and into a tall black limousine, whose driver rushes to open the door as soon as he sees them in the side mirror. Gerhard sits on the soft seat; he is enveloped by their breathing, their sharp evil-smelling sweat. He sniffs himself; he doesn't smell like they do. Is it because he's young, or because he's not afraid? This is perhaps the last moment without fear, he thinks, watching streets in the evening quiet as they pass. A minute can be a lifetime if one lives it intensely, if one pays careful attention to the passing houses, the people, if one knows that one has done what one wanted to do. What would he have gained had he not been arrested, holding out until the final victory? Nothing. A repetition of what had gone before. And as for other experiences, such as new places, new people, a woman he might have desired, they are insignificant compared to this sense of certainty growing within him. To solidify that feeling, Gerhard opens his mouth and begins to sing loudly the first song that comes to mind, the one his mistress was singing in the cellar the night before, after they made love, her head on his chest, in her steady metallic alto, "Midőn Mexikóban hajóra szálltam én," from the film "Juarez," which he otherwise considered a simple-minded, sentimental apology for monarchy.

The departure of Slavica Božić to the village of Gajdova, at the insistence of her second husband, the veteran noncommissioned officer Veselin Djurašković, who had been released from the army as an invalid and given a house there. Packing into chests, secretly, out of Veselin's sharp sight, all Milinko's belongings, down to the last objects, his little comb, pencil, sharpener, because when he comes back to her, he must find it all. She is certain that he will come back, that he is alive. She has received no official notice of his death, as have the parents of the other boys who went into the army with him and perished in the offensive in Slavonia. He has disappeared, yes, because she has had no news of him for three years, but two of his comrades, Stevo Crnobar, who took part in the attack on Dravograd at Milinko's side, and the company commander, Marko Orlović-Dečko, said that as they retreated from the overrun position on the canal beneath the bridge they saw Milinko—left behind by the others, probably wounded by a mine—being put on a truck by German soldiers. The Germans very likely thought that he was one of them, because, the day before, the commissar gave him a uniform taken from a dead German soldier, to replace his civilian clothes, as a reward for good conduct and bravery in battle. But that eye-witness account, now that the war is over, has not led to any trace of Milinko, despite requests for information made to the Red Cross and more recently to the Yugoslav Military Mission in Berlin.

This worries Slavica Djurašković and has made her bitter, but her conviction, prompted by instinct, is not shaken. She would think of him, dream of him, in a different way if he were no longer alive. Concealing her thoughts from her new husband, who wants her to be continually attentive and cheerful, she broods secretly about Milinko: where he might be, whether he has enough to eat, whether he has shoes and clothing. When it's cold, she remembers how sensitive he used to be to the cold. But her anxiety is always for one who lives, and whenever a doubt creeps in—"perhaps he is no longer . . ."—the doubt is instantly cut off, because she knows, trembling and triumphant, that he is alive, that somewhere he exists, and, in answer to her fear, a warm wave of his presence floods across the space separating them.

The departure of the three Kroners is unusual, because it leaves behind a member of the family, who is protected by her origins and her husband's generous decision not to urge her to accept his faith. That fourth member prepares food and clothing for their journey in self-effacing silence, like the servant she once was, when her masters went on an outing or a vacation. But she has been cut off anyway from the three Kroners by her liaison with the NCO Hermann Arbeitsam, pulled back down to the lower class. The lower class, however, is now protected, while the upper class moves higher, to heaven, and the irony of this gives an edge to the preparations. The food, packed by a servant who never really became a lady: chunks of cold meat, cheese, and lots of bread. "Do you want the child to be poisoned? And is she to carry all that with her?" Kroner sneers in disgust, his eyes wide in his dark face, not blaming his wife for this piece of stupidity, but for her ignorance of their fate, even though he has only a premonition of it.

A premonition of death, of no return to this oppressive home weighed down with lies and mistakes, a home that, even so, he experiences as the last solid ground before the plunge from a high crag into a chasm. Tomorrow he will step into the street with a haversack over his shoulder, taking with him his mother and his daughter, whose protector he ought to be, in obedience to an order that is illegal by the laws of humanity, the product of a deranged mind. Obeying instead of rebelling, as Gerhard did. Gerhard was right. Kroner acknowledges it once again, and with bitterness feels rising in him his son's passion for survival, which he once disparaged and condemned. To live in the present, for the moment, while one is still master of one's actions, and after so many years he wants once again that redhaired woman whom he took for her body, but who now is leaving him for another man.

"Don't you know better?" he shouts at her, sweeping the clumsy bundles to the kitchen floor, where they fall apart like dead frogs. He replaces them with foods he has selected: bacon, cubes of sugar, bars of chocolate. "Wrap that up!" In exasperation he pushes her back to the table, surreptitiously feeling her arm, thigh, buttock, and his eyes fix hungrily on her neck, on her calves. She is still desirable and warm, and he ought to get her into his room, in the evening when everyone retires after a long day, and take her like a whore one last time. But he is too afraid now even for that. He stands there, the sweat of fear and humiliation pouring down his face.

Vera sees this unseemly lusting, the way her father's eyes play over her mother's body, and is revolted. Ah, to escape! That's what she has always wanted to do, but escape is impossible now by virtue of her birth and the fact that she will be carted off to a place created for her, another prison. But perhaps—she isn't sure—it will be a better place; perhaps, in some lower, half-animal, day-to-day existence, such as accounts of the camps promise, unprecedented peace awaits her.

Her support is her grandmother, not her father, whose desire for life has flared up so inappropriately. For food, which he shovels into his thin body or wraps into small packages with the precision of a shop assistant, and for his wife, her mother, around whom he prowls like a tomcat. Her grandmother does nothing; she prays. Aloud, on her knees, banging her head against the floor, in words dredged up from a remembered language rich in guttural consonants. Vera takes lunch and dinner to her—her last—in her part of the house and pushes the food into the old lady, who, like a sick animal, distractedly and reluctantly chews at it with broken teeth, letting whole mouthfuls drop into her lap. Vera sees a model for herself in this distraction and abasement, and when the moment of departure comes, she takes her grandmother's bundle along with her own. Keeping at a distance from her father, bidding a tearless farewell to her mother, who stands at the gate trying to press superfluous things on them and offering ridiculous advice (they should write, they should try not to catch cold), Vera sets off at a slow pace, suited to the old lady, to the synagogue, from where they will all be detailed, so they have been told, and assigned work to redeem their crime of being Jewish.

Vera's departure will influence the way Milinko Božić leaves home. He watches from a distance, long since removed from the stage and powerless to help, disarmed, in this collision of fire-breathing dragons which, roaring, consume their victims. Six months later, when only memories remain of those taken away, one of the dragons suddenly pushes its furious head forward and offers Milinko a ride. Join the people's army, drive the Germans out: such is the exhortation on the posters in newly liberated Novi Sad, bustling with public speaking and peasants' carts.

Milinko has no use for those overheated promises and passions; they remind him, as have all other excesses, of his father's drunken boasting, whose outcome he had experienced. Milinko's model is still the quiet wisdom he encountered in the Kroner household during those evenings he spent sitting with his host surrounded by books, knowing that Vera was nearby, Vera, whom he would win through his own quiet wisdom. Now he considers it his duty to revenge the defilement and annihilation of what he held most precious.

That it should be by the violent means the enemy employs saddens him, of course. The thought of doing violence to someone's body, someone's thoughts, someone's will horrifies him. And he dreads pain, which also seems a deviation from dignity and reason. But now he must go to meet chance bullets, throw himself among explosions, expose his throat and belly to the jabs of sharpened metal. He does not feel equal to this ordeal, nor does he believe that he will come through it unharmed; he is more like a nonswimmer who plunges into the water to save a drowning man.

When Milinko first started visiting Vera's house, Kroner lent him a German novel about the First World War, in which, of all the horrible episodes, he was most affected by a short description of the death of a secondary character in whom he immediately recognized himself: a soldier who does not see the sense of fighting, of killing in order not to be killed, and so lacks the instinct common to hunter and hunted, which turns yesterday's civilian into a willd beast which crawls, hides in ambush, fires, and finds cover. The character perishes clumsily, absent-mindedly; knowing that he will die, he moves like a sleepwalker toward that inevitability from the very first battle. Reading the book, Milinko was certain that if he was forced to fight, he would share that fate, and felt the character's wounds in his own flesh. The identification was so strong that it acquired the force of prophecy.

His mother, too, because she lost her husband from a bullet, because Milinko is all she has, and because he is so good, has a presentiment of doom and tries to mobilize her contacts, not highly placed but numerous, to find her son a position that will shelter him from immediate danger. But just as the brother-in-law of one of her old customers, a Partisan commander, Veselin Djurašković, moves in with her and promises to find Milinko employment in a military warehouse not far from town, Milinko enlists as a volunteer for the front. When he tells his mother what he has done and hears, among her lamentations, of the opportunity now missed, he feels drained of blood, seeing this as a sign that his fate has been decided. He will take nothing with him, not a change of underwear, not even a book to read, for he is certain that he is descending, despite his high principles, into an abyss of savagery and blood.

Chapter 19

They kept us in the synagogue three days, from the twenty-fifth to the twenty-eighth of April. On the fourth day, at dawn, they woke us, ordered us to gather our belongings for a journey, but not to make noise, because the town was still asleep. We hurriedly collected our bags and tied them securely, then filed out into the street, where the guards formed us into ranks and marched us down the middle of the road to the station. It was still dark. Those who wept were told to be quiet, those who could not control themselves were silenced with rifle butts. Outside the station, on a siding, was a long line of freight cars with doors open and guards all around. They ordered us to get in. The cars quickly filled, but the guards forced more and more people to climb in, hitting them with their rifles. Finally, when we were all in, they shut and bolted the doors. In the darkness there was shouting, confusion. Some called for help because they were injured, some cried out for air, children screamed as their mothers tried to hush them. On each side of the car was a small window strung with barbed wire, and everyone pressed to get near them. Those who could not stand any longer sat on their luggage, but that encroached on the space of others, so there were quarrels. We seated our grandmother on our bags, and my father and I stayed next to her. Gradually people grew quiet from sheer weariness. Outside, it was getting light. When would we leave? Where would we go? No one knew. We listened to the voices of the guards outside, and the people standing by the windows reported on what they could see. Hours passed. Suddenly the train jerked into motion, and some began to weep again. Whenever the train stopped, those standing by the windows read out loud the names of the stations. We were moving north. Sometime in the afternoon we by-passed Subotica and stopped in an open field. The guards were shouting, banging, and our door opened with a crash. Out! We grabbed our bags and stumbled out, glad to be in the fresh air, filled with the hope that perhaps this was the end of our ordeal. In the front of the train the guards formed us into a column, led us across the rails to a road, and in about half an hour we reached an empty mill, in which we were shut up. Inside the mill were several thousand people from Subotica and the surrounding area. There was not enough room for them, and now we climbed over them with our baggage, trying to make space for ourselves. There was almost nowhere to sit or lie down. The floor was concrete. We had brought two blankets with us and now spread one of them for my grandmother, covered her with the other, and huddled close to her, my father and I, sitting in our coats. The people from Subotica told us we wouldn't be staying there, we were all going on to Germany. At night the children—there were hundreds in our room—took turns crying, and those who had to go to the bathroom trampled over the rest of us. There was only one toilet, two taps. Wherever you went, you had to get permission and be escorted by guards, and for everything you waited in line. So we saw the dawn arrive. In the morning, we were given boiled chicory, and during the day we ate what we had brought with us, which was soon consumed. We spent two weeks in that place. One morning, they told us to pack our bags and formed us into ranks. We waited until the afternoon, the stronger among us standing, the older and weaker sitting or lying on the ground, without water, because no one was allowed to leave the ranks. Finally they took us to the train. Once again, the loading, the crush in the car, the heading north. The train passed Baja, and again we stopped in an open field. When the door opened, the sky was dark, though it was still daytime. The wind hurled dust, the clouds rolled above us, cold and heavy. The guards, agitated, ordered the old people and children to one side, ordered us to put our bags down. People rushed to one another, said their good-byes, redistributed their packages, shared comforting lies. The guards, angry, struck with their rifle butts indiscriminately. Finally we started, and as the storm neared and the wind turned icy, we were harried along at a trot. When the camp came in sight—a barbed-wire fence in front of two large wooden barracks—it began to pour. Prodded and cursed, we rushed through the camp entrance and straight for the closer barrack. It had an earth floor that hadn't been watered down, so our feet raised a thick cloud of dust that made us choke and cough. Somebody screamed that it was a gas chamber, and for a moment we all believed that. More people pushed in behind us, soaking wet, raising new waves of dust, until the barrack was packed with people coughing. Outside, it continued to pour. The roof began to leak, and water fell on us, so we took off our coats to cover our heads, but the water came down in streams and soon covered the earth floor, covered our shoes. We spent the night standing in mud. In the morning, they herded us out of the barrack, and we were not allowed to go back until evening. The old people and children they drove out of the other barrack; we saw them staggering, heard them weeping, but were not allowed to go near them. We sat on the ground and tried to figure out what was going to happen. After the storm it became hot. There was no shade, no grass, and the blankets we could have used to shelter ourselves had been taken away when we left the train. We gathered odd pieces of wood, stuck them in the ground, spread our coats over them like tents. We were hungry, thirsty. The guards brought soup in huge cauldrons but we had no cups or plates, they were in the bags that had been taken away from us. We went back and forth, begging, borrowing, the guards relaxing the harsh discipline somewhat. In the early evening, I sneaked across to the other barrack to look for my grandmother, but couldn't find her in the crowd. I returned quickly for fear I would be found out and punished. They herded us back into the barrack, into the mud, and ordered each of us to occupy a sleeping space of forty-five centimeters. People measured with their feet, with their hands, but there was not enough room. Then the guards rushed in and ordered us to lie down as we were, and they said that anyone who made a noise or moved would be killed. We squatted through the night. The next day, they again drove us outside. Again I managed to get across to the other barrack without being seen. Pushing

my way through a mob of people, I saw my grandmother sitting half-conscious, her arms around a concrete pillar. She must have clutched it before sliding to
the ground. I begged for some water, obtained a few
drops with great difficulty, sprinkled her face, got her
on her feet, and smuggled her across to our group.
Somehow we managed to hide my grandmother, keeping her with us for all the ten days we were at Baja. She
listened to us, suffered patiently, almost as if unaware,
and only occasionally moved her lips in prayer. But my
father found the disorder, the hunger and thirst unbearable, and particularly the crowding in the evening,
when quarrels broke out in the barrack and the guards,
with blows, made us huddle in a heap. He became irritable, cursed our neighbors, then would hold his head
in his hands in remorse. During our last night in the
barrack, I woke up and heard him weeping, but said
nothing, thinking it better for him to be alone with his
trouble. In the morning, when the command to move
was given and we rose and lined up, my father spread
his coat on the ground and lay down on his back with
his eyes closed. I ran over to him in a panic and begged
him to stand up. Not opening his eyes, he told me to
leave him. He couldn't go on, he said, couldn't take it.
The soldiers noticed us, pushed me back. I joined my
grandmother, who did not know what was happening,
and the column continued on its way, walking around
my father. Leading my grandmother by the hand, I looked
back and saw guards gathered around my father, who
still lay on the ground. I heard two shots, and then we
were outside the camp. We were marched back to the
railroad track, where a train was waiting. The day was
hot, the cars like an oven from standing in the sun, the

windows no longer strung with wire but boarded up. Our car was filled, but the guards kept loading in more people, until we were packed solid. The doors were shut. We thought we would all be suffocated, that this was indeed the end we had all feared from the guards' threats and the whispers of our prophets of doom. Sweat poured from us. The children, again with us, cried for water. Feeling along the bottom of the car, someone came across buckets of lukewarm water. There was fighting, pushing, shouting. One of the women suggested that the children be given sleeping pills, which some had brought along. Each child was given half a tablet, and finally they grew quiet. The train did not move until the evening. It traveled all that night and the following day, and not once were the doors opened. Again the children cried, and the old people fell from exhaustion, making the already cramped space more cramped. There was some air in the car while the train moved, but people needed to relieve themselves. One of the buckets, which we had emptied, was used for that purpose. The car stank. Someone covered the bucket with a coat, but people were going to it all the time, until it became too full and excrement flooded the floor. We had no more water. Hardly any food. All I had left in my pocket were a few lumps of sugar and one small piece of bacon. My grandmother and I took turns chewing it, saying nothing. On the evening of the second day, the train stopped. The car door was opened, but our attempts to jump out were met by Hungarian policemen's threats and bayonets. An officer told us that we had reached the frontier and would now be handed over to the Germans. "Up to now you've had it good, you dirty Yids, but that's all over. So anyone who has anything of value, gold, rings, bracelets, anything you've hidden, cough it up. If the Germans find that someone's held on to the smallest trinket, they'll kill the whole carload without mercy." He hurried off down the length of the train. There was urgent whispering. Although our bags were taken from us at Baja, we all had managed to hide a small thing of value, in case there was the possibility later of buying something with it. Some people thought it was dangerous to hand over anything, because that would be proof of our deception, but others said it was dangerous not to obey the order. Finally, we collected several articles of gold in an old man's hat and gave that to the police. They seized the hat and, right there in front of the car, before our eyes, distributed the gold among them, then pulled the door shut on us. After perhaps an hour, the door scraped open again. Now German soldiers stood in front of our car with flashlights fastened to their chests. Two or three of us cried out in German, begging for water and to be allowed out of the car to go to the bathroom. "Shut your mouths!" was their answer. One of them announced that we would be searched, and if even one of us was found to have anything of value, everyone in the car would be shot. It was our last chance, he said, to surrender what we had hidden. Someone dared to reply that we had given all our remaining possessions to the Hungarians. At this, the Germans swore, but did not let up in their demands: "Collect what you have, scum, or we'll search you one by one, and then you're done for." Again, reluctantly, several gold objects fell into a handkerchief, and I gave up the ring I had sewn into the hem of my grandmother's dress. The door was shut; the train moved on. From weariness and hunger, our legs gave way, and we would have collapsed if we had not been held up-right by other bodies pressed against us. The old and the sick fainted, raved, prayed, and the children whimpered with fatigue. We guessed that we had passed through Austria, though it no longer mattered. We would have exchanged our state for any other. On the third day, we stopped. The door of the car was opened, and we heard shouts of "Los! Los!" Outside, the daylight was blinding, the air sharp as we poured out of the car and, pushing or carrying the weak, fell on the ground. Dogs barked, German shepherds on leashes held by healthy young pink-faced German soldiers, and we, like refuse, crawled at their feet, gasping for air and rest. But we were ordered to stand up. "Los! Los!" And the men had to go to the left, the women and children to the right. There were farewells, weeping, my grandmother and I made our way with the women to the right. They pushed us forward, I held my grandmother around the waist, because she could hardly move her legs, until we reached a tall officer who was separating the women left and right with a thin stick. He lowered the stick between me and my grandmother, she slipped off to the side, to the ground. I bent to help her, but the officer's stick pushed me to the other side, and the guards herded other women after me. That's how I left my grandmother. I didn't have time to look back, and I never saw her again. We were arranged into ranks of five, and I found myself with four strange women. Marching along a path lined with soldiers and dogs, we came to a high barbed-wire fence; behind it were hundreds of people the like of which I had never seen in my life—emaciated, gray, with huge, bulging eyes and hairless heads. Waving rags in their shrunken hands. "Madmen!" someone whispered, and for a moment we believed that. The guards opened the gate, and we entered among those apparitions, who now made incomprehensible signs or pointed with their thin, dirty fingers to their mouths. We passed them, and passed prisoners using the brief time they had after washing themselves to dry whatever clothing they had washed, too, surreptitiously, by walking back and forth, which we would do ourselves the following day. Then we were in front of a large brick building. Two well-dressed women in German military caps came out and ordered us to strip for a bath. We left our clothes in separate little piles and waited, naked, holding our shoes in our hands, until we were let into the building. After showers, which sprinkled us with only a few drops of lukewarm water, the German women pushed us into the next place, where we were received by men in striped prison clothes, watched over by a soldier. They shaved our heads and bodies, sprayed a stinging liquid between our legs, and pushed us on to the next place, where we were given clothing from a heap—oversized, bedraggled, torn, so that for a moment we looked like a band of revelers. They quickly lined us up and marched us to a barrack. There were three rows of double bunks, no blankets, only bare boards. We had to lie down five to a bed and could hardly move. In the evening, they took us out for roll call, counted us, recorded us, but gave us nothing to eat. We complained of hunger, but the trusty of our barrack, a young Slovak woman, told us that we would get no food tomorrow either, we were not on the provisions list until the day after. We lay down on our cramped beds, our stomachs aching, delirious from the desire for food. In the morning, we were awakened at two-thirty—it was to be the same every day—and given half an hour to relieve ourselves and wash, but since there were only two latrines for all the thirty-two barracks, and only one wash basin, people were still pushing and shoving when the order for roll call was given. We had to stand in place until late morning, when the Lagerälteste arrived to inspect us, a woman in uniform escorted by SS men and dogs. Before she came, some of the women fainted, and the trusty hit with a stick anyone who tried to help them. After the roll call, we all collapsed in exhaustion. We were not allowed back in the barrack, and so spent the day lying on the ground, twisted with hunger. In the evening, roll call again, until late into the night. Now there were dozens of women unconscious. We were ordered to drag them to the roll call and lay them out in rows of five. After the roll call we had to drag them back into the barrack. The next day, we got up in the dark again, again ran to the latrine and the wash basin, and went to roll call. Then our first breakfast, a soup of pine needles. We had no spoons, no dishes; we drank the sickeningly sweet but warm liquid from a single mess tin, passing it after each mouthful. In the afternoon, turnip soup and a piece of bread. In the evening, a little marmalade, a slice of brawn. The minute we swallowed the food, our hunger, unsatisfied, would gnaw at our stomachs worse than before, but then it would go away while we stood, half-asleep, half-unconscious, at roll call. We grew weak, we could hardly move. But we knew what awaited us if the last of our strength went; we saw what had happened to the camp inmates before us. One day, they herded several hundred women into the barrack next door, all skeletons who had trouble putting one foot in front of the other. In the evening, after roll call and after we had just got to sleep, we were awakened by shouting, barking, screaming. We went to the windows and saw closed black trucks in front of the other barrack and German soldiers forcing the skeleton women into them. The women resisted, they yelled at the top of their lungs that they didn't want to go to the ovens, they were still strong, they could work, and their fear gave them new strength, they clutched convulsively at the door frames, the windows, at anything they could, and some even climbed on the roof of the barrack. But the searchlights from the guard towers located them, and the soldiers and dogs pulled them down and threw them into the trucks, which took them away. The following day, we began to be sorted for the ovens. Two SS men came into the barrack with a woman doctor in a white coat and the trusty. They set out narrow planks in the middle of the floor and, stripped naked, we had to run the length of them, from end to end. If anyone stumbled, lost her balance, touched the floor with her foot, the doctor made a tired movement with his hand, and the SS men grabbed her like a sack and tossed her, no matter how much she struggled, outside, where the black truck was waiting. I didn't stumble, but something else happened. The SS sergeant, Handke—we tried to avoid him, because he enjoyed hitting us at roll call for no reason—was there, and when I ran across the planks, he beckoned me over with his finger. He looked me up and down, pinched my arm to see how quickly the flesh recovered, then repeated the test on my breasts and thighs. He told me to wait by the door. He did the same thing a little later with Klara, a girl from Užgorod. After the inspection was over and the black truck was on its way, the trusty took our numbers, gave us dresses, and Handke, with the other SS men, escorted us out of the barrack. He took us to be bathed and disinfected, just the two of us, then through the camp and to a fence that separated the camp from the administration building. The soldier at the gate stood at attention. We passed the Kommandantur, the workshops, and went as far as the hospital, on the other side. There, they handed us over to prisoner nurses. We were told to undress and were given clean hospital gowns. They took us into a room with a row of cubicles, put each of us in a separate one, and told us to lie down. A strong light was shining. Two nurses came in, told me to spread my legs wide, then gave me an injection there that hurt terribly. Soon I went numb. They came in again, helped me to my feet, and dragged me past the cubicles into the operating room. Klara was already on one of the tables. They strapped my legs to a metal frame, tied my hands to my body, and a doctor wearing a mask and rubber gloves came in. They all bent over me. I saw a long drill-like needle that ended in a corkscrew, then felt a burning between my legs and, despite the numbness, a sharp pain deep inside, in the womb, as if it were being pulled out. They withdrew the needle and untied me. I was bleeding heavily, and they packed cotton wool in me and carried me back to the cubicle on a stretcher. I asked what had been done to me. One of the nurses hissed through his teeth: "It's so you won't have a baby, stupid." I was feverish. But in the evening they brought me food, a soup much thicker and tastier than anything I had had so far in the camp. The next day, while I was being bandaged, a nurse pulled the gown off my shoulder and tattooed something across my left breast. This time I didn't even bother to ask what it was. I was half-delirious. Later, when I felt better, I read it. My convalescence lasted about a week. The bleeding stopped, and Handke came to fetch me. He brought a dress for me, which I had to put on right there in front of him. He motioned to me to follow him. We went out of the hospital and to a building nearby, which was called the "house of pleasure." It was a long room with cubicles like those Klara and I had been in at the hospital, except that each cubicle was closed off by a white curtain. Each had a bed. Klara was not yet there, but there were women in the other cubicles. We were eighteen in all. We could sit or lie down, but were not allowed to leave the cubicle except three times a day and all together. The commandant of the house of pleasure, Gisela, was a German woman who had been found guilty of poisoning her sister. Her cubicle, the last, had a door instead of a curtain. She wore a uniform, boots, and had a whip attached to her right forearm. When the soldiers came, from either our camp or a nearby garrison, or from units passing through on their way to the front, Gisela would shout, "Everyone out!" We would stand, each in front of her curtain, and the soldiers would look us over and choose. The girl chosen was supposed to go into her cubicle, take off her clothes, and make herself available. Gisela warned us that we must be nice to our visitors, satisfy their every wish, and that any girl who did not would be beaten to death. One by one she called us into her cubicle, undressed us, and showed us, herself undressed, what we had to do with the soldiers, but at the same time it was her way of getting her own pleasure. We had more food than in the camp, almost enough food, we were cleanly dressed, we showered every day, our heads were no longer shaved. But we were terrified at every visit, because we knew that we would not be able to defend ourselves against any accusation that we had not satisfied. Klara and I, in fact, replaced two girls who had been punished—that was what my neighbor, a Czech Jewess, whispered to me across the cubicle partition. I myself witnessed one such punishment. The victims were two sisters, Leah and Tzinna, brought into the camp from a Polish ghetto, probably no more than fifteen or sixteen, still undeveloped, and always terrified. Perhaps they didn't know what to do in bed to satisfy the soldiers, perhaps Gisela just decided that they were not suitable or not to her liking as women. One morning, we were ordered into the circle in front of the administration building, and from the other side of the camp they brought hundreds of inmates right up to the fence, all of them stumbling skeletons, just as we had been before we came to the house of pleasure. Then the Germans emerged from the administration building, from the storerooms and guard posts, their uniforms unbuttoned, without their weapons, to watch the spectacle. Handke carried out the punishment. Two wooden horses were brought out, like those used in gymnastics but without the padded top. Gisela led the two girls up to them. The girls were holding each other by the hand, weeping. Handke, almost gently, separated them, suddenly ripped the dress off one and then the other, and deftly tied them tight to the horses, each arm and leg separately. A soldier handed him a stick, perhaps a meter long, and thick. Handke stood behind Leah and with all his might hit her on the leg below the knee. She screamed, but we could hear the crack of the bone breaking. Then he hit her on the other leg. Then on both her legs above the knees. Leah was still screaming. Then he stepped to one side and hit her across the base of her spine, so hard that her body, even though tied down, bounced. The next blow was to the middle of the back. Her head was now hanging—she had lost consciousness—but Handke kept hitting until he smashed her head in. After that, he stuck his stick under his arm, unbuttoned his jacket, and lit a cigarette. We watched him smoke and walk up and down the row of us, looking at us with a smile on his face. Tzinna, too, watched him, followed him with bulging, glassy eyes. He went up to her. He did the same with her. Then, brandishing the stick, he walked to the administration building with measured strides, and the Germans, as he went past, clapped him on the back. They led us back into the house of pleasure while some of the prisoners came with handcarts to take Leah and Tzinna to the ovens. Eventually Handke killed and replaced all the women except Regina, a girl from Košice, my neighbor Helena, and me. He had already told us that we would suffer the same fate if Germany lost the war, that we had no hope of living to see it. But we still hoped, each to herself, although when together we repeated Handke's threats. There were frequent alerts because of Allied planes flying overhead, but we couldn't leave the building. Gisela locked the doors from the outside and took shelter at the Kommandantur. It was at those times that we could make our plans. But we were careful, for Gisela had the habit of questioning us separately about what the others were saying. The only one I trusted was Helena, and during the alerts she came into my cubicle or I went into hers, and we plotted how to stay alive when the Russians or the Americans arrived. We talked nonsense:

We would attack Gisela, tie her up, and use her as a hostage; or we would seize the weapons from the nearest guard post. But when the moment of liberation came, we had no chance to do anything heroic. The Germans emptied the camp in stages: They took the surviving prisoners into a field, where they mowed them down with machine guns and set fire to them, because the ovens couldn't handle such a large number of bodies. Meanwhile, they themselves were leaving—the storeroom people, followed by the hospital people and the administration, until only the guards were left. No one visited us anymore, and we were given hardly any food. Gisela stuck a revolver in her belt. One morning, after we were allowed to go to the latrine, we heard hurried orders, a guard rushed up and shouted to Gisela, and she shouted to us to get back into the house of pleasure at once. Instinctively, I didn't obey. I heard the women's footsteps leaving the latrine, but then realized that they would find me missing and come to look for me. So I left the latrine, sneaked around the building, and lay on the ground behind a wall. I heard agitated orders, men running, shooting. I pressed my head to the ground and waited, determined not to move, to wait for my death there. The shots grew more frequent; whole bursts of gunfire could be heard, and the sound of men running. Then silence, then running feet again, the clatter of weapons, shooting. Suddenly, in the distance, the sound of many voices in a long shout that sounded like a shout of triumph. I didn't dare believe my ears, I stayed where I was. The noise got nearer, then petered away. I heard something being broken nearby—it had to be the windows of the administration building. Again silence. I couldn't stand it any longer. I raised my head and crawled out. There was no one around. I went into the latrine. Then I thought that a German left behind might find me there, so I went out again. Where should I go? I didn't dare go into the administration building or the storeroom. The door of our house of pleasure was wide open. Inside, everything was smashed, the curtains were torn and bloodstained, and the women were dead in their cubicles, in pools of blood. I heard a groan. It was Regina, she crawled out from behind her bed and collapsed at my feet. I turned her over; she had a wound in her neck. I tore off a piece of curtain and bandaged it. She said, "It was Handke," and pointed to her legs, which were wounded, too. I tried to drag her out by the shoulders, but she groaned, so I put her down and ran outside. There I came upon two prisoners, who were carrying bloodstained shovels. I asked them to help me carry the girl into the abandoned Kommandantur. I stayed there with Regina and took care of her until the Soviet army arrived, fed us, and arranged for our transport home.

Chapter 20

Sredoje Lazukić viewed the Occupation with the vindictive pleasure of a descendant viewing the corpse of his haughty ancestor. Yesterday's circle of constraint, though he had not seen it then as constraint, was broken. Law and order were no more, because they were maintained by an invader with a machine gun across his chest and pale eyebrows and a frown beneath the rim of his steel helmet. Respect was no more: hunger and fear had destroyed it. Patriotism was no more: shame had made a mockery of it.

Belgrade, the great metropolis, the capital described in school textbooks, the residence of the monarch for whom every Sunday prayers were said in church, was spread out before Sredoje like a junkyard. The surviving inhabitants poked around the still-smoking ruins, retrieving an undamaged picture, a chair in one piece, a jar of jam miraculously unbroken. Worried housewives, their shoulders hunched, roamed the marketplaces, which the peasants warily avoided, buying their food instead in doorways and alleyways at three times the normal price. The taverns were empty, as were the movie houses and the station waiting rooms, because word had got around that the Germans were seizing people at such places of assembly and putting them to work clearing the streets of rubble.

People sat in their apartments, said nothing, sighed, looked out the windows, drank slivovitz from their meager reserves, and played cards without paying attention. They slept badly, cursed, ground their teeth. Hatred said they should have nothing to do with this gloomy, disrupted new life, but empty stomachs said to hell with hatred, and empty stomachs won. So the people came out, exposing themselves to police seizures and insults, and they observed the curfew, became accustomed to seeing the bodies of hanged men on Terazije Square, and breathed grateful sighs of relief when they reached home. They located the offices of the new authorities and submitted applications for identity cards and ration books. They submitted requests for work or to be given their old jobs back. They curried favor with those who had been the first to associate with the Germans and to gain their confidence. They began to learn German.

Nemanja Lazukić and his son spent several days at the apartment of his old friend Spasoje Gigić, who was a tax assessor. In that time, Lazukić said almost nothing, opening his mouth only to sigh. Then he set off to make the rounds of those of his acquaintances in Belgrade who had family in Novi Sad, to try to get a message to his wife and learn about the situation there. He came back distraught, but more animated: On its arrival in the town, the Hungarian army had shot a hundred prominent Serbs. This confirmed his fears. But he had outwitted the enemy.

In the houses where he had sought news, he met refugees like himself, men faced with the inevitability of starting a new life; they had need of his advice and even his help as a lawyer. He obtained a few papers for them, helped with two or three formalities in court, and for this received valuables from them in payment. In the evening, he discussed with Spaso and Spaso's portly wife, Živana, who had problems with her legs, how to convert these articles into ready cash, because he wanted to relieve the couple of the burden of his and Sredoje's keep, though for form's sake they refused at first. Finally they established a number of contacts for him, and from then on the chain of transactions that led from legal services to money assumed a certain regularity. Then the chain shortened: watches, jewelry, and cameras could be used directly as barter, without the necessity of going to the Town Council and court offices. The lawyer became a pawnbroker.

He got up later now, and stayed in the apartment virtually all day, since people in need brought their possessions to him, and he persuaded potential buyers to come as well. But all this clandestine traffic frightened Gigić's sickly wife, and as a result of her remarks, tension grew between the old friends. Lazukić looked for a separate apartment for himself. By that time—September 1941—he had good connections in the new underworld of the Occupation; so he succeeded in moving into a bachelor apartment that belonged to an Industrial Bank partner who had been arrested. The place was on Dobrnjac Street, and the furniture was included in the bargain, massive, dark, carved pieces that filled the large single room with shadows. But Lazukić, in keeping with his new profession, which he had unexpectedly taken a great liking to, lowered the blinds halfway, and this made everything still darker.

He would sit in an armchair behind the desk and, squinting dubiously to left and right, pull out the deep drawers and sift through the items to be sold: rings, gold chains, watches, cuff links, gold and silver brooches with precious and semiprecious stones, all jumbled together. He already had an exact record of every piece in his head, but liked to run them through his fingers. If anyone rang the doorbell, he would rapidly and noiselessly put everything back, lock the drawers, drop the keys into his trousers pocket, go to the door, and after a precautionary look through the peephole, let his customer in. He would cough pointedly in Sredoje's direction, for him to leave, having no wish to involve the boy in any unpleasant consequences of this unauthorized commerce.

At first Sredoje was reluctant to forsake the comfort of the apartment, especially in bad weather; and, each time, Lazukić had to bribe him with extra pocket money. With this bounty the young man roamed the streets of Belgrade, in search of the pleasures to which he had become accustomed in Novi Sad. But he had no idea where in Belgrade such pleasures were provided, and without friends his own age he had no way of finding out. So in his wanderings he kept his eyes open and followed his instinct on what direction to take. Sometimes this was decided for him when he saw a suspicious character, with a bundle under his arm, walking with a step as uncertain as his own; sometimes it was a woman in a short skirt, who, looking over her shoulder, suddenly ducked into a doorway; sometimes it was a group of men gathered in front of a tavern, which Sredoje would enter.

As a rule, he would find himself in a small, gloomy

room with a few bare tables and a counter, behind which the unshaven proprietor or his slovenly, bad-tempered wife was drying glasses and pouring drinks. Sredoje would sit down and wait patiently. Before long the door in the back would open, and a girl or a woman with heavily painted lips and cheeks, and that look of both indifference and questioning he knew so well, would walk in, neatening her hair. He would order another drink, light a cigarette (he had begun to smoke by then), and study the girl with care: her legs, breasts, neck, hips, and, from her movements and expression, her temperament. He sweated in indecision, afraid that if he approached her, she might laugh at him coarsely and turn him down, because Belgrade, after small, well-mannered Novi Sad, seemed aggressive and direct. Then the woman, at the first, barely perceptible, invitation, would sit at some other customer's table, ready to drink, laugh, and allow herself to be pawed, allaying Sredoje's fears when it was too late for him to take action. He continued to observe what went on at that table, noting every gesture, every wink, listening to every word, deriving a masochistic pleasure from the expertise of the other man, whom he envied and hated.

More and more often, green uniforms made their appearance among the clientele; Sredoje watched these men with special curiosity. The German soldiers usually came in twos, stiffly, as if out of duty and not for enjoyment. From the doorway they saluted the room in general, took off their caps and placed them neatly on the rack, sat at an empty corner table, and ordered beer, which they took a long time drinking. Finally they called a woman to the table, and after coming to an agreement with her, more by gestures than by words, one of them went out with her while the other stayed to hold the table. Then they changed places. They were incredibly quick in the sexual act and obviously well organized: they didn't get carried away, didn't get drunk. When both were finished with the woman, they sat and finished their beer, talking together and nodding.

Sredoje was fascinated. He admired them for being so sure of themselves, so composed, for being able to take their pleasure so deliberately, matter-of-factly, without fuss. But what really enchanted him was the thought that their being in this tavern, this evening, was transitory, that tomorrow they would be in another town, or in a battle, and would be killed. Sredoje sensed that they would all die, for now the conflict with the vast Soviet Union had begun, and there was no doubt but that eventually Germany must go down in defeat. Yet this only increased his admiration for them: warriors condemned to death. He felt the need to talk to them, to offer his assistance in understanding what for them was an unfamiliar language, to make friends with them, and learn, from the horse's mouth, where their strength of character came from. But he never approached them; that would have drawn upon him the hostility of his compatriots, who blinked at those uniformed intruders with an affability that masked the same contempt and hatred that they in turn inspired in Sredoje.

In any case, Sredoje's wish was soon fulfilled, and without any effort on his part, because the German soldiers—the officers, particularly—found out that articles of value could be bought "under the counter" from his father and began to come to Dobrnjac Street. At first the lawyer did not like to let them into the apartment, but his reluctance disappeared after several profitable deals.

Since he spoke no German, on such occasions he did not dismiss Sredoje with a cough. Sredoje began to translate for his father: simple sentences that were easily repeated in the other language. "How much is it?" "Can you make it a little less?" "What else do you have?" But the lawyer was delighted with this modest demonstration of his son's knowledge. Several months later, even after he had picked up enough of the language to bargain with the Germans himself, he still insisted on Sredoje's presence. During the negotiations he would sit to one side, deep in the shadow, and from there, nodding his head in satisfaction, would watch and listen as his proposals and answers were turned into foreign words and finally into an agreement.

His opinion of the Germans underwent a change. Sometimes, after a customer departed with a piece, having paid well, Lazukić would compare German gentlemanly largesse and Serbian tight-fistedness, occasionally going so far as to regret his earlier prejudice, for which—he maintained—the local Germans of Novi Sad were responsible; they were dull and small-minded, obviously degenerate, not like these "real" Germans.

He took a special liking to Captain Dieter Waldenheim, who appeared on the scene as a buyer in the following year, 1942, shortly before the lawyer received the news that his wife, Sredoje's mother, had been killed in Novi Sad during an air raid. The death of that meek woman, whose whole life was lived in the service of her family, lay between father and son for days, like a black cloud. They had given her too little in return for her devotion and, by leaving her, bore some of the blame for her death. Waldenheim sensed something wrong the moment he stepped into the apartment, where he was no longer a stranger, and asked what was the matter. Lazukić mumbled and waved his hand; Sredoje was silent. But Waldenheim, as he examined the articles the lawyer had set out on the table, asked again, until Sredoje, with no prompting from his father, blurted out what they had heard. Lazukić began to weep. Waldenheim, who was a lawyer, too, did not rise from his chair to express condolences or try to console them; he simply asked if the news was certain, then offered to find out the truth of the affair through his official contacts in Hungary. Lazukić, distressed, thanked him warmly, and after Waldenheim left, he even entertained the hope that by some miracle he would hear from the German that his wife was alive. But that was not to be. Two days later, a soldier rang the doorbell, saluted crisply, and delivered a folded piece of paper, on which was written, in tiny handwriting, in German: "The information has been verified and is unfortunately correct. Waldenheim."

The next time the captain put in an appearance, with no mention of the message or of what had passed between them, he was received as a family friend. He, too, felt this unmistakably and visited Lazukić more often, not only to see what was for sale and also to buy, which he did without haggling, and sometimes just to talk. He came with a bottle of slivovitz under his arm and a box of foreign cigarettes. He would take a comfortable position in the armchair, cross his legs, light a cigarette, and, sipping brandy from the glass Lazukić poured for him, ply his hosts with questions. What were they doing? What was new in the neighborhood? In the world of business? How did Sredoje occupy himself? Gradually, Waldenheim penetrated to their past—their life in Novi

Sad, Lazukić's career as a lawyer, and his politics. But he spoke little of himself, and when Lazukić reproached him for that, he laughed. "What you find out about me will be of no use to you. I am not a typical German. I do not drink beer. I do not carry with me a photograph of my wife and children; in fact, I have no wife and children." And he went on to discuss the character of his countrymen, their habits, even their defects—above all, their coldness and arrogance. "We are still provincial," he said. "We are not mature enough to rule. Instead of earning respect, we often arouse hatred through ill-considered actions."

It was Waldenheim's view that the Germans should win the confidence of the people they had recently begun to rule by adapting themselves to the local ways of life. "Like the British," he added. If the talk turned to the shooting of hostages and to arbitrary requisitions, he would sigh, lifting his eyes to the ceiling. He didn't hide the fact that as an intelligence officer he had to take part in reprisals against the resistance movement, which was gaining ground in Serbia, and in an almost humble tone he begged his new friends not to take part in any disturbances, especially Sredoje, whose youth could easily lead him astray. Lazukić was touched by this expression of concern for them, but Sredoje laughed to himself, because in his wanderings in search of carnal pleasure it had never occurred to him to shoot at the Germans. He wondered if he should confide in Waldenheim, tell him of his secret love for Germans, but he never had the chance to be alone with him, and besides, he didn't completely trust him. Even physically Waldenheim was different from the Germans Sredoje saw in the streets or in the remote taverns on the outskirts of town. Blond, stocky, and not particularly neat in his dress, with cigarette ash on the pockets of his creased jacket, he had a gentle, almost mocking smile, which played around his full lips and twinkled in his wide blue eyes. Whereas the other German officers and soldiers ignored the civilians in the streets, or kept their distance from them with a disgust they did not bother to conceal, the captain's blue eyes, looking slightly misty, rested on Sredoje with warmth and attention. But somehow this acted as a warning instead of inspiring confidence.

However, when, at the beginning of summer, it was his age group's turn to be enlisted in the Serbian National Guard, which he had not the slightest wish to join, Sredoje, at his father's insistence, approached Waldenheim for help. The German once again was understanding and discreet, passing over in silence the young man's motives for getting around the law, and said that he would look into it. The next time he called on Lazukić, he had a solution: he could get Sredoje, who knew German, a job as a police translator, which, because of the service's importance, would exempt him from the grueling and perhaps even dangerous duties of the National Guard. Father and son looked at each other and hesitated—the police under the Occupation were despised as traitors—but this consideration was outweighed by the evident and immediate advantage, and they accepted the offer gratefully. Waldenheim took a calling card bearing only his name and rank from his pocket and wrote "Sredoje Lazukić" on the back in his familiar small hand. The next day, Sredoje presented this laconic recommendation at the Police Department, which was located in a grimy old three-story building.

They gave him a number of forms to fill out, and

he had to be photographed and go out twice for tax stamps, but evidently everything had been arranged beforehand, because after ten days an official letter of acceptance came in the mail, engaging him as a junior clerk with the city police. He arrived for work on the top floor of the building where he had submitted his application. It was a long, bright room, which could easily accommodate a desk for the new arrival, in addition to the desks of the two men already there: Rudi Streuber, a German from the Banat, who was in charge, and Peter Kilipenko, a Russian émigré, who was a clerk. Young, brilliant, but lazy, Streuber gave the orders, and industrious old Kilipenko would hunch over his documents and battered dictionaries. The two were translating from German all the German Command orders for the Southeast and the orders of the German Military Police, and into German the decisions of the city police, which they sent in three copies to the department secretary, who passed them on.

There was not a great deal to do, a few notices and three- or four-page information bulletins a day, a relatively simple job, since the documents contained much the same vocabulary. Kilipenko jealously guarded every paper until he had translated it roughly in his hooked, clear handwriting, and it was left to Sredoje to polish the language and sometimes retype. He spent a good part of the eight-hour day smoking and reading the newspapers, but when he realized that Streuber, himself not overzealous, had no objection if his new assistant, recommended from higher up, disappeared when there was little to do, Sredoje left the office to take walks, the kind of walks he had taken before from home.

In his new circumstances his lust became more deliberate. In place of occasional pocket money he now had a salary, by no means negligible; he was protected by his position, carrying a card complete with photograph; and he also carried in his pocket, out of a kind of bravado, since joining the police, a snub-nosed revolver, which someone had pawned with his father. Only now did Sredoje realize how timid, anxious, and even risky his earlier excursions had been. But that was in the past. He no longer entered taverns with the feeling of committing a crime, but with the confidence of the elite, almost like his heroes, the German soldiers. When he caught himself imitating them, he smiled. It was easy for him now to start conversations with women there, and with some of them he even had amorous encounters. But the constraints and banalities of the main rooms were carried over, however much he tried to avoid it, into the little rooms to which the women took him for their hurried embrace. This ceased to satisfy him. Led by instinct, he ventured farther afield, prowling the town more boldly.

He would follow any unescorted woman who seemed unsure of herself, rejecting her only if she turned her back on him sharply when he accosted her, or if she disappeared into a house where he was not bold enough to go. He explored unfamiliar streets, memorized faces, took note of details. His eye became practiced.

As a diver, after plunging numberless times into the darkness of the deep, finally puts his hand on the iron bar that reveals the position of the sunken ship, so Sredoje, one evening after work, on the street in front of the railroad station, suddenly became aware that the women who appeared to be standing there by chance or walking beside its walls were exactly what he had been imagining in the course of his long search. He looked one of them over; she returned his look. Holding his breath, he approached another, and saw that she, too, had spotted him and made him aware of it by a movement of her shoulders. A number of other men loitered around the street with their coat collars up and their hats pulled down on their heads. One of them exchanged a few words with the first woman, then left her and stood a short way off. Sredoje, as if pulled by a magnet, took the man's place, mumbled "Good evening," and the woman, turning to him and pretending surprise, returned his greeting. He asked her where she was going; she said nowhere. He suggested they go for a stroll together; after a careful look around, she agreed. They chatted. The woman said she was thirsty, so they went into a nearby tavern and each had a brandy at the counter. In the light, Sredoje saw that the collar of her coat was worn down to the lining and that her brown hair was greasy, but his eyes were drawn to the wedge of fair skin between her bulging breasts, taut beneath her coat. He asked her abruptly if she needed money, they agreed on a price, and she led him out. They walked some distance, she half a pace in front of him, and then, near the quay, she knocked at the door of a low house, where a stooping old woman in a head scarf rented them a stifling little room.

The novelty of this encounter held so much charm for Sredoje that he went right back again to the street in front of the station. And every day from then on. He went further to the left and to the right, to see how far this hunting ground for women extended. For it was a hunting ground, as opposed to those cages of the taverns, where he had felt almost as trapped as the women there. But here the women came from all directions and of their own free will, like wild animals drawn to a watering hole, and new ones came, some out of poverty, some out of habit, some out of inclination. They were not yet crushed; they still had some pride, and, unlike the tavern girls, no one was their master, their pimp. But also there was no one to protect them. Like game in front of guns in ambush, they exuded that mixture of boldness and fear which excited the hunter. They strutted before the eyes of their enemies and partners in the game, making their inevitable surrender more delightful.

Sredoje now discovered that not only bodies beneath coats and dresses were laid bare, but souls as well. With a hungry passion he questioned the women who risked the street: Where did they come from? For what reason? He observed their fear, a fear equally of punishment and of scandal; he observed the moment when, crossing the threshold of the rented room, they cast off the mask of self-confidence with their clothes, abandoning all resistance, as in ardent love, but without the burden of responsibility that love imposed.

Their very submissiveness was exciting, their trembling setting of limits. As he possessed one after another, Sredoje wondered how far he could go in his amorous demands without meeting a refusal. The police card was burning a hole in his pocket. He toyed with the idea of dumfounding some woman with it, of breaking her down further, to a surrender that was total. For some time he hesitated, knowing full well that it was wrong, illegal, to use it, that he would be plunging into danger, which would result in his fearing as they feared. But he longed for that fear, too, his own, which would add to the excitement.

One evening, when it was snowing, he stopped under a streetlight with a tall, black-haired girl in a thin dark coat. The moment she quoted a price for her services, he pulled out his card, unfolded it, and shoved it before her panic-stricken eyes. "Do you see this? I'm placing you under arrest for prostitution." He expected an argument, or that she would read the document carefully and say that it did not give him the power to arrest, and he would then try to laugh the whole thing off as a joke.

But, instead, the girl's thick lips quivered, and tears from her wide eyes made shining streaks down her face. "Don't do that to me, please! My family would kill me!" And she seized his hands in hers, which were soft and moist.

He pulled his hands away. "Not arrest you? Ha! And what will you do for me if I don't?"

"Anything. I'll do anything," she said, again grabbing his hand, as if she wanted to kiss it, and looking at him with terror in her eyes.

"Very well," he agreed, his throat tight with lust. "Let's go, and then I'll decide."

She was rooted to the spot, as if unable to believe that her crime had been so easily pardoned. Then, afraid that he might change his mind, she ran quickly into the darkness. He followed, stumbling over the cobblestones, his legs weak. She took him into a big old house, up a creaking narrow wooden staircase to the top floor, to a door on which hung a rusty padlock. Her hands shook so much, it took her forever to unlock it. Once inside, she fell on her knees before Sredoje. He dragged her to the bed, which showed white in the faint light from the street, a lifeless doll with which he could do absolutely anything.

He played the same trick on other women on the streets around the station. He practiced, perfected the details. At the start he would try to establish how independent or intelligent they were, how experienced in their trade, and how advanced the self-destruction that accompanied it, so that his attack, delayed until the moment they were alone, would be neither more brutal nor more considerate than necessary: to destroy the woman's confidence while leaving her with enough hope to beg and obey. He trembled as much as his victim, trembled on the brink of achievement and in the fear that one of them would see through his deception. He felt himself sinking into this new addiction as into madness, felt it changing him, making him incapable of any other approach to a woman. After each one of his intoxicating bouts he swore that he would never do it again, telling himself that it was dangerous, that he had had enough experiences to last him a lifetime, that it was time to put them behind him, to keep them as no more than an incredible memory. But the temptation was too powerful. Sitting in the office or lying around at home, he would suddenly recall a posture of supplicating submission, or, better still, think of some form of violation he had missed, but which he could do the next time, and he would get up, his blood hot and his knees wobbly, to rush off to the streets where the women assembled.

He had the gnawing suspicion that he was being seen too often around the station, that the women had exchanged information about the rapist with the police card, or that they had already reported him to the police. A noose, he felt, had been thrown around him and was being tightened. Even so, he could not stop himself; he realized with horror that only a disaster could stop him. That was in fact what happened.

One evening, he came upon a young girl with an unusually firm body. After the deception with the card had worked and he had undressed her and enjoyed her in an attic near the quay, he discovered that her dark-pink body, so supple and strong, still tempted him, and he regretted that his threats ruled out the possibility of their meeting again. Thinking feverishly as they were getting dressed, he asked for her identity card. She dug it out of her dress pocket and handed it to him with a worried look. "I'll keep this," he said. "If you want it back, come tomorrow to the place we met today, at the same time." At home he examined the card; although the photograph did not live up to the girl's freshness, it was a pleasant reminder and made him want to see her the next day. But that, he knew, would be a mistake, it would be crossing the line of risk, which so far he had not crossed. He should throw the identity card away and not go. But he went.

The girl was where he had told her to be, in front of a pastry window, but as he approached her, a small man in a worn suit and crumpled hat suddenly appeared at her side. An older brother? An uncle? Certainly not her father. Raising his worried-looking, pointed nose, the man asked in a thin voice, "And why, sir, did you take this girl's identity card?" Sredoje went cold, produced the card from his pocket, and gave it to the man, intending to walk away in silent disdain. But a thickset young policeman appeared out of the nearest doorway. "What's going on here?" Untroubled, the small man answered at once, confirming Sredoje's suspicion that there was complicity between them: "This man took the girl's identity card from her." And he held it up. "Indeed?" drawled the policeman mockingly, turning to Sredoje. "And who are you, sir, to be taking people's identity cards from them? Can I see your papers?" Sredoje thought quickly. If he took out his own identity card, he would be subjected to further questioning. He decided on the police card. The policeman unfolded it slowly and read it, his eyebrows raised in surprise. He looked hesitantly at Sredoje, at the photograph, examined it again, then folded it and returned it with a salute. Sredoje walked away.

He stopped going to that part of town, but it did not help. He knew he would be called to account. Several days after the incident, Streuber stood in front of his desk and nervously informed him, "I've been ordered to tell you not to leave the office during working hours again without my express permission." And two days later, no less abruptly, "I've been ordered to send you to Captain Waldenheim for a talk. At once, please."

At the German Military Police headquarters, whose grim, steel-helmeted guards he had often watched from a distance, with a shudder of curiosity, he was expected, and the duty officer took him up to the second floor. Waldenheim was alone in a large office, with a pile of papers and books on his desk. There were several bottles and small glasses on a circular table, and around the table, leather armchairs with seats sunken from use and covered with cigarette ash.

"Sit down," said Waldenheim and sat himself, sinking deep into the chair. They sipped brandy, lit cigarettes. "It's my job to reprimand you," said the captain, clicking his tongue as he put down his glass. "Of course I have no intention of doing anything of the sort. But if you are asked what we talked about, say that you were roasted over a slow fire. And now let's turn to something more sensible." He asked Sredoje how he was, what his father was doing, and if there were any interesting new items for sale; he listened carefully to Sredoje's answers and promised to drop in on them soon. "I think you've spent enough time in my office for a thorough tongue-lashing. I'd keep you longer, but I have a lot of work to do." He held out his hand and kept Sredoje's in his own for a moment. "Even so, don't let yourself be caught again in any more of your little pranks. If you're bored, I'll try to find something else to amuse you when the weather improves."

And indeed, he soon began to invite him—through Streuber, Sredoje's immediate superior—to accompany him on his official trips, as an interpreter. They went to small towns in the interior of Serbia, to Topola, Smederevo, Milanovac, Niš, where Waldenheim had things to do in each local Military Police section. They usually set off in midmorning—Waldenheim liked to sleep late—in a small gray Opel, which first picked up Sredoje on Dobrnjac Street; it returned the same day, in the evening, early or late, depending on the distance and the amount of work Waldenheim had to do. They were always driven by Hans, a young, blond soldier with a long face and thin arched eyebrows, taciturn and extremely attached to Waldenheim. The captain had Sredoje sit in the front next to Hans, while he sat on the back seat, as though on a couch, smoking, chatting, or dozing.

These outings, which continued through the spring and summer of 1943, were extremely pleasant for Sredoje. They took him away from the oppressive heat of Belgrade, from the dusty office, which, since he had been forbidden to leave it, he felt was a place of punishment. A few deft movements of Hans's hands on the steering wheel, and they would be out on the main road, where Sredoje was overwhelmed by new images—vegetation, villages, people. The wind blew the freshness in through the open windows; Hans drove, stepping on the accelerator with silent precision; Waldenheim chattered away, often teasing Hans about his fast driving and his reticence, sometimes tickling his bare, sunburned neck or jokingly tugging at his ear, and the trip would pass quickly, in exhilarating motion. They would stop in the middle of a town, and Waldenheim would put on his jacket and get out of the car, usually specifying the time he was to be picked up. For a few hours Sredoje and Hans would sit in front of a small tavern in the shade of vines and drink beer, Hans, silent, knitting his brows, Sredoje watching the peasants, the children, who cast mistrustful looks at the two of them. If they had more time, as soon as they dropped Waldenheim off, they would drive to the nearest river and, taking off their clothes, go for a swim, then sunbathe on the stones. At the appointed hour, refreshed and replete with silence, they would drive back to the police post and wait for Waldenheim. Then they would race back to Belgrade.

Waldenheim was interested in how they had spent their time, laughed at Sredoje's descriptions of peasants at the taverns, and late in the evening delivered him in front of the building on Dobrnjac Street, calling, "Good night! Regards to your father!" before driving off. In his bed Sredoje breathed in contentment, as if dreaming, and he did not regret that he no longer stalked the area around the station for fallen women. Yet he had not entirely relinquished that passion, he simply curbed it until a more favorable moment, just as he had never completely lost his distrust of Waldenheim. He continued to find something alien to his notion of a German officer in Waldenheim's relaxed behavior, in the warmth of his friendship.

Toward the end of August they went to Požega. It was a hot day, one in a succession of hot days in late summer. There was no movement in the air; dust hovered above the trees that bordered the road, turning their tired, overabundant foliage gray. At a crawl they drove into the town, which was thronged with people, vehicles, German soldiers with bayonets on their rifles. After they delivered Waldenheim at the Military Police post, on a street off the main square, and were told the time to pick him up, Hans turned the car around and, skillfully avoiding the people walking in the middle of the road, made a circle and came out at the river Skrapež.

They looked for an isolated spot, parked the car in some bushes along the bank, undressed, and jumped into the river, which was shallow and rapid. They splashed about for some time; feeling cool, they stretched out on the stones in the sun. As usual, they were silent, except for an occasional grunt of pleasure in the sun's heat. Sredoje propped himself up on his elbows, looked at Hans, and noticed that the soldier had a green, heart-shaped stone pendant on the gold chain he always wore around his long, muscular neck. Sredoje's father, not long ago, had had the very same pendant displayed on the table for Waldenheim. "Hans," he said, looking at the pendant again, to make sure he was not mistaken, "where did you get that green heart on your chain?" Hans opened one eye, gray as the sand, and looked down at the thing Sredoje had mentioned. "From a girl" was all he muttered.

After a while they went into the water again, and when they came out, Hans walked over to the car, took his wristwatch from his shirt pocket and said that it was time to go. Instead of lying in the sun again to dry, they ran around and rubbed themselves with their palms; still damp, they dressed and got into the car. Back in the town, they found the streets strangely empty, but when they neared the square they saw a crowd of people, with their horses and carts, pressed close together, all standing still and looking in the same direction. Hans sounded the horn, but no one turned around. A German soldier with a rifle and bayonet motioned him sharply to move away. Hans backed up and, taking empty side streets, approached the square on the opposite side, by the police post. Here, too, was a wall of people. Sredoje stayed in the stuffy car for a minute or two, then got out and joined the crowd to find out what was going on.

He stood on tiptoe but saw nothing, so he pushed his way between two peasants, who were craning their necks. In the center of the square was a space cordoned off on all sides by Germans and soldiers of the National Guard. There was an unusual silence, as if no one were breathing. The smell of human sweat spread from man

275

to man, in stifling air already thick with dust. "What's happening? Why is everyone waiting?" Sredoje asked the peasant beside him. The peasant started, glared at him, as if Sredoje had interrupted something important; then, his eyes returning to the center of the square, he said quietly, his throat tight, "You'll see. If you're a Serb."

Sredoje heard a shout, distant—it sounded like an order—and on the side of the square, in front of the Town Hall, there was movement. Through a wide passage that had been left open, a squad of National Guard soldiers with rifles on their shoulders stepped briskly into the square. A second order rang out, and they halted. Sredoje could now see clearly who was shouting: a broad-shouldered young officer with short bandy legs encased in boots, standing in front of the detail with his sword drawn. The squad fanned out, pressing with their backs against the crowd, until only three figures remained in the center: two soldiers and, between them, a small, burly civilian, bareheaded, in wide gray trousers and a darker gray jacket that was too big for him.

The officer waved the gleaming sword in the sunlight, the two soldiers each pulled on a clanking chain, and the civilian was jerked first one way, then the other, as if dancing with tiny steps. This went on for some time. Impatient, the officer waved his sword and several times even helped pull. The crowd murmured. At last the ends of the chain were in the hands of the soldiers, who stood at attention as if they, too, were now chained. The civilian stood straight, his legs apart, and began to rub his wrists slowly, first one, then the other. There was an awkward silence. The officer looked around, as if searching for someone, made a sign with his sword and beckoned with his free hand. But instead of anyone stepping forward, the monotonous drone of a voice was heard, its source invisible. Now and then a whistle came from the crowd and a shout of "Louder!" but the speech went on in the same low tone. After a while Sredoje was able to make out phrases he knew by heart: "Communist hireling," "crime against the Serbian people," and "death by hanging."

He broke into a sweat, even though this was really what he had expected. He thought of leaving, but a cold curiosity rooted him to the spot. The peasants next to him stared ahead without blinking, and the one Sredoje had spoken to stood with his mouth half open, showing his pointed upper teeth.

The squad moved to the right, and Sredoje now noticed, directly in front of the Town Hall, a wooden frame, a rope hanging from a crosspiece, not a thick rope, but ending in a noose. The squad came to a halt beneath the noose, the officer waved his sword, the two soldiers took hold of the civilian and lifted him up, and suddenly he was standing, higher than everyone, on a stool. The civilian's face was plump, with high, rounded cheekbones, heavy lips, big, dark eyes, and bushy eyebrows. Those eyes expressed both fear and disbelief, but most of all, Sredoje thought, a mute, tense appetite for life.

Next to the civilian's head a second head appeared, beneath a forage cap, with thin, drained features, and a long, bony hand took hold of the noose, hurled it up, and dropped it deftly over the civilian's neck. Then the head with the forage cap was gone. The civilian shuddered, as if the noose burned, raised his stubby hands to his neck to pull it off, but suddenly the hands jerked out in terror. He sank, the rope went tight and began to swing, and the stool lay overturned.

The man's legs pumped as if on an invisible bicycle, he spread his arms wide, drew them to his neck, frantically threw them out again, and his face took on an expression of childlike petulance, turned dark, then the eyes bulged, wanting to pop from their sockets. Another shudder, a shiver, and everything was suddenly still. Arms and legs hung loose, and the short trunk to which they were attached swung slowly back and forth. The head was turned to one side; the face, now purple, was longer. The jaw had dropped to show a lolling blue tongue, and the eyes, expressionless, looked like buttons sewn on in an inappropriate place.

Sredoje was staring at these dulled eyes when a hand fell on his arm, making him jump. Was it his turn next? He looked around and found himself face to face with Captain Waldenheim, whose misty eyes regarded him with tender concern. "You shouldn't have watched that," the captain said, shaking him as if Sredoje had been asleep. "Come. We've decided to stay for supper with my colleagues here. You'll like them." He squeezed his arm in encouragement, and Sredoje followed, not entirely grasping what was expected of him. He was still mesmerized by the sight of a simple rope transforming a live body, a body that had walked, rubbed its wrists, and looked with avidly longing eyes, into a crooked, sagging carcass.

He let Waldenheim lead him back to the Opel. A group of German officers stood behind the car, near a long blue limousine he had never seen before. Automatically, he sat in his usual place next to Hans, and Waldenheim got in behind, next to a tall young officer with a hooked nose. "Let me introduce you," said Waldenheim, leaning forward, and Sredoje turned around and held out his hand to the cross-eyed officer, who greeted him stiffly. Above the rumbling of the engine, Sredoje heard himself described as "our young friend, who is working for us." They drove through the streets of the town, which were once more filled with people, people hurrying home, and came out on the dusty, empty highway. The cross-eyed officer directed Hans along country roads. As they climbed into the hills, the sun disappeared for a time; when it reappeared, it lay, weary and distended, upon a low, flat ridge.

They stopped in front of a two-story building of stone and wood, which looked like a hunting lodge. A guard with a rifle stood in front, and beyond him several soldiers, without weapons and bareheaded, ran around carrying crates and light cane furniture. Waldenheim and his companion got out and invited Sredoje to do the same. Sredoje was still unsteady on his feet. In front of the building a wire fence stretched at chest height, and beyond the fence, between it and a country well with a winch, was a yard shaded by ancient trees, beneath which the soldiers were setting out tables and chairs. Still farther back, they had a large fire going. There was the drone of an engine, and around the bend appeared the blue limousine, which parked behind the Opel. Several German officers sprang out and, with loud laughter, hustled the group that had arrived earlier through the entrance in the fence, where the sentry, standing at attention, saluted. The tables had been placed end to end and covered with white tablecloths. A soldier crouching in the grass filled kerosene lamps.

The guests sat down at the tables, the soldiers opened

bottles of beer, and from the other end of the yard came the smell of grilling meat. The kerosene lamps were lit and hung on nails hammered in the trunks of the trees. As it grew dark, the officers filled their glasses, clinked, and drank. Sredoje sat at the end of the table, next to Hans, and together, in silence, they sipped their beer. The rest of the company was noisy, celebrating the birthday of the cross-eyed officer with the hooked nose, who sat next to Waldenheim. Perhaps, too, they were showing off before their superior from Belgrade. They praised the beer, praised the spot under the trees, and, when the meat arrived, praised the skill of the military cook, who in answer to the loud summons of all present appeared in a long white apron spattered with grease and blood.

Red wine in liter bottles was brought to the tables, along with clean tall glasses. A young and chubby second lieutenant stood up and toasted his colleague on the occasion of his colleague's twenty-sixth birthday, and everyone had to empty a glass of wine. The tall, cross-eyed officer responded, announcing that it was an honor for him to celebrate his birthday in the presence of the esteemed Captain Doctor Waldenheim, at which they all again drained their glasses. Waldenheim stood up and quietly, deliberately proposed a toast, and referred to the delicate position in which they found themselves, in a foreign country where there was not yet sufficient understanding of the German aim to introduce a civilized way of life. Everyone applauded and again drank. Sredoje, this time, only wet his lips with the wine, but the chubby second lieutenant shouted across to Waldenheim that his interpreter was shirking, at which Sredoje, with a forced laugh, raised his glass and drained it. Now everyone wanted to speak, to drink, to clink glasses. Sredoje suddenly felt the wine rising in his throat; he broke into a sweat, and his stomach began to churn. He got up and rushed to the far end of the lawn, to the well, around it, and to the wire fence, where by a wooden post he vomited in one dense stream. Now he was empty, sober, but exhausted.

He stood panting, pulling himself together, wiping the sweat off his face, as the soldiers eating around the spit and the grill watched him. The officers' wild laughter reached his ears. He had to return. He walked back in the shadows cast by the fading fire and came into the lamplight right next to his seat. A full glass was waiting for him, and the second lieutenant, the minute Sredoje sat down, clinked glasses with him, winking. Sredoje shook his head; he could not swallow another drop. The second lieutenant called across to Waldenheim, who, conversing with the cross-eyed officer, turned distractedly to Sredoje and raised his hand. Everyone fell silent. "You're not feeling well?" he asked Sredoje across the table in a soft voice. Sredoje shook his head. At that, Waldenheim snapped his fingers, called over one of the soldiers serving at the table, and whispered in his ear. Then he turned to Sredoje with a look full of understanding. "He'll show you to bed. Is that all right?" At Sredoje's thankful acceptance, he turned to the other officers and said, "Our young friend is not accustomed to ordeals of this kind," and clinked glasses with his neighbors. Everyone was now shouting, drinking. No one paid attention to Sredoje, who got up and followed the soldier.

He thought they would go to the lodge, but the soldier led him out through the gate and by the fence that went parallel to the tables. He walked at the soldier's side, taking care not to stumble in the shadows of the tall trees. They left the circle of light, plunged into darkness, and the air was suddenly cooler, fresher. Sredoje breathed more easily. But he could see nothing until the soldier switched on a flashlight, revealing an uneven path. The sound of laughter grew fainter and, after they rounded a small hill, ceased completely. Only their own footsteps and breathing could be heard. The soldier stopped, swept the darkness with the flashlight, and its beam fell on a small house, on the door of the house. He pushed a key into the lock, and the door creaked open. When they stepped inside, Sredoje almost fainted from the hot air that hit them. But the soldier seemed not to notice. In the room, the only pieces of furniture were beds and a small white chair next to each, like the chairs on the lawn of the hunting lodge.

Turning, the soldier said over his shoulder to Sredoje, "If you need to go outside, go while I'm here."

Sredoje was surprised. "No, I don't need to. But why do you ask?"

"Because I've been ordered to lock the door." And then, as if to justify it, he added, "We don't mount guard here." He waited for a moment to see if Sredoje would change his mind, then murmured "Good night" and left, taking the flashlight with him and slamming the door shut.

Sredoje heard the key turn and the soldier's footsteps receding. In the silence, he was sorry he hadn't asked the soldier to wait by the open door a while, for the room to air, but it was too late now. He looked for a window, though he did not remember seeing one in the brief sweep of the flashlight. He felt along the walls

282

with his hand and came upon wooden shutters. He groped for the bolt, found it, turned it, but the shutters would not open. He pulled it, rattled it, but nothing happened. Passing his fingers along the edges of the shutters, he discovered that they had been nailed in place with large nails. He gave up with a groan. His legs shook with fatigue; his head was swimming. He walked to the middle of the room, felt around for a bed, sat down. He took off his jacket, threw it across the back of a chair. The revolver he carried in his inside pocket knocked against the seat. He took off his trousers and shoes, collapsed onto the pillow, and was instantly asleep.

He woke, dimly aware that something had disturbed his sleep. His head ached, his body was bathed in sweat, all he wanted was to sleep, but whatever it was that wouldn't let him was fumbling between his legs. He put his hand out and caught hold of someone's hand, pushed it away, and in the same moment, relieved, sank back to sleep. But he woke again: the hand was touching him. He pushed it away again, harder. It did not occur to him to wonder whose hand it was or why it was touching him; he only knew that it prevented him from sleeping and that he had to go back to sleep. Sleep was like an animal swallowing him. He slept and again started, bewildered: the hand was back, stubbornly pulling him out of the peace into which he had just settled. He didn't want to move, such was his longing to return to that peace, but he had to. He found the hand and, turning from his back to his side, shoved it far away, to the neighboring bed. It must have left him alone longer after that, because it was a deep, heavy dream he came out of when the hand intruded again. Sredoje felt that he had no more strength to resist it, yet he could not allow the hand to continue, because what it was doing was something so unnatural that even in his sleep he fought it. He turned over on his back and without opening his eyes felt for his jacket, slipped the revolver out of the pocket, and, relieved that he had found a solution, slid it across his body to his other side, and pulled the trigger.

There was a deafening explosion and a flash that penetrated his eyelids, though they were shut tight. The hand jerked away, he heard a scream, and when he opened his eyes, there was complete darkness and the sound only of his own breathing. He jumped up, wide awake. He realized that he had wounded, if not killed, someone—Waldenheim, probably. He walked across to switch on the light, but remembered that there was no light in the room. And did he want to see the wound, see a dying body? He must flee, he thought, trembling. He pulled on his trousers, stuffed his feet into his shoes, grabbed hold of his jacket. He rushed for the door, but collided with a wall instead; he searched back and forth until he felt wood and the lock. A huge key was sticking out of it—the first moment of relief in this nightmare. He turned the key, pushed at the door, and dove into the free cold night air.

Before him, low in the sky, hung a round white moon, showing every blade of grass. He stopped, listened, could hear only the loud music of the crickets. He started to run, crossed the path and climbed a steep hill. He continued to run blindly all through the night. At the first sign of light he crawled under some bushes at the edge of a meadow and fell asleep. He was awakened by the sun and thirst. He didn't know where he was. In the distance he caught sight of a man reaping and debated whether or not he should go up to him and ask for water. Perhaps he could persuade the man to give him shelter and even take a message to his father in Belgrade. But the man might turn him over to the authorities, instead.

Sredoje crept out of the bushes and moved on, keeping low, hoping to come across a spring or stream. He started at the least noise, the crack of a twig, the distant bark of a dog, and kept looking over his shoulder. In the evening he came to an isolated house and well in the middle of a field. His lips were parched with thirst and his stomach ached from hunger, but he didn't dare approach. He slept, listened, retreated from the house in panic, approached it again cautiously. He sheltered in a small knoll overgrown with brush and wild trees, where he could keep watch on the house, the well, and the surrounding area.

In the morning, he saw an old man emerge barefoot from the house, urinate, and then go back inside. Shortly thereafter, a sturdy young woman appeared, went to the well, drew water, poured it into a pail, but left the pail, half full, on the edge. His eyes were glued to that pail. He was so thirsty that he decided, despite the danger, to go over and drink. Several times he left his shelter, but then took fright and crawled back. The old man, meanwhile, went in and out of the house, or sat on a bench in front; twice he ate something. More than once the woman left, stayed away for a while, then came back. Sredoje thought that the old man had spotted him, but wasn't sure. When it got dark again, the old man and the woman went into the house.

Sredoje made up his mind to go to the well this time, and he calculated how long it would take them to go to sleep. But while he was waiting, he dozed off himself. He was awakened by the cracking of twigs. Before he could spring to his feet, two hands pressed him to the ground.

"Shhh," he heard someone whisper, the breath hot against his cheek. "Who are you?"

Sredoje could not speak.

"Are you the one who killed the German in the hunting lodge?"

Sredoje nodded before he had time to think.

"Do you have a weapon?"

At last his throat loosened up. "No."

The hands relaxed and slid deftly over his chest and thighs. "Come on out, but don't lift your head!"

He obeyed and, crouching, followed the shape, a silhouette, through the bushes. Then the shape split into two: one half continued on in front of him and the other fell into step with him. Sredoje looked at them furtively. The man in front, tall, thin, was wearing a long sweater and nothing on his head; the one beside him was shorter, broad-shouldered, with a cap pulled down over his ears. Both moved quickly, lightly, while Sredoje stumbled. They went uphill and downhill for what seemed to Sredoje an eternity. Every few moments he thought of asking them to let him rest and drink some water, but he didn't know who they were, though their caution made him sure that they were not on the side of the Germans.

When he thought he couldn't go any further, his escorts stopped at the foot of an unusually steep hill. They talked softly with someone, though Sredoje could see no one, then they pulled him up the slope, onto a plateau, and under a clump of trees. All around, men were lying, some asleep and some, awakened by their arrival, clutching the coats with which they were covered. Sredoje and his escorts made their way around them and proceeded toward a hollow with fewer trees, then came to a house. A sentry appeared under the eaves. Sredoje's escorts exchanged a few words with him in a whisper, and he went into the house. After a short wait, the sentry came back and led Sredoje and his escorts inside. They stepped into darkness and the smell of confined bodies, and heard snoring. Then there was a crack of light, a door opened hesitantly, and Sredoje saw a burning candle in front of a face whose eyes were puffy from lack of sleep. The man had a mass of unruly black hair. Sredoje went in and, stopping at a table on which stood an earthenware jug, asked for some water. The disheveled man pointed to the jug, and Sredoje picked it up in both hands and drank deeply.

After that, nothing mattered to him, he felt relieved, safe. The man—the commander of a Partisan detachment that had just formed and was hiding from the Germans—asked how and why Sredoje had killed the German captain. Sredoje told him. Then his escorts took him out and put him in a shed behind the house, blocking the door with a stone. He slept the night on the ground. In the morning, he was let out to relieve himself, was given a piece of bread, an onion, and more water. Later they took him back into the house, where next to the commander sat a man with a round head and bluish lips, the detachment intelligence officer. The two of them interrogated Sredoje along much the same lines as the commander had done the previous night. The intelligence officer was less inclined to believe him than the commander, or pretended to be so, suggesting that Sredoje had been sent by the Germans to infiltrate them. But the fact of Waldenheim's death put that theory to rest, and in an angry voice the intelligence officer ordered Sredoje to write down everything about himself and the incident on several sheets of typing paper, which he produced from a briefcase on the table. "But this time the truth," he added, rolling his eyes.

Sredoje was locked up again. He was not worried about the accusations, knowing they would be refuted. What troubled him were the damp ground on which he sat and slept, the dirt he had picked up on the way, which made him itch all over, and his hunger. But those were troubles of the body, not the soul, and they brought him closer to the men among whom he suddenly found himself. It was strange the way it had all happened, but if he looked back on it—and he spent all his time doing just that; they had ordered him to remember—he saw that what had happened was in fact perfectly logical, and even inevitable. His life in Belgrade had become unendurable, a sleepwalker's trance between the perils of wartime reality and his own wild desires, desires that mirrored Captain Waldenheim's secret vice. One of them had to come to grief. That it had been Waldenheim seemed to Sredoje proof of his greater strength, of the accuracy of his instinct, and at the same time proof of the superiority of these rebellious men to whom that single shot had joined him. It was as if that shot had roused him from a sick dream.

The Germans, on whom he had looked with admiration mixed with fear, could not establish their cold, premeditated rule as long as the people on whom they tried to impose it were stubborn, independent, hardy, resilient. He, too, was like that; the shot was proof of it. He belonged among them. But between him and them still lay the intelligence officer's suspicion. Whenever Sredoje emerged from the darkness of the shed, blinking his eyes, and found the men lying on the ground eating or getting ready to go somewhere, their eyes met his with curiosity, but also with distrust. It was not until three weeks later, when news came from Belgrade that Lazukić the lawyer had been seized and shot, that the suspicion lifted from him. Although, once again, no one informed him of this; he would find out much later, when he secretly read his own file.

They let him out of the shed and assigned him to a Partisan group as an unarmed auxiliary. From then on, he slept with the others under the trees, or, when he was lucky, in the entryway of the wooden house. He shared their scanty, usually dry food. But despite the fact that the most serious accusation had been withdrawn, his unusual past was an object of derision: the killing of the German captain (the story told with stifled laughter), his service in the police, his education.

The detachment, which had been in the woods around Zlatibor for nearly two months now, was made up of local peasants who had joined in fear of reprisals following Partisan actions. The "schoolboy," as Sredoje was called, and the commissar, a former teacher, away at that time, complemented their limited experience and wish for immediate vengeance. On the move from hill to hill, with a piece of bread and cheese in their pockets, the peasants suffered because they were not at home with their girls or loving wives, and because hiding took them into unknown regions, into dangers from which they might not return. Sredoje, on the other hand, considered those hardships natural. For him, there was no return to the past, to what was left behind; he thought, instead, about ways to improve things. Therefore, although a newcomer, he was a better and more able soldier than many.

He showed his mettle in the very first skirmish. It came about unexpectedly, with the arrival of a German unit that had been drawn into the mountains by the deceptive promise of an easy victory. In the general confusion, Sredoje was ordered to carry ammunition to the machine gunner, but when a bullet hit the machine gunner's hand, after an instant's hesitation Sredoje took the man's place and pulled the trigger. He did this when he saw green uniforms jumping out from behind the trees. If they captured him, they would torture him and kill him. But his action was also spurred by the fascination he now had for killing, for violent death, which he had had a taste of in the hunting lodge and in the square in Požega, too, that same day—a vivid memory of every movement, every sound, charged with the horror of how thin was the line between life and death and how easy it was to cross it.

Now he fired and was being fired at. Would he be the first to be hit by a bullet, or would his bullet hit the man who was aiming at him, trying to make him the victim? And suddenly that man, so threateningly alive, so intent on him—Sredoje—as if they were linked, the two of them, would fall and cease to be, with his strength, his consciousness, including the images he carried within him, the image of Sredoje, too; and there would be nothing left of him, like a splinter from a tree that the bullet on its murderous course broke off in passing. Sredoje wished to repeat, to experience again and again that passage, that risk, that excitement, and this, combined with his new sense of belonging, would sustain him through the hardships and illnesses of the Partisans, and bring him, after a radio operator's course and a transfer to a Vojvodina unit, back again, on October 27, 1944, as a liberator, to Novi Sad, where there was no trace of his former existence, with the exception of Anna Drentvenšek's diary.

Chapter 21

May 4, 1935

With God's help.

May 6

For Orthodox Serbs today is a holiday. Only four lessons, so more time for rest and reflection. I don't feel too well, a slight fever as usual. Still, I have decided, though not for the first time, to begin my diary today. Perhaps these words will bring me consolation when all this is done, when youth has passed—a youth I can still feel sometimes coursing through my veins, but sometimes it seems that the thread of life is getting thinner. If it breaks, no one will shed a tear over me. A coldness in the depths of my heart, like ice. God in Heaven, send the sun to shine into my weary heart. My life until now has been a deception. If only I could lay down my weary, tormented head to rest. But where? Beside Kleinchen? Dear, sweet Kleinchen, I have found you again, only to realize that I will never obtain what I desire. I think of you day in, day out. I can't wait for the day you will come—soon, soon. Today is the 6th. A few hours of happiness then, when everything around me turns to brightness. But never over the *line*! No, I must remain virtuous, for your sake and for my sake! You, you, is the cry inside me. In a short while I'll see you—only to suffer again afterward. You! You!

May 16

Disappointment again. No Kleinchen, though I was sure he would come. A night full of sadness. My heart was in pain. My life—what emptiness! How awful it is to be awake in the middle of the night! I feel that I have lost something precious, though I never truly possessed it. You! You! How am I to get over you?

I have my work. My work will help me to survive. Why can't I find what my weary soul has been seeking all these years? To be kind, kind to everyone, particularly to him! But he was noble, and could behave no other way. How he kissed, how he held me, without asking for what every man wants! If only I could see him, see his dear, intelligent eyes! Hard days of struggle lie before me. But God is with me.

May 18

Gloom, gloom! Yesterday I waited, today I hoped—for a word at least. Now I have given up hope. He could have written a letter, a note. Kleinchen, I don't reproach you, because I love you! I would give my life to see you! No, I mustn't despair. I knew this would happen. I must be strong, that's all. But I feel so weak!

The school year is nearly over. Soon I'll be free. Then I intend to recover—if I can. Go off somewhere and forget. Where, I don't know. Victor Hugo said poverty makes a hole in the heart and places hate there. But I won't hate you. May God help me to forget! But it's so hard. I love him. My heart is filled with pain.

May 19

Today I feel unwell. Yesterday I worked hard, but the worst of the pain is over. Kleinchen was here. Asked for me. Unfortunately, I was out. It doesn't matter, for now I know he doesn't despise me, that he will come again. I would love to see him! Or is that a lie? Ah, the plant has put down deep roots.

May 22

Today Kleinchen was supposed to come here, he promised. Now it's eight o'clock, the bells are ringing— no sign of him. Kleinchen, why did you not keep your promise?

If only God had made me tougher. Why must I be so sensitive? Why must I suffer like this? God in heaven, give me the strength to forget. Kleinchen, my heart weeps.

Sunday, June 2, 1935

For a few days I stopped writing. I felt wretched in mind and body. Next week I'll see a doctor. I must. God only knows what will happen to me. Let no ill befall me, let me carry out what I have planned. Now there are only a few lessons to give, but I am weary, terribly weary. I'm afraid of the day that is drawing near. . . . Why did I choose that day? Thirteen is an unlucky number, but I will not give in to that. The 13th will certainly open up old wounds. God, I wish for only one thing—to know what he thinks of me. Almighty God, do not abandon me.

The summer holidays are near. How will I spend them? I would like to see my native region, press my wounded heart against the cold tomb, on my knees pray to the dear Mother of God, to pray endlessly. I would like to see the ocean, travel, travel to forget. I know there are great struggles ahead of me. The struggle for my daily bread. The struggle with my heart. The struggle with death. If I could weep aloud just once. A weight on my chest. I don't know for sure what it is. Loss, worry, everything chokes me. Father, dear Father in Heaven, give peace to my weary soul. Heavenly Father, don't let me be ill. Hear my prayer.

June 11

Whitsun passed without joy. I hoped that I would receive some token of remembrance from Kleinchen, a greeting, as for Easter, but nothing. Often my eyes fill with tears, because, in addition to everything, I must keep my promise. I swore on my own health that I would not call him again—but it has to be. The 13th draws near, one more day, and then, God willing, I start my journey. I must go away, collect my thoughts, rest. On my journey I will learn much, I will visit all the places I loved—visit them for the last time. It will be autumn soon. But the hardest thing is my heart. It yearns, suffers, poor empty heart. I would like to have my own home, someone to understand me. Dear God in Heaven, be with me. Let me be good and worthy.

Ten more days of teaching.

Dear, dear Kleinchen, may God bless you and give you happiness. I wish you that with all my heart.

June 13

Tonight I dreamed of you, Kleinchen, you were with me, I was in your arms, and I wondered, dreaming, if the dream was true. When I woke up, my arms were empty. Dearest one, come today; today is the 13th.

No, you won't come. You won't come, however much I want you.

Today many difficult hours are ahead of me.

June 13

It's nine o'clock in the evening, the bell announces the time and also the end of my dream. Laying my desire to rest in the grave. Kleinchen, dearest one, farewell. Farewell forever, and may God bless you and with you all those dear to you. I can't, I won't, be angry with you, because it's not your fault. Lord, miraculous, invisible Force that directs and rules us all, do not abandon me! Give me consolation, take pity on me! Grant my wish and give me peace, rest. Kleinchen, I write this with my heart's blood.

June 26

I haven't written anything for thirteen days. And what was there to write? My heart is a throbbing wound. I have conquered, but I cannot forget. As I leave, Almighty God, help me! I will visit my father's grave, but also want to do something for my health. Whenever I take up this book, my eyes fill with tears. I did what I swore to do, but God, how empty my life is.

July 5

The fifth day of my travels. I'm here at Kustošija, at Klara's. They are both good people, but I'm afraid of being a burden to them. I still feel terrible. I can find no peace. I would gladly continue on my way without a pause. God in heaven, be with me. There's a bitterness in me, as if I hated everyone. Heavenly God, hear my prayer, you know what would bring me tranquillity.

July 14

When I began my travels, I thought that I would write something every day in this little book, but things have turned out differently. I'm tired, I sleep a great deal, and that is for the best. To sleep and not feel anything. I haven't gone to a doctor yet, afraid of finding out the truth. This week I must go back, unspeakably difficult for me, but I must. For the last time my eyes will take in all the dear places where I was once happy— but also terribly unhappy. Almighty God in Heaven, do not abandon me!

August 11

It's almost a month since I jotted anything down, yet so much has happened. The first thing was that I went to a doctor and, thank God, he gave me a favorable diagnosis. He told me that he wished all his women patients were as healthy as I was, and assured me that I was in no danger. With that illness, he said, you can live a hundred years. And then: Be brave; when you feel the pain, come to Kárpáti. And walk, walk a great deal, move around a lot, and, most of all: love. That's what the kind little doctor said. I like thinking of him, of his soft eyes. How charming, the way he hurriedly lowered them when I looked at him. He said: Women don't find understanding in men, which generates neurosis, and neurosis, in turn, generates all sorts of illnesses. He was right. I will follow his advice, and I'm so grateful to him—and glad that he found pleasure in looking at me.

And now—Egon.

Egon, little Egon, handsome you are not, but there is something about you that excites. You're not honest, not sincere, but what does that matter: you kiss well. Passionately. I love your kisses. You want to drink the glass to the bottom, but it didn't work out for you. Be my friend; a friend is what I want, nothing more. Nothing more, because I saw into you, saw through you—poor little fool. But it was good. I had several fine hours with you, I won't forget them. You made promises and swore by many things, but it was all deception. Silly little Egon.

I'm over it. Yesterday I suffered, today I'm singing. But in the depths of my soul, God only knows. Now off to the theater.

August 13

I woke up happy. Yesterday I was with Egon. He was kind and sweet, but now I must leave.

A good vacation, but too brief.

Egon, your kiss on my hand burns.

You don't deserve it but *I love you.*

August 16

Home again! How miserable, to be here. Alone. It's all over. Unspeakable pain, that everything must end this way. My departure from Zagreb was bleak, my future is bleak. Almighty God, you must not abandon me. Give me the strength to forget. My hardest hours are ahead. Will Egon answer? I can hardly believe he will, because I wounded him. It was partly his fault, though. I did spend some happy hours with him, but a woman needs more. But it was my fault, too, because he was sincere—sincere in a sense. When I think of his vows, it hurts. No, I must forget.

August 25

I've been at home for ten days. The workmen are putting insulation in my room, so I'm practically without a place to live, which makes me nervous. But that's not the worst of it. I have other problems. God in Heaven help me. I hope next week will bring a little relief. On Wednesday (the 21st) I received another postcard from Egon. I didn't answer it, since he has not answered my letter. Perhaps he lost interest, not obtaining what he wanted. But that's unimportant now. My conscience tells me he's not the right man for me. Inconstant. It's true that I am drawn to cheerful dispositions, but Egon is not sensitive enough for me. Disagreements would be inevitable. I must be sensible. But it's all in God's hands. I must be brave, I must go on. And where is Kleinchen now?

I've been to three lectures. Professor K. spoke wonderfully. About poetry, the indefatigable Leonardo da Vinci, and yesterday Christ and the Jews. He said the Jews are the greatest materialists, but without them it would be hard for the others to survive. They are the mortar between the bricks. Without Jews we would not be able to think logically. They are the creators of science. He went on to say that the greatest anti-Semites were themselves the greatest Jews. He spoke marvelously about Marx, Freud, Adler, Einstein. And then about judging people. His opinion is that we should judge only after we know the essence of a man. We should approach everyone with respect, for in every human being there is something noble, which must be explored.

October 1

Dear little book, how long you have lain untouched. I've been very busy, and was ill, a slight infection of the bladder. But I'm better now. Protect me, Almighty God, from illness.

My work helps me surmount everything. And helps me forget. Only when reading Egon's letter do I feel a gentle pain. I cannot understand how a person can be so imperfect. It is a question of morals. I don't want to be angry with him. Perhaps I will see him when I go to Zagreb. But I have become indifferent to him.

And Kleinchen, where is he? I won't call him, although I would like to see him. That, too, will come.

Thank God I have a lot of pupils. Perhaps I will even make enough to go away for Christmas. That would be marvelous. I must go away more often, otherwise I will become completely cut off from people. But we shall see.

October 21

Monday. One o'clock in the garden, a splendid autumn, very hot, as if it were August. I'm weary, so weary, but reading my letters takes my mind off things. Egon has written again. His tone, after my letter, is cold. Silly little Egon. He says that he is old but his heart is young. I had to laugh out loud. Klara writes regularly and is glad that we will be seeing each other again. I, too, am glad.

October 28

Dear little book, you are my solace and my torment. When I open you, my eyes fill with tears, but sometimes, too, with a little joy. Life is so empty and sad. Yesterday I went to Dornstadter's with two ladies. It is chaff we thresh! Is there nowhere a man who can understand me? God in Heaven, help me, bless my work, fulfill my desire.

November 1

All Saints! The bells are sad, so sad. I've just returned from the cemetery. I saw Kleinchen there, talked to him. God, open wounds! Only now do I realize what you meant to me.

His eyes sought mine. Ah, Kleinchen, if I could tell you my troubles! And then, today, being given notice! What will happen to me? Dear God in Heaven, do not abandon me.

November 20

New lodgings. I am once again dissatisfied. But what can I do? I must eat.

I don't know what's wrong with my students. I've already lost two. I should go back; that would be the best solution. Once again, struggle. Yesterday, a letter from Egon. Difficult for me to go away for Christmas, much as I would like to. Egon waits in vain.

November 25

Home once again!

I call this little room home. And that is what it is. My home. How glad I am to be here.

Egon sent me a photo. Good to know that he still

thinks of me. That he still hopes. Perhaps, God willing, at Klara's for Christmas. Tonight I dreamed of Kleinchen.

December 13

I always intend to write, but am so busy. Work up to my ears, thank God. Today I woke up joyful, and when I saw the gray sky, I was overcome by a real feeling of Christmas. Christmas! It's been so long since I was a child. Again I dream of going away, how happily I would go, if it were only possible. Egon has written to me, but I know he's not sincere. But let me go on dreaming. I've broken off with Madame; she was unkind to me. But if everyone hates me, God is with me.

December 25

Christmas. The word echoes in me like a cry of pain. Such an empty, sad Christmas, and for so long I was looking forward to it. Why can't I make happiness for myself? It's my own fault. But it's Egon's fault, too. In his last letter, he wrote only: Do as you like. That was all he said. When I look at the beautiful blue sky, my heart weeps. How splendid it would be to be there with him! We would take long walks, side by side, like children. Little book, my true friend, only you know my torment. Today I'll write to Klara. If only Christmas were over.

Today, Böske's wedding. The bride was very pretty, the Jewish ceremony very pleasant, even though it all means nothing. What are all the vows, promises worth, when people get to know each other only afterward? Still, my heart was empty and sad, especially when the groom asked me pityingly: Why are you alone here? He's right, I am alone, alone.

Christmas—on the table are red carnations, red as blood. How I love flowers!

God in heaven, do not abandon me.

December 26

Second day of Christmas. I had a nap this afternoon. Last night I went to the cinema. Gustav Fröhlich was very good.

There was quite a scene yesterday. Hirschl saw Egon's postcard and bellowed like a bull. Threats. I see now that he's worthless, as coarse and vulgar as a peasant. The devil take him. But I'm not going to get myself worked up about it. Let him go.

I'll do my work, and God is with me. But I wish I had a companion—a friend who is kind, and who understands me.

December 30

Christmas is over—thank God. It brought me no joy, but that was my own fault. It could have been different. Where did I go—to the cinema and to F.'s. Yes, to F.'s. It was enough to make one want to run away. The atmosphere was miserable. I didn't see Kl. Christmas with no brightness, no joy, so be it. Yesterday I went to a tavern with Miss Sch., a boring Gretchen who wants to get married. May the devil carry her off to the matchmaker's.

I ought to have worked today, but my students also seem to want to prolong the holidays.

Tomorrow I will work. Today I'm tired, lazy. And inside, emptiness.

January 4, 1936

Wonderful days, like spring. This morning I saw a beautiful rainbow. What does it mean? Let us hope for fine weather at Easter, so I can go away.

January 12

The marvelous weather is still holding.

January 19

Beautiful days, just like spring. If only it could stay that way. Nothing new with me, except that unfortunately my health is poor. I have a bladder inflammation again. I must go to the doctor. God in Heaven, do not abandon me!

January 28

The weather is still pleasant. I went to see Dr. Kerner, who said more or less what Kárpáti said. He's treating me. I hope I'll be all right for a while, please God.

Poor little Kárpáti, I feel sorry for him, but people should not be so greedy. Money is the root of all evil. I live alone and I will always live alone. How empty is my little room.

April 7

It's been such a long time since I saw you, my dear little book! Why is that? I don't know. I write, I suppose, only when I feel the need. What should I write? My health, thank God, is tolerable. Easter is almost here, but it's cold and unpleasant. There have been so many expenses, I haven't saved a penny. E. writes rarely, as do I. Everything has a beginning and an end.

Sunday. In the house, peace and quiet. It's good to be by myself at last. But I'm so somber. Easter passed, joyless, and the weather is bad. Work again coming to an end. Summer holidays, how shall I spend them? In Zagreb, God willing. Egon hasn't written since Easter. Since I wrote him that I'm no longer thinking of marriage, he has cooled off. He himself brought it up, proposed, hoping in that way to get what he wants. But he's mistaken! Should I allow him just for that? No. Let him get it from others, from those who want only that. I seek friendship, deep and sincere. God will help me.

May 4

Nothing new. E. is silent. I was right. I don't like his kind. Especially Jews. I went to the cinema, saw "The Merry Widow." Excellent! Very amusing. There is an honest woman. She acted well. Love conquered her. I, too, would like to be loved—just a little—but all that is over. Autumn is at the gate. I don't really want to see it.

May 30

Tomorrow, Whitsun. Nothing new. Klara wrote; her words hurt me. Last night I dreamed of L. Wearisome nights. I long for love!

Next month I go away. May God help me.

June 30

Since the 26th I've been here in Zagreb. But how forlorn I feel! On account of E. I see now what a liar he is. Dear God, help me! You alone see how unhappy I am. But why, why? Can no one be trusted? Never mind!

He's not worth thinking about. I won't think about him!
I want to forget and I will forget what I've heard.

July 13

Here I am, ill, my will broken. What have I done?
Yesterday, Dr. G. I yielded to him. He overcame me.
Never mind. I learned something, a good lesson for me.
I don't despise him—it's his nature. And dear E.? I broke
off with him! It's better this way. I will remain alone.
G. told me the truth, but not the whole truth.

I spent some lovely hours with him, lovely, but to
what purpose? God help me, I no longer believe in anything. I would weep if I could, if I were alone—but I'm
not. Only my heart is alone.

Lord, do not abandon me!

August 30

Back home three weeks already! Tomorrow, with
God's help, work begins. Deliver us from holidays without joy, without pleasure. But luckily everything can be
forgotten. And I have forgotten. I love my work; all my
reward is in it.

December 30

Little book, dearest friend, how long is it since I've
seen you? And what bitter hours. The worry of earning
enough to eat. What can I say? Lament my troubles?
No, I have put lamenting behind me. Serbian Christmas
is almost here.

January 15, 1937

Another year has passed.
The festive season is over, joyless. I received nice

gifts, but nothing makes me happy. I am cold inside, my nerves are terrible, I am so tired. I don't want to hear anything about the past. God grant that my pupils learn and get good grades. Klara writes rarely. The holidays are approaching again. Very cold today. Otherwise, nothing new. God, do not abandon me.

January 26

Blizzard. It's impossible for me to leave my room. The elements are as angry as we are. How dismal life is! My health is not good. Lord, give me strength to get through this! The days pass without happiness; my pupils are often rude.

February 12

Extremely pleasant weather. But I'm very tired. Mila was here Sunday. That's how it is when you have a sister but don't really have a sister. I know that I'm an old maid and will remain one. Nothing but conniving on all sides. God, help me.

March 28

Easter! Cold, vile weather, which suits my mood. But no, sunshine would cheer me up. Many times I wanted to write and complain to you, dear little book. I had much to say. For the moment, thank God, there's enough work, but the students are poor. I'm taking on too much; that's why I have so little energy. Once again the school year draws to a close. A gloomy, vacant year. God grant the next one will be better. I must make a new schedule.

Klara has invited me to go to Rogaška Slatina: I'll see. I must look for a new home. Pleasure, sunshine, happiness, where are you hiding? Come out, come to see me just once!

April 22

Rain for four whole weeks. Melancholy has taken hold of me. And my work is not going well. This year I took on too much. I mustn't let that happen again. The results are not nearly as good. If fewer students show up in the autumn, I mustn't forget that I swore to work less. This is beyond my strength. I can feel it. Dear, kind God, make everything end well. Sun, where are you?

August 15

The next to the last day of my stay here. I have learned something, seen the people I wanted to see, done what I wanted to do.

But with no pleasure.

October 20

What can I say? Everything is the same. My health, thank God, is all right. My work is difficult. Klara's friendship has cooled. No matter. It's all in the past. Wonderful weather, as in midsummer.

November 13

Terribly windy for three days now. This sudden change is unpleasant. I've had a chill since the 1st. I haven't been out of my room. Everything is a struggle. God, just give me my health! I've gained weight this year, more than four kilos, I'm looking better. I have to laugh when men's eyes linger on me—me, already in the autumn of my life. I have no regrets, but if only the sun would shine on me just once more! On the night of November 1st I dreamt of my father. He was playing the piano. He lifted me up and said: My poor unfortunate child.

January 10, 1938

Christmas, holidays, again without cheer. New Year's Eve at F. Feith's, but otherwise working. Yesterday to the theater, the day before to the cinema: "Der Pfarrer von Kirchfeld." Awakens an aching longing for my native country. The people, nature, loving eyes. I know now what it is I miss. Worries, serious worries on account of my students. Almighty God, give me strength. Since December 21st, extreme cold.

January 27

St. Sava's Day. A national holiday this year. I was working.

Sunday, I made a new acquaintance—Albin. Dark eyes. We have known of each other for a long time. He kissed my hand. A sweet memory. I spent several good days thinking about him. Small pleasures. His words, "I should like to see your beautiful eyes once again," fill my heart.

September 11

It's been a long time since I saw you, my good little friend. I had nothing to write. I spent the summer in Zagreb, uneventful. I've been back here since August 1st, and am already working. A lot of work. I rarely see A., but on the evening of September 5th I saw the one with whom I spent the best days of my life, K. He was so handsome, his eyes sought mine, our eyes met. As the national anthem was played, we looked at each other.

A moment of inexpressible beauty. I feel that I love him and that he still loves me. I'd like to talk to him—I'll call him—perhaps. Tonight I dreamt of him, we were kissing, he took me away. My dear, my dear. I love you.

I must think of the future. I'm forty-two, and when I look at myself in the mirror, I am amazed. Is this a woman on the brink of old age? My eyes shine, my cheeks are fresh. Merciful God, give me happiness just one more time!

October 23

I've been in my new lodgings for a few days now. Sad days. I hope I'll soon calm down.

Father in Heaven, do not abandon me.

January 9, 1939

Christmas has come and gone, the New Year also. I stayed at home. To the cinema occasionally, good films. Otherwise, nothing. The weather is fine, a lot of snow— for our Christmas and for the Orthodox Christmas, too.

I must get back to work.

What can I say? I am unhappy, but I work.

January 27

Saint Sava, 1939.

Here I am, dear friend, with you again. But what will I write?

Mila was here. Perhaps I shall buy that house. I work. Work progresses, to quote Berberin's messenger. But I've caught a chill and my head aches. Time goes so quickly, my students are lazy—today I had only four lessons. My loneliness is a curse. I must do something, I have a plan.

June 12

Ill since February. A lot of pain.

My God, God in Heaven, do not abandon me.

August 1

Still sick. The holidays are almost over. Don't know where to begin. On Sunday I was at Vinkovci. The house is not for sale and I have lost my money, but I made an acquaintance—Rakić. I shall never forget it. The animal proposed marriage just to get what he wanted.

Dear God, I'm at the end of my strength. Be with me!

October 20

There are days when I feel better. I've gained 3½ kilos, thank God. But I'm still very ill. My work goes well, though I'm doing less. God preserve me.

November 1, 1940

The bells ring out sadly. All Saints. A new illness. Dear Father in Heaven, do not abandon me. Dear Father in Heaven, restore me to health.

Chapter 22

The end of the war, like its beginning, long expected yet sudden when it came, was announced by gunfire: soldiers joyfully turned the muzzles of their rifles skyward and pulled the triggers.

The salvo found Sredoje in Koprivnica, and when he ran into the street and saw the red trails of the tracer bullets against the May sky, he understood their meaning, that he had been made a gift of the future. With emotion he loaded his radio equipment onto a requisitioned peasant cart, jumped on with his three assistants, and at full speed, whipping the horses and singing, in a night and a day covered the road to Celje, their new destination. They merged with a flood of soldiers and prisoners there in the streets, which were pleasantly warm in the milky sun and wild with rejoicing.

The town was his. He deposited his radio equipment in a barracks building outside town and set off to look for a place to sleep. He found it in the first house at whose door he knocked: in a town that had lived under the Germans, no one would refuse a Partisan liberator.

And before long Sredoje was a Partisan with silver

stripes. The relaxation of standards in the suddenly expanded army brought him the rank of sergeant and membership in the League of Young Communists. This meant new advantages and new responsibilities. The recognition filled him with pride—he had succeeded, he had not lagged behind others—but it came as no reward for his convictions. Rather, it now required him to have convictions. He had to profess a loyalty he did not feel, even impose that loyalty on others, and this put him in a foul mood. He went to the Party meetings with his stomach in knots, and returned home feeling as if he had been plunged in deep water and held down to the limit of endurance. There was no air to breathe. He found air where his mind could be emptied, and where there was even a demand for such emptying: in fornication.

For a soldier, all of Celje was one great fornicating ground, as the instinct for survival strove to make up for wartime losses. And to whom could its treasures be opened more freely than to those who had by some miracle survived? In those days girls and women walked the streets like bitches in heat, trailing the scent of lust behind them; it was simply a matter of stopping them, asking them. Secretaries on their way home from work, peasant girls passing through, women waiting for their husbands to return from battle, young girls, and divorcées who had long ago renounced love to preserve their honor and their peace of mind—all now unhesitatingly stepped across the threshold of Sredoje's room, in an apartment that belonged to a young mechanic with four children, and surrendered themselves, their hearts beating with the hope that in him they would find a man for the life that was beginning anew.

He disappointed that hope, of course; he changed women constantly. At three o'clock, after lunch in the mess, he was capable of persuading an attractive woman walking by to go home with him, and then, after he had had his enjoyment and got rid of her, of going into town again in the early evening and finding another to waken his desire. Exhausted after a day of panting and sweating in bed, he would drag himself to the park in front of the railroad station and rest on a bench. There were always people there. Women with bundles would sit down on benches nearby, and again he would stir, ferret, introduce himself, boast of his sufferings, show his wounds, and into the bushes, instead of taking her back with him to his little room, which was permeated with the smell of sperm.

The predictability of his encounters began to irritate him. He realized, also, that he was participating in something that had been arranged beforehand, arranged by the women themselves, that he was their instrument as much as they were his. He took them with anger, contempt, caused them pain, yet they rose from his bed with a smile of understanding, perhaps even finding excitement in the humiliation they suffered, and soon went on to the beds of others, driven by their own glands, their own needs. He disliked negotiating with them, disliked the wordless, impatient escortings to his room. He moved to a room nearer the park, in the house of a retired accountant on a street facing the station, but after five weeks looked for a third place, something that would vary the routine of these rendezvous.

His attention was drawn to a cul-de-sac that crossed his own street, and a two-story house set back in a small but well-cared-for garden. Here, not far from the bustle of the station, a profound silence reigned. The silence of a trap, he thought. He lifted the latch on the iron gate; it swung open noiselessly. But the door of the house was locked. He rang the bell. A young woman with brown hair opened it, and he told her that he needed a room. She stepped aside, and he entered a cool hallway from which a staircase led up to the second floor.

"Who lives here?" he asked.

"Downstairs there's only me," said the woman, "and upstairs an elderly lady."

Sredoje stepped past her and took a look around. To the left, underneath the stairs, a door opened into a small room with a blind lowered over the window, so that he could just barely see a low bed, a wardrobe, a table, and chairs. To the right was a larger bedroom and, beyond it, a very clean, bright kitchen and bathroom. He took a minute to make up his mind, walking up and down in the hallway, on tiles that rattled faintly. Then he pointed to the room he had looked at first. "I'll take this one." When the woman nodded, he turned toward the entrance, said he was going to get his things, saluted, left. Intrigued not only by the room's cavelike tranquillity in that cul-de-sac full of flowers, but also by the submissiveness of the young woman, he hurried to the room he currently occupied, threw what few personal possessions he had into his haversack, knocked on the kitchen door—the landlord and his wife always sat in the kitchen, so as not to dirty the rooms—told them he was leaving, and a few minutes later was back at the house nestled in the garden.

Entering quietly, he walked down the hallway and

found the doors to both rooms wide open. In the room he had chosen, in front of the open wardrobe, the young woman stood with ironed white sheets in her arms. Surprised by his rapid return, she froze and stared at him wide-eyed. He set the haversack on the table, took his belongings out, and turned to put them in the wardrobe. But the woman's sudden stiffness and her gaze, which was drawn despite herself from him to the shelves, made him look more closely inside. Behind the white stacks of linen he spotted something silver; bending down, he saw a German officer's cap, with silver braid around its shiny visor, on top of a carefully folded green uniform.

Sredoje straightened and looked at the woman; she looked back at him with large pleading eyes. He threw his things on an empty shelf, turned, and left. But he did not go to the park to find a woman with whom to try out the attractions of his new room; he was too taken with the recent discovery and the woman's eyes, which promised much more than a surrender achieved through negotiation and persuasion. He went to the center of town and wandered, waiting for evening. At the mess he had supper, then stayed to watch a chess match played by two NCOs after the tables were cleared. He was delaying his return to the house, as a gourmet postpones a meal to whet his appetite.

When the clock on the wall struck nine, Sredoje got up and left. The little street was lit by a flickering street lamp; the house in the garden was quiet and dark. He pushed the latch on the gate; it opened, but when he shut it behind him, his fingers touched a key left in the lock. He locked the gate. It was the same with the door, and he locked the door also. In his room he switched on the light and found the bed made with clean sheets. He went to the wardrobe: the uniform and the cap were gone. He undressed quickly, went to the bathroom and washed, but on the way back, instead of going to his own room, he entered the room opposite. Its door was unlocked. In the bed by the window, in the faint light from the street lamp through the cracks in the blind, the woman lay with her eyes open. He got in beside her and spent the night with her.

He did this every evening, in the same silent way. Only gradually did he find out things about her: that her name was Dominika, that she was from a neighboring village, that she was twenty-one (his age), and that she worked in the town's land registry, which was where the Liberation found her. He never brought up the German officer's uniform, not wanting to dispel the secret that chained her to him, and she volunteered nothing about the man (a lover? a relative?), perhaps because she no longer wished to break that chain. They lived side by side with the secret between them. He left the house in the morning (as she did), ate in the mess, had his laundry done, and only at night, like a stranger, went into her room to perform the ritual of love.

Winter came, bringing winds and blizzards; the streets were deserted. Sredoje spent his free time in the mess, reading the newspapers or watching the chess players. With the arrival of spring and warm weather, promiscuity did not return to the streets with the walkers and idlers: lust had quieted down; young men and women chose more constant partners or else withdrew into their former shells. Nor did Sredoje feel his previous hunger for novelty in love. He still occasionally struck up a quick acquaintance and continued it in the afternoon in his room. But across the hallway was the silent Dominika, and he sensed her presence even as he embraced the other woman. It made him feel, somehow, less the predator, which detracted from his pleasure. He thought about moving again, but then he realized that he would be leaving the very thing that he had been searching for: a lair with his victim assured. He stayed. But he was not satisfied. The monotony ate at him. He had the feeling that his life was over and that there was nothing to look forward to but repetition.

The barracks, where he had to go every day, lay outside the town on the main road; the gray buildings, large and cold, were separated by empty paved courtyards. His duties were the classroom instruction of the first postwar recruits—at the end of their basic training in the surrounding hills in all weather—in the handling of radio equipment, which was relatively easy for him. But the instruction included political lectures and meetings—for Communists, for non-Communists—all of which he had to attend, and they were geared to the low level of understanding of the majority. Moreover, the commissars and secretaries, who had come of age during the war, were not much better educated than the recruits newly arrived from the villages.

At these interminable lectures and meetings, where words were mispronounced and professions of faith were made without substantiation, Sredoje alternated between acute boredom and the urge to shout out, to challenge what was being said. But even his hypocritical silence, he realized, was not worth the effort, since he could not hope for further promotion on account of his dubious past. He began to think of leaving the army, of beginning a new life, perhaps as a student, though he felt that he had lost the habit of intellectual effort.

In the spring of 1947, he put in his application to be demobilized, but it was refused, after a delay of four long months, on the grounds that he was irreplaceable. He decided, in revenge, to stop being irreplaceable. He withdrew into himself, changed from a comrade in arms to a cynical soldier: his instruction became half-hearted, openly ill-humored; he avoided political meetings by vanishing after the roll was called, on the excuse that he had to repair something, or with no excuse at all.

Soon, drawn by his boldness, a group of malcontents began to form around him: Master Sergeant Vukajlović, who for three years now had an unhealed wound on his leg and who had also not been granted a release from the army; Corporal Saboš, from Srem, with the thumb of his right hand missing, many times wounded and decorated, but with poor promotion prospects because of his quick temper and sharp tongue; Junior Sergeant Perišić, big and handsome, homesick for his native mountains; Sergeant Simović, whose older brother had been shot by the Partisans as a Chetnik. Their meeting place was the NCOs' mess, a converted tavern in the center of Celje. There, with wine brought in from next door (alcohol was not served in the mess), surrounded by cigarette smoke, they discussed the brigade, inveighing against their fellow NCOs and their superiors as oafs, imbeciles, toadies. Each recounted the unpleasantnesses accumulated in the course of the day, and the others waved their arms and muttered in indignation and sympathy. But from this daily airing of grievances, spurred by alcohol, they proceeded to criticize the army and the country itself, where it was no longer courage and ability that were valued but blind obedience and careerism.

Sredoje participated in these discussions, but with only an occasional remark or amusing anecdote, because injustices that did not affect him personally did not interest him, and more and more the subject tended to be not their small circle, but the general situation, all of Yugoslavia. At the same time, as if in counterattack, newspaper editorials and speeches delivered in town squares trumpeted the justification of every decision, every position, and this wave of unanimity, driven by invisible hands, entered the barracks, too. Political meetings became more frequent; many young Communists were accepted into the Party without the usual lengthy procedure—among them Sredoje, despite his obvious indifference.

At last the reason for all this noise and haste became apparent. At a Party meeting, after a short word of welcome to the initiates, the secretary, Major Vukoje, in a hoarse voice, sweating, read out the Cominform resolution signed by Stalin and Molotov and called upon the membership to respond to the accusations leveled at the Yugoslav Party. Several speakers came forward immediately, clearly old-timers; prepared in advance, they refuted, article by article, the lengthy, convoluted indictment, and the meeting concluded, late at night, with a unanimous rejection. But now, those who before had hesitantly asked questions or else suppressed their qualms of conscience were being told, by this, that it was possible and perhaps even necessary to argue. In the mess, instead of half-joking and complaining as usual, Vukajlović and Simović quoted the resolution from memory, Perišić attacked it, and Saboš, almost permanently drunk, stared at the coat of arms on the far wall above the clock and mumbled that perhaps tomorrow they would have to trample what today was sacred.

At first Sredoje found this new intensity entertaining, and he encouraged them, but before long he found his friends' rigid opinions, their inability to go beyond the level of faith and loyalty, disgusting, tedious. He sat at the malcontents' table now only out of friendship, but the moment tempers flared, he would take his glass and move to the table of the chess players.

One evening, Vukajlović, Simović, and Saboš failed to appear in the mess. Sredoje asked Perišić, who was gloomily draining his glass, but Perišić didn't know where they were, so Sredoje went to watch the chess players. The next morning, the duty officer at the barracks gate informed him of the battalion commander's order that he take over the instruction of Vukajlović's section, but, inexplicably curt, refused to explain why. In the evening, when Sredoje returned home from the mess (and now Perišić was not there) and switched on the light in the hallway, four men jumped out, two from his room, two from Dominika's, and put handcuffs on him. They drove him to the local Celje prison and locked him in a cell alone. In the morning, he was taken before the investigating officer, a red-faced young Slovene civilian, who questioned him about his past, particularly his wartime service in the Belgrade police, and then about his participation, as the Slovene put it, in the plot with his fellow conspirators from the mess. Sredoje denied the latter allegation and signed a statement. In the afternoon, he went before a second investigator, a Montenegrin captain, who demanded details about the leaflets he, Sredoje, had received from Simović and distributed. Sredoje denied this allegation, too, at which the investigator, apparently with the aim of confounding him, described a series of incriminating conversations in the mess with great accuracy, though misrepresenting the remarks Sredoje had made, and especially Sredoje's failure to reject Saboš's suggestion that the national coat of arms be taken down and trampled.

The captain summoned Sredoje several times a day: first he waved the confessions of others before his eyes, though he never allowed him to read them; then he threatened to widen the inquiry to include Sredoje's treachery during the Occupation. After three weeks, worn out and fearing worse, Sredoje gave in and made a full confession of his participation in the plot against the people and the state—with the exception of the leaflet episode, about which he indeed knew nothing. The inquiry was now reduced to the rounding out of his statements; he could breathe again.

One December morning he was shaved, given a fresh shirt and a jacket without stripes of rank, and driven to the military court, where he saw Perišić, Vukajlović, Simović, and Saboš for the first time, their faces pale and lined, as was his own, though he was not aware of it. The accused were escorted into the courtroom: at the far wall, the captain awaited them, and two majors and a lieutenant colonel sat at a raised table. One of the majors read out the charges. The main charge against Sredoje was based on his irreverent statements in the mess; only Simović and Vukajlović were charged with distributing the leaflets. Simović and Vukajlović were sentenced to five years in prison, Sredoje to one, Saboš to eight months, and Perišić to only three, the duration of the inquiry. They were taken back to prison together but then separated, and Sredoje never saw any of them again.

After ten days, he was transported by truck to Lepoglava. There he spent the winter in a cell with sixteen other prisoners, freezing and eating poor food. At the beginning of April 1949, he was taken by train, with one other prisoner, a gold smuggler, to Sremska Mitrovica. There they were given sufficient food and sent to work in the fields, and Sredoje quickly recovered. At last, on October 12, he was released and given a train ticket to Celje. At nine in the evening, he arrived at the house in the cul-de-sac. Dominika was not there. The housing authority had moved her out a few days after his arrest, but the new occupants, a large family, knew her address and gave it to him, staring with curiosity. Sredoje found her on the outskirts of town, in a small house that belonged to a retired teacher and his wife. Dominika had been allocated a room on the ground floor. She was already in bed, asleep; she came out drowsy, in her nightgown, but showed no hesitation about taking him in. So he began to live with her again.

Early in the morning, she would go off to work, while he stayed in bed. He would get up much later, eat what she had left for him, read the newspapers, smoke, listen to music on the small old radio. When Dominika came home, they would eat a meal together; then she would do the housework, which made him feel out of place in her single room. After the housework, Dominika cleaned herself, combed her hair, applied creams to her skin, washed her underclothes. He didn't like watching all these activities having to do with her body, which he was accustomed to possess at night in all its naked simplicity. And it annoyed him that her personality extended beyond that body, a personality he was only just discovering: her neatness, thriftiness, the way she examined every object with a prudent, careful eye, as if she were near-sighted, even every mouthful of food, before accepting it and using it. Impatient, he wanted to shout at her, but restrained himself, believing that it was not she who upset him but the claustrophobic memory of his stay in prison, from which he had not completely recovered.

Another problem arose: once the teacher and his wife got over the surprise of Sredoje's arrival, they became unpleasant, and one day the old man confronted Dominika when she returned from work and threatened legal action unless her lover—an unauthorized lodger—moved out. They thought about what to do. Dominika was ready to risk going to court, but Sredoje found that he did not want the circumstances under which he had come to live with her to be held up to public scrutiny. He decided to move to a rented room nearby, from which he could easily come to see her. She agreed, but it quickly became apparent that she could not afford to pay for two lodgings. He promised to look for work. But he could not look for work any more than he could go to court, and for the same reason: it would require him to give an account of his past, of his ridiculous disgrace, to strangers. Time passed, the deadline set for them drew near. Then both came up with a solution that each had been thinking of in secret: to get married.

The necessary documents were assembled, and Dominika arranged for the registry office to make it official without delay, so she could show the teacher the marriage certificate, which would keep him quiet. But the legal bond left them, apart from a sense of relief, with a bitter taste in their mouths. Sredoje suspected that he had been lured into a trap, while Dominika was disappointed that he, as soon as their difficulty was resolved, dropped the idea of looking for work. She let him know, at first in a roundabout way, then openly, that she had no intention of supporting him all his life; he, infuriated by her nagging, mentioned the German officer, whom she had certainly put up with. The spell of their mutual secret, broken, no longer restrained them. They quarreled, looking at each other with hatred, their faces distorted, amazed that they could ever have thought of spending their lives together.

Now they avoided each other. The minute Dominika got home from work, Sredoje would leave the house, returning late in the evening, when there was little time left for arguing. But it was winter, he had no money, and the streets of Celje, through which he sloshed in low shoes and the coat Dominika had bought him when he first arrived, were far from hospitable. He frequented small taverns, and if he had a dinar or two—extracted from Dominika in their less strained moments—he would order a glass of wine and sit over it for hours. If his pockets were empty, he would hide in a corner, preferably at an already occupied table, where the waiters would not notice him for a while. He felt that he was rapidly going downhill; his clothes, which he never changed, were crumpled and worn thin; his face and hands had grown furtive, coarse.

But the thought of looking for work, of explaining to personnel officers why he had been in prison, was unendurable and he pushed it aside. He considered an earlier idea: to return to school. A diploma, a profession, a new life free of the past. He began to read the announcements of the different universities in the newspapers, wondering which one would suit him best. But what was the use of selecting a school? To study, he needed money—enough, at least, to begin with, for traveling to Ljubljana or Zagreb and renting a place. His plans, wreathed in tobacco smoke and alcoholic vapors, moved into the purely financial realm. He thought, in turn, of a well-organized robbery, of buying a lottery ticket, of asking for a substantial loan from simple-minded people who would be moved by his story, of an unexpected inheritance.

At inheritance, he stopped. His parents' house in Novi Sad probably belonged to him legally. It was worth going there and filing a claim of ownership; if his ownership was recognized, he could sell the house and with the money go back to school. The prospect woke him from his lethargy; once again he felt young, capable. He unfolded his plan to Dominika, who agreed with it only as far as the house was concerned. His going back to school was out, she said, because she had married a grown-up man and—here her lips twisted unpleasantly—she was pregnant now and needed a breadwinner around, not a student. Feeling his life closing in on him, he promised Dominika that as soon as the inheritance business was over, he would look for work, but when he packed, he packed all his personal belongings. In April 1950, Sredoje left for Novi Sad.

The town spread out before him, gray with dust, resigned, the walls of its old houses marbled with moisture. Creaking and groaning, a streetcar took him to the center. Opposite the stop was the Queen Mary Hotel, now called the Vojvodina, and he took a room there.

The porter, drawling in a way Sredoje had long lost the habit of, asked how many days he was staying. Sredoje didn't know. The porter told him that he could not stay more than five days—that was the regulation. The town, which Sredoje had once considered lively, and in the rush of the Liberation wild, now seemed abandoned, sleepy. He went to his parents' house. It had, again, new occupants, who were scornfully indifferent to his announcement that he intended to reclaim his right of ownership. He went to the Town Hall. The official he had to see was not there.

He made several trips with the same lack of success. When he grew angry and began to shout, an aged clerk, looking at him over his spectacles, outlined in vengeful detail the kind of petition that had to be submitted. All this Sredoje did, but no one could tell him how long it would be before he received an answer. His time in the hotel had run out and his money was rapidly dwindling; he had to look for accommodations. Subconsciously his steps led him to the places he had frequented in his youth, and soon he found himself in front of the house of Milinko Božić. He went in, but was told that his friend had not returned from the war and that Mrs. Božić had remarried and not long ago moved away.

Wandering around uncertainly, Sredoje arrived at Fräulein's lodgings, passed them, and in a decrepit little back street not far away caught sight of a handwritten sign: "Subtenant wanted." He went in and, since a month's rent was less than three nights in the hotel, took a furnished room. The landlord was a peasant with a mustache and a potbelly, who had sold his land and bought this house in order to send his two sons to school in the town and avoid paying taxes; he worked as a

327

night watchman in a factory. Sredoje spent his days in the courtyard in front of his unheated room (to save money) and ate cold food, which he bought from the shop next door. With nothing to do, and almost against his will, he observed the life of the small community: the tiny but wiry lady of the house, old before her time, who cooked and kneaded in the kitchen; her scrawny sons, one ten and the other twelve, reluctantly doing their homework under the trellis; the two subtenants and the landlord, who came home from work at different times, ate, slept, then went back to work again, they in the morning, he in the evening.

Out of boredom, Sredoje would occasionally correct the children as they read aloud and recited uncomprehendingly; he would explain to them or drill them. The landlord, at his wife's prodding, came to him one afternoon and asked if Sredoje would coach the children regularly until the end of the school year, and in return offered to put him up rent-free. Sredoje at once accepted. But he had no money now to buy food; so he wrote to Dominika and meanwhile borrowed some cash from the landlord. Dominika sent him money and a letter in which she asked him to return immediately and find work; he could no longer count on her assistance because she was soon to give birth.

Instead of answering her letter, he went to the Town Hall again. This time he found a helpful official, an educated young shopkeeper-turned-clerk, who, after patiently rummaging through the papers on his desk and in a file cabinet, found a document he was looking for, read it, his two plump hands clutching his forehead, and finally said that Sredoje needed to support his claim by the affidavits of two witnesses. Sredoje went in search of people who had known his parents. Most of them were no longer around—they either had left the town or were dead—and the only ones he could come up with, a retired civil servant and the widow of a prewar officer, refused to appear as witnesses for fear their testimony would be viewed as an attack on property that was now state owned.

On the horns of this dilemma, Sredoje decided to seek the aid of a lawyer. He remembered a name, Dr. Karakašević, learned from the telephone directory that he was still practicing, and went to see him. The small, balding old man, whom he had never seen before, received him far more cordially than anyone else had done, but when Sredoje finished explaining, he shook his head: "No, young man. I would never take up a cause that is already lost. This state gives nothing back." Sredoje left the lawyer, dejected, and abandoned his claim.

But he did not return to Celje. He continued to work with his two charges and waited, as if spellbound by indecision and the sudden onset of the hot, oppressive summer of the plain. As a result of Sredoje's efforts, the landlord's younger son passed all his final exams and the older son improved several poor grades, failing only his exam in history. Sredoje went on coaching him, and parents from the neighborhood, unschooled, unfamiliar with book learning, and worried by their children's lack of success in competition with the children of the old middle class, started to bring their own confused sons and daughters to him for instruction. Sredoje began to support himself.

In August, just before the school placement exam, a telegram arrived for him: Dominika had had a daughter and was asking him to come home. He put off the decision until the exams were over, and then, since he had remained silent for so long, could not decide to break his silence. (Several years later, he would receive another letter from Dominika, with a photograph of a round child's head and a message: "To Daddy on my fourth birthday—Vali." He would often look at the photograph when he was drunk.) In the autumn he continued to coach the pupils whom he had helped through the placement exams, along with a few new pupils. Every day he spent seven or eight hours over their untidy notebooks. In his free time he rested in his room, or went out for walks, though rarely. On one such walk, his eyes were drawn to the silhouette of a woman ahead of him. Her slightly stooping gait seemed familiar. Then, seeing the red cascade of her hair, he knew that it was Vera Kroner. He ran up to her and took her in his arms.

Chapter 23

On his first visit to Vera, Sredoje presented her with Fräulein's diary. She was thrilled; she grabbed the little red book, opened it, pressed it against her chest, but Sredoje retrieved it from her for long enough to show her the place that had caused him to take it and keep it: Vera's own entry, with the date and circumstances of Fräulein's death. Vera looked at it, said that the handwriting, although she didn't deny it was hers—she remembered well that she had written it—was strange, completely unlike her present style. She wanted to show him. She looked around for a piece of paper, asked him for a pencil, and sat down to write. Leaning over her as she wrote, he insisted that she was wrong, that the two scripts were the same. They fought over the piece of paper—he trying to take it, she not letting him—until they almost tore it in half. They laughed, they were like children, teasing and chasing around the table, and when they caught each other, they forgot what they intended to do, lost their breath, fell on the couch, on the floor, with their arms entwined, and kissed.

They kissed for hours. Sredoje pressed a thousand slow kisses on Vera's hair, shoulders, arms, and, with special tenderness, the indelible black letters on her breast, which Vera for the first time made no attempt to hide. Lowering her rust-colored eyelashes and with a lost look, her face pale, she accepted and counted silently those thousand kisses, each the same, each different. Her blood did not quicken, nor did his; rather, it was as if, thirsty, they were drinking of some bottomless cool liquid, which left them with a greater thirst. Their chasteness amazed them, and again they laughed like children as they lay in each other's arms for hours, kissing without desiring, without demanding that their embrace culminate in the way they had both long ago mastered.

Sredoje said this was because of the strength of their love, which, he had read somewhere, could dull or completely eliminate lust. Vera didn't like his explanation, not because she did not believe it, but because his talk of love and lust made her uneasy. She wanted only to play, not to think or analyze, pretending she had gone back ten years or more. She was even unwilling to hear Sredoje's dreamy memories of the attraction they had felt for each other years before. Better for their love to have no past and be all in the present. And when Sredoje made her recall the snowball fight, how he had saved her from her attackers and then kissed her, she refused to believe it. No, boys had never attacked her with snowballs, and he hadn't kissed her, and at parties she had danced with Milinko, her boyfriend, and with no one else. That was their first disagreement.

The second was about the diary. After they had touched and caressed it as an object precious to them both, and opened it at random to a familiar word, a familiar sentence, one afternoon they sat down to read it together from beginning to end. They were surprised—first, by how short it was. And, read aloud, word by word, many passages were unclear, confusing, something they had never noticed when they read the diary to themselves.

They wondered who Kleinchen was, Fräulein's great love. The man Sredoje had seen once when he arrived for his lesson, who sat at a distance from the table with his hat in his lap? But the stranger had seemed awkward and old, unkempt, possibly even unshaven. When Sredoje saw him, he felt that he had intruded on something extremely private. Or was Kleinchen one of the people around her to whom they never paid attention, but whom they had seen show up at her funeral? And what did the word mean? Was it a diminutive of the surname Klein, as Vera thought, or a term of endearment, "little one"?

Klein was as a rule a Jewish name, Sredoje observed. Had Vera noticed the anti-Semitism in the diary? Vera denied that. Sredoje picked up the notebook and leafed through it until he found and read to her the entry for May 4, 1936: "I don't like his kind. Especially Jews." Vera retorted that he hadn't understood it properly: Fräulein didn't like men who told lies, particularly if they were of a different origin, not *because* they were of a different origin. Besides, Klara, whom Fräulein visited, most probably her landlord's daughter (who was a Klara, Vera remembered), was also Jewish, as was Böske, whose wedding Fräulein attended. Then there were the lectures she went to at the Novi Sad Cultural Club, which had Jewish patrons.

Sredoje ascribed that to a snobbish inconsistency

on Fräulein's part. He cited her liking for "The Merry Widow" and "Der Pfarrer von Kirchfeld," a film he remembered as highly nationalist, and which had drawn from Fräulein the exclamation, "The people, nature, loving eyes!" Vera insisted that that meant nothing. Anyway, the Jews *did* have some unpleasant traits. She, a Jewess, knew that better than anyone. But to criticize them for these traits did not mean anti-Semitism.

In this way the war crept into their conversation, and it was inevitable that they should share with each other their experiences of it. Sredoje told of his life as a soldier, the circumstances surrounding the deaths of his parents, and Vera told of Gerhard's suffering in prison and how her father, her grandmother, and she were taken to the camp. They became exceptionally attentive to each other: Vera met Sredoje halfway when it was time for him to visit, and he brought her small gifts— candies, or pretty buttons, which he searched for in the shops (he noticed that she changed them often on her dresses), or a pack of cigarettes.

When winter arrived, each tried to soften it for the other. Since Sredoje's room was chilly (he told her this; he never took her there), they agreed that after the lessons with his pupils, he should spend his free time in her room. Vera made sure to light the fire early to warm the room; she found an old woolen plaid scarf and gave it to him carefully washed and ironed. Sredoje drank less. Through the father of one of his pupils he even managed to get some coal for her. In the evening, it was their custom not to light the lamp, but to watch, their arms around each other, the red glow of the fire through the small cracks in the door of the stove. They said little. Their whole effort now was to combat the winter, which seemed to them an angry giant, for it was the first time in their lives that no other danger threatened them, the first time they had someone to care for. They covered each other, warmed each other with their breath and the palms of their hands. "Are you cold?" they would ask. "Are you comfortable? Do you need anything?" And when they parted, they exchanged advice on how to keep from catching cold.

Suddenly it was spring, with a sun not strong enough for them to do without heating but bright enough to make the closed-in room oppressive. They opened the windows wide to let out the smoke from the stove and the cigarettes, which burned their throats. They paused at a window and, hugging each other, watched the passers-by. But they avoided going out together, by unspoken agreement, reluctant to show themselves in public places after the humiliations they had suffered.

The streets were full of bustle that spring: people venturing out, paying more attention to their clothes. Brightly colored fabrics fluttered in the wind as motorcycles went by, and occasionally these were overtaken by a shiny new car. This modest burst of ostentation, of luxury, distressed Vera and Sredoje; they felt that they were being left behind, they felt the need to keep in step with life. Sredoje spoke of going back to school, Vera of finding work again. But they were afraid to put these words into action, afraid of losing what they had so unexpectedly gained, this companionship that scorned the world, this peace unassailable from outside. So they fell silent, but there was reproach in their silence. Sredoje looked at Vera out of the corner of his eye, at the object of his love, which separated him from his future, and he saw someone dear to him but not her worth.

And Vera looked at Sredoje and shared in the dissatisfaction. They paced the room.

Once again they picked up Fräulein's diary, turned the pages, read passages, and discussed them. There was one completely incomprehensible allusion to "Berberin's messenger." Sredoje said he would look up the name in an encyclopedia in the public library, but he never got around to it. And who was Mila? Apparently Fräulein's sister, whom she didn't like very much, it seemed. And Egon, who replaced Kleinchen at one point? And Hirschl, who saw Egon's postcard and "bellowed like a bull"? Sredoje said that Fräulein, if one read the diary carefully, was constantly surrounded by suitors—some platonic, like Egon, others aggressive, like Dr. G., who apparently had taken liberties with her during an examination. Thus there were both honorable and dishonorable admirers from whom she could have made her selection. Yet she chose none of them, not wanting to go "over the *line*," as she put it in one place. At the same time, she complained of loneliness, and that no one would shed a tear over her. Didn't it seem to Vera that Fräulein's diary, for all its tragic tone from beginning to end, was a farce if read against the background of the horrors that Fräulein had escaped? Because, when all was said and done, she had made her choice, whereas many—millions—had been given no choice.

In answer Vera shrugged and said that happiness and unhappiness could not be measured by fact but only by feeling, by the state of mind.

Sredoje could not accept that. If it was only a matter of state of mind, there would be no justice or injustice, no good or evil. What would Fräulein have said if, instead of the deprivation she imposed upon herself, she had been forcibly deprived—whether by others or by society—of the experience of love? Or if, the other extreme, she had been forced to accept love against her will, as Vera had been forced?

Vera said nothing.

Did that mean, Sredoje went on, that Vera considered herself less unfortunate than Fräulein?

They were two different kinds of misfortune, Vera answered suddenly and without hesitation. They couldn't be compared.

But Sredoje persisted: Didn't indecision in love seem laughable when compared with rape, just as death from an illness developing within us, limiting the span of our life, seemed tame, almost idyllic, compared with death by violence?

It amounted to the same if one was not resigned, Vera said, but this time uncertainly.

Resigned? Both surprised and thoughtful, Sredoje repeated the adjective, as if tasting it. And had she, Vera, been resigned to the embraces that had been imposed on her?

With a shrug Vera said that perhaps she had been resigned. She survived, didn't she? She suddenly burst into tears. She cried her heart out, lips twisted, face streaming; her body racked with such sobs that the couch on which she was sitting creaked. "It was an insane asylum," she blubbered, "where the guards were more insane than anyone. The screams, howling, blows, the crowding and shivering with fear, and the roll calls, over and over again; it made you resigned. How resigned? So resigned, so obedient, that you smiled and opened your arms to the soldiers who came in like wolves, and when one of them chose you, you trembled with gratitude, you hugged and kissed him and rolled your hips so he wouldn't complain later, so Handke wouldn't kill you with his stick."

Full of remorse, Sredoje sat down beside her and took her hands to comfort her, but she pulled them away and shook her head.

"That's what I was, Sredoje, obedient, cheerful, because I had resigned myself. Yes, I was resigned!"

He took her in his arms and kissed her wet face, her hands, shoulders, breasts, first one, then the other, and gradually the embrace of consolation became an embrace of love, sensual, unrestrained, because now that the face he knew so well was contorted, there arose before him another face, and beneath it another body, shy, helpless, the body he had imagined and desired as a boy, which now ran to meet him, naked, innocent, enslaved, across a wide, empty space, along a plank as perilously narrow as the line between life and death.

He pressed, sculpted, formed her body into the one of his dreams, and it yielded, opened, molded itself to his need. Out of breath, they sat up, not looking each other in the eye. Then again they lay down and joined, this time deliberately, slowly, exciting each other with experienced movements, until their whispered endearments turned to cries of pleasure. Afterward, they lay there smoking, silent, and, since it was warm in the room, completely naked.

Now that the days were long and it was light until midevening, each could see every detail of the other's body. Their bodies were no longer in their first youth: Sredoje had put on weight, while under Vera's white skin was a network of blue veins, and sudden motion made her thighs shake. But these bodies were the only future their bond held for them, and Sredoje and Vera, having exhausted the pleasure, became aware of this.

For several days they would not see each other; then they would arrange to meet on a definite day and at a definite time, blaming the interval on the time of year, the end of the pitiless winter. Sometimes, when Sredoje came to see Vera, he found her in a bad mood, stubborn, and once half drunk. He lectured her, even though he himself drank. She retorted, finally, that she knew a place where she could drink as much as she liked, and when he raised his eyebrows, she reminded him with a self-mocking laugh that her mother owned a tavern in Germany. Sredoje, who had expected a worse, more shameless answer, lowered his eyes and asked if she wanted, then, to go to her mother. "Why not?" Vera said spitefully. He thought of dissuading her but realized that he had no right to do so, since he had no future to offer her, and when she saw that Sredoje was hesitating, she began to consider seriously the possibility she had thrown out offhandedly. She concluded that apart from making love with Sredoje there was nothing for her in Novi Sad. She said as much to Sredoje, but he was silent.

As a first step, which did not obligate her and from which she could always draw back, in a moment of alcoholic decisiveness Vera wrote to her mother, and since the answer she received was encouraging—though accompanied by the carefully reiterated condition, not at all to her liking, that she must help with the work— she made up her mind. She renewed her passport and, on the basis of her mother's written invitation, registered and attested to at the Frankfurt Town Hall, obtained a visa and, through a travel agency, a ticket valid for two months. Her departure was fixed for September 14.

Now they both waited for that date, waited for it with the unspoken wish that it would never come, for notwithstanding the clear awareness each had of the other's imperfections, each still desired and loved the other. But neither Vera nor Sredoje had the strength to take the responsibility for changing the decision; so time carried them inexorably to their last meeting, which was the afternoon before Vera boarded the train.

Sredoje postponed two lessons to the next day and arrived on time. Vera was dressed for the journey, and next to her on the floor stood Mitzi's old suitcase and the tartan traveling bag she had brought with her from Germany. She looked around to make sure she had not forgotten anything, and in her agitation stuffed a few more objects into her open bag, a Turkish coffeepot, a hand towel, then changed her mind and took them out, placing them back on the table or the nearest chair as useless, of too little value. Fräulein's diary still lay on the table.

"What will you do with it?" asked Sredoje, whose eyes had kept straying in that direction.

"Nothing," said Vera, although until that moment she had no idea. "I'll leave it for you," she decided.

"For me? But it's yours."

"No, it isn't. You found it."

"In your house, in your cupboard. With your writing in it. It's yours."

Vera shrugged. She wanted to say that the house was no longer hers, but such words were irrelevant now, so she said vaguely, "Why should I take it with me to Germany? There's no point."

340

Sredoje thought for a moment, then suggested, "As a memento?"

Vera pursed her lips. "As a memento of whom?" And she looked at him in surprise, because she had expected, thinking of the diary, that they would argue, instead, over who would keep it, and that such an argument might even unite them at the last moment. But at the sight of the packed suitcases she realized that without Sredoje she had no need of the diary, and that Sredoje, without her, had no need of it.

"Shall we destroy it?" Sredoje asked.

Vera slowly nodded. "That was what she wanted. For it to be burned."

Sredoje hesitated, finally got to his feet, picked up the little book from the table, and looked around for a suitable spot to carry out this decision. He moved slowly, as if hoping that Vera or something else would interfere, preventing the disappearance of the last thing that bound them together. Vera, too, hoped for that, but no hindrance, no disagreement arose. Their throats went tight; they would have shouted to each other that what they were doing was madness, but their voices wouldn't let them. Sredoje's eyes fell upon a corroded tin tray on the window sill; he walked over and picked it up. "May I use this?" he asked, looking at Vera.

"You may," she said, fixing her eyes on the tray.

He placed the tray on the table, the diary on the tray, and took out some matches. He lit one and again looked questioningly at Vera, but she kept her eyes steadily on the tray; then he lifted the front cover of the book with the gold lettering "Poésie" and brought the lighted match to the first page, which had opened with the cover. The flame caught the corner of the page, crawled toward its center, then went out. But now, paying more attention to what he was doing, Sredoje took the book and stood it with the pages spread, lit another match and put it to each page one by one. A dozen little flames flared up, ran along the pages and into the heart of the book. But there wasn't enough air for the fire, so Sredoje had to spread the pages more with his fingers. The little flames burned him as he pulled apart the book with a vengeance, pulled as if driven by a need, a conviction. Vera, frowning with impatience, watched the fire on the tray. Finally the flames caught on, licked around the covers, curling them and blackening them, joining in a single reddish-yellow flame, which flared and shot up high, then slowly sank, trembled, and disappeared, leaving behind nothing but ashes and cinders.